Education and Belief

Brenda Watson

Basil Blackwell

©Brenda Watson 1987

First published 1987
Published by
Basil Blackwell Ltd
108 Cowley Road
Oxford OX4 1JF
England

British Library Cataloguing in Publication Data

Watson, Brenda
  Education and belief.
  1. Religious education
  I. Title
  200′.7′1   BV1471.2

ISBN 0–631–15208–3

BSD CS7

Typeset in 11/13 Sabon
by OPUS, Oxford
Printed in Great Britain by Page Bros (Norwich) Ltd

To the Hon Robert Wills, founder and chairman of the
Farmington Trust, and to all colleagues and staff at the
Farmington Institute, Oxford, without whose constant support
and encouragement this book could not have been written.

Acknowledgements

The author gratefully acknowledges her debt to a great many people, especially to Dora Ainsworth, Charles Barnham, Hilary Elgar, Molly Gogarty, Roy Niblett and her father John T. Watson for reading the text and offering many valuable suggestions; to Catherine Elgar for considerable help with the figures and mind-maps; to Betty Colquhoun and Pam Stone for typing and proof-reading the text; and to all the many teachers and students, discussion with whom over the years has helped to clarify her understanding of the purpose of education.

Thanks are also due to W H Vanstone for permission to quote extensively from an article which appeared in the *Quarterly Review of the Community of the Resurrection* No. 332, 1986.

The author and publisher would like to thank The Reader's Digest Association for permission to reproduce 'The Night I Met Einstein' by Jerome Weidman, which appeared in *Readers' Digest* March 1979, pp 99–102.

Contents

Preface

This book should be of interest to all who are concerned about the state of education today, and especially to those involved in curriculum planning and development. It argues forcefully for the value of education at a time when many are challenging it.

The first part of the book seriously considers the mismatch between education and what so oftens happens in schools. It suggests some fundamental reasons for this, and puts forward a strong case for a different set of priorities applicable right across the curriculum.

Education cannot avoid questions to do with belief. Value judgments underline the organisation and ethos of schools and what is taught; these value judgments are based on beliefs, whether acknowledged or not, chosen or imbibed. Schools need to explore ways in which they can help people to reflect on the content and validity of beliefs within a framework of mutual respect. This book argues for a mode of education which sets out to initiate young children and older students into responsible self-education. This involves sharing with them the purpose of education, alerting them to the dangers of indoctrination and conditioning from whatever source, and introducing them to those skills and attitudes which can enable them to develop their full potential.

Having discussed education and belief in general terms, the book goes on to look in some detail at one particularly contentious area of the curriculum which is centred on beliefs – Religious Education. The only subject legally required in our schools, Religious Education has gone through a tortuous series of chameleon-like transformations in recent years to make it fit modern thinking and become acceptable in a predominantly secular society. The book discusses what kind of Religious Education is needed for it to make its distinctive and significant contribution to education.

What this involves in practical terms is set out in the third section which seeks to dispel possible criticism that the approach advocated is unworkable. Chapters 15 and 16 are concerned only with primary education but contain much material which middle and secondary school teachers may adapt for older age-groups. Similarly, the two corresponding chapters (17 and 18) on secondary education may furnish primary school teachers with a greater appreciation of how vital their role is in Religious Education.

Brenda Watson
Director of the Farmington
Institute, Oxford

A ON EDUCATION

1 Schools and Values

Education in the West is at a critical point. Many seem to have lost faith in it altogether. Despite vast expenditure, education does not seem to be delivering the goods. Complaints range from low standards in the '3 Rs' to absence of vision and the lack of a sense of responsibility. Universities as well as schools are criticised for failing to expose students to values and turning out 'knowledgeable barbarians', who have no real understanding of their society.

In Britain the point of education is being questioned even within the teaching profession itself, at present in considerable and serious disarray. Low morale among teachers is coupled with the anxious search for new courses, new methods, new approaches to assessment, more relevance, more awareness of the needs of society and increased efficiency. At the same time industry, central government, pressure groups, governors, parents and children continue to protest, in one way or another, about the quality of education.

Is education failing, or has it indeed been tried? Perhaps what commonly passes for education is really something else. What indeed is education?

Values in education

The Chief Education Officer for Oxfordshire, Tim Brighouse, when addressing a recent conference at Westminster College commented: 'The first ingredient of an excellent school, in which relationships are good and learning happens, is a shared value-system.'[1]

He went on to say that such a system enables young people to be comfortable in handling ideas and teasing out prejudices; without this ability people succumb to a mental form of slavery.

A shared value-system gives a sense of direction without which no school can operate efficiently. Shared values encourage vision. In underlining the importance of what the school is about, they help to develop – in all concerned – a proper self-respect.

Yet any consensus as to what such values are, or should be, is increasingly difficult to sustain in a world remarkable for its intermingling of convictions and life-styles. There is no longer any 'gold standard'. Values are widely regarded as purely subjective; the possibility is rejected of there being any absolutes to which people should seek to relate their views and their behaviour. In this situation values logically become an arbitrary matter of agreement between people who happen to be thrown together. Yet the divergence of opinions to be accommodated makes this 'holding-the-ring' exercise ever more problematic.

Awareness of how important and how difficult such questions are seems to be becoming more widespread. Roy Wake (recently Senior HM Staff Inspector for Secondary Education in England and Wales), considers that there is 'a take-off all over the country in the study of values and attitudes in education, and in those held by teachers in responsible positions'.[2] This is very encouraging.

Difficulties in reaching agreement on values

The search for shared values, however, is no light undertaking. In addition to the diversity of views already mentioned there are a number of other considerations.

First, society does not wait for consensus before transmitting values, and neither do schools. They convey values every day, knowingly or unknowingly, both at the more explicit level of what is taught, and at the less openly-acknowledged level of how the school is administered. The latter constitutes a largely hidden agenda which determines, in no small measure, the content of the schooling experience.

Second, schools often convey conflicting sets of values. Figure 1 refers to a school, typical of many, where contradictory signals are given, and neither staff nor students know where they are.

Third, it is often not easy to ascertain what values are being transmitted because of the distinction between what people *say* and what they actually *do*. Paying no more than lip-service to some ideal can be due to laziness, hypocrisy, or lack of understanding, as well as to other factors outside a person's or a school's control. Such lip-service is therefore not infrequent.

Fourth, there is of necessity something of universal significance about the term 'value', even if a subjective view of values is held. We cannot choose values as we choose a coat, or plants for the garden. They are not a matter of mere preference, nor even of what is personally important (in the way that music can mean a lot to some people and football to others). A statement such as 'I value honesty and integrity' implies some kind of obligation laid not only on the speaker but on everyone – irrespective of whether they choose to acknowledge that responsibility or not.

Fifth, in any community there has to be some accommodation of differing points of view. This process of accommodation should not be a compromise, nor be seen as such – still less a matter of expediency. Rather, it should be a conscious choosing of priorities, based on the awareness that not everything

Figure 1   The importance of shared values

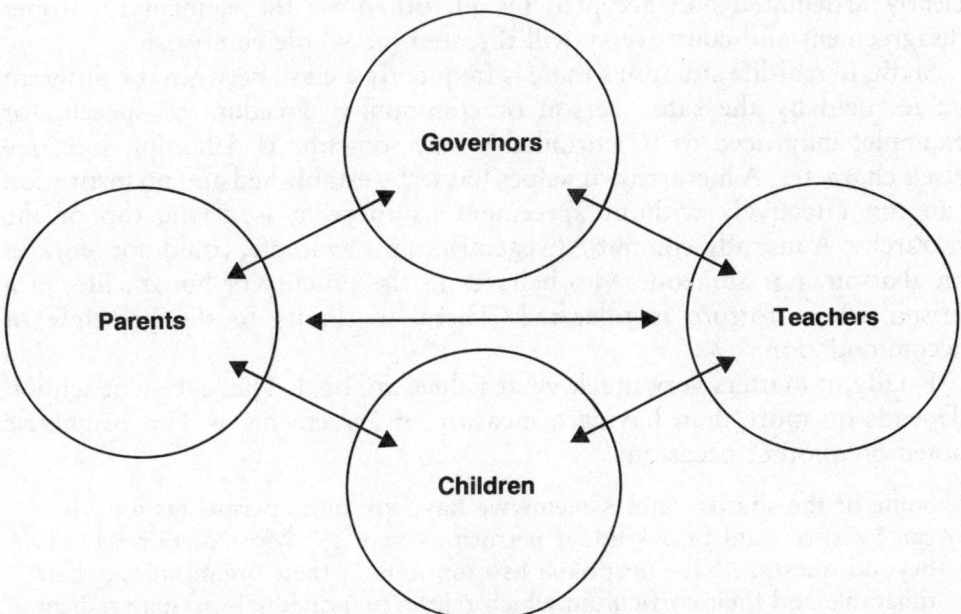

a A school with shared values showing good relationships

b A school (known to the author) without shared values, showing confused communication

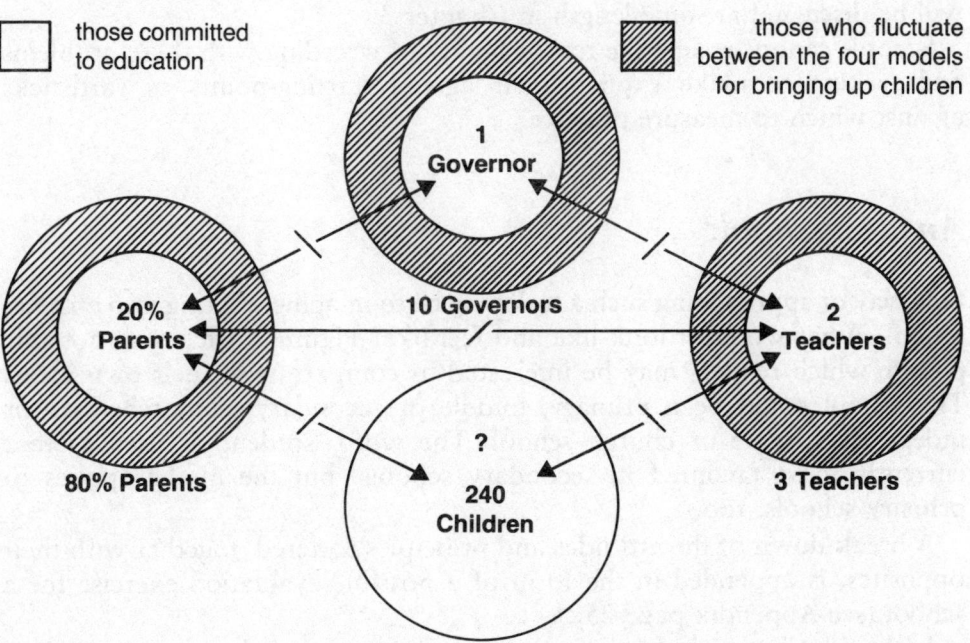

can be done or agreed. Ovid's maxim *Discors concordia* – agreeing to differ – points to a necessary ingredient of being civilised. Yet this is only possible on the basis of some viewpoints being held in common. These need to be clearly articulated and accepted by all, otherwise the element of proper disagreement and controversy will threaten the whole enterprise.

Sixth, in real-life situations there is frequently a clash between the different values held by the same person or community. Freedom of speech, for example, may need to be curtailed where someone is defaming someone else's character. A hierarchy of values has to be established and no institution can run effectively without agreement as to what is at the top of the hierarchy. A morally-committed vegetarian, for example, could not work in an abattoir, nor someone who believes in the sanctity of human life, in a prison where torture is tolerated. There are limits to the principle of accommodation.

Finally, it matters very much what values are held. The 'excellent school' depends on more than having a measure of agreement, as Tim Brighouse noted on another occasion:

> Some of the shared value-systems we have are quite pernicious and they can be successful in a kind of pernicious way ... Most of our schools beyond question have unspoken assumptions in their organisation, their timetable and their curriculum which reinforce individualism, materialism and minimise the need for co-operation.[3]

This is a challenging observation and the question of prevailing assumptions will be discussed at some length in Chapter 3.

Schools cannot escape the responsibility of wrestling with these problems and seeking to make explicit their agreed starting-points as yardsticks against which to measure practice.

An ideal school?

One way of approaching such a task may be to imagine walking into an ideal school. What would it look like and feel like? Figure 2 offers one possible picture which readers may be interested to compare with their own ideas. The school could be a primary, middle or secondary, comprehensive or independent, state or church school. The word 'student' is used as that currently most favoured in secondary schools, but the model applies to primary schools, too.

A break-down of the attitudes and principles fostered, together with their opposites, is appended in the form of a possible evaluation exercise for a school (see Appendix page 252).

In the 'ideal' school, the shared value-system would help to unite staff and students in one common aim. The values would not be constantly talked

Figure 2 An ideal school

Appearance

Visually attractive – evidence of thought in design and use of colour, shape, furnishings, pictures, plants, flowers and display of students' work; well-cared-for impression free of rubbish and clutter; creatively-designed grounds – car parks and cycle-stands well-hidden and areas for people to sit or walk around quietly and for younger children to explore and enjoy

General atmosphere

Lively but without sense of pressure – a place where everyone can find some fulfilment; timetable generously planned so that students and staff have some time each day to pursue their own studies in an atmosphere of learning; emphasis on individuals gaining real understanding not on superficial covering of a lot of ground; all areas of curriculum have high status; competitive element played down and examinations not regarded as be-all-and-end-all; extra-curricular activities highly valued; focus on wider community development.

Integrity

No discrimination against individuals; everyone able to express views; widespread discussion of controversial issues in order to get beyond prejudice and mindless opinions

Staff

Aware of influence of example in dress, speech and general manner – not role-playing but exercising leadership without being dogmatic or pompous; courteous to students and each other and willing to listen; careful in staffroom not to *enjoy* criticising people

Head

Enthusiasm and drive without over-imposing own personality; open to ideas yet prepared to take decisions; creating atmosphere in which everyone feels important and part of running of school; honest and fair avoiding favouritism or victimization; concern for seeing proper respect for the school

Students

Self-disciplined and attentive out of interest or because they understand importance of what they are doing; able to organise much of their own learning themselves; avoidance of sense of failure and under-achieving but also of self-importance and cocksure attitudes; evidence of proper self-respect without need to hide behind false image

Teaching methods

Variety, including some team-teaching; individuality and non-uniformity appreciated because of

Organisation

Minimum of meetings but decision-making people alive to views and reactions because they see to it they

Discipline

Uniform approach throughout school beginning with earliest age-group so that students

awareness that people need to approach education differently and make different claims	have time and skill for informal listening; no undercurrent of bad feeling allowed to develop; opportunity always available to voice grievances and these carefully investigated; good system of communication so that everyone is aware of what is happening	aware they help to create atmosphere; disruptive students treated justly and firmly but with reasoning wherever possible

about or paraded in any obvious way, but they would form the backcloth to everything that happened.

Possible reactions

I suspect that there may be at least three possible reactions to this picture of an ideal school. Some may view it as ludicrous because so far removed from what actually happens and so transparently unattainable. Such ideals do indeed frequently feature in the aims and objectives for courses in schools, colleges and universities. Yet the teacher facing a row of apathetic, gum-chewing, weirdly-dressed, ill-disciplined teenagers in the secondary classroom, or coping with the increasing numbers of primary school children whose behaviour is disruptive and whose span of attention appears minimal, may well laugh at this imaginary projection of what a school could be like. The difficulties are indeed enormous and must not be underestimated. The rhetoric of high-minded educational theory is one thing, the reality is another.

It is, however, the purpose of ideals to act as stars to guide a course. What matters is not their unattainability, but the inspiration and discipline they can give. It can be argued that when the situation is grim, idealism assumes even greater importance as a means of raising people out of their rut. In this sense idealism becomes the only realism. It is also the case that stars are seen best on a dark night, but the eye has to get accustomed to the darkness before being able to appreciate them.

Others may find fault with my ideal school because they prefer an alternative blueprint – perhaps one where streamlined efficiency and preparation for the world of work receive first place, or where particular cultural traditions are inculcated, or where students are sent out with a mission to reform society in a particular way. If pressed far enough, this objection may not simply spring from a difference in emphasis but may be a fundamental attack on the concept of education itself. Discussion of this will form a large part of Chapters 2 and 3, where I examine what is distinctive about education and what is corrosive of it, why the latter is unsatisfactory, and why I regard education as desirable.

A third possible reaction is that expressed to me by Charles Barnham, a Senior Adviser for Secondary Schools who has just retired:

I agree with everything you have written. It describes a situation which many of us in teaching have given our life's work to achieve. . . It has been achieved to some extent in some primary schools, but never, I think, in secondary education. WHY?[4]

Notes and references

1 Tim Brighouse: address given at a Farmington-sponsored conference, Westminster College, March 1985
2 Roy Wake: opening address given to School Curriculum Development Committee Seminar, May 1986 entitled 'Contentious Issues in the Curriculum'.
3 Tim Brighouse, speaking at a meeting on Education in Beliefs and Values, held at Farmington Institute, October 24 1985
4 I am grateful to Charles Barnham for this comment on an earlier draft of this chapter

2 Cross-purposes in Education

One major reason why the educational ideal is so often not achieved is because it is not thoroughly understood or is confused with other views about the purpose of education. Confusion can occur at a basic level because the word 'education' is used in ordinary speech with two quite distinct meanings which are, or should be, related. The first meaning loosely describes what schools, colleges and universities are about. Education in this sense is synonymous with schooling. There is, however, a far deeper meaning, one which is concerned with developing the potential of individuals to become persons in the fullest sense of that word. Schooling can only give impetus to the process, for education can and does happen outside schooling altogether. It is with this second use of the word 'education' that this book is primarily concerned.

Another, more serious, cause of confusion lies in the failure of so much educational provision to educate. It is necessary to make a radical distinction here. So wide is the gap between the two meanings that some people even argue that schooling is contrary to education. Schooling can do great harm when it teaches rigidity, boredom and uniformity; it can kill the natural instincts of curiosity, delight in learning and creativity which are normally present in early childhood.

Could it be that most people who are disappointed and disgruntled with education are really referring to the products of *schooling* rather than rejecting education in our second sense as an ideal? So much schooling is in fact taken up with concerns other than education. We need, therefore, to try to identify and examine these concerns.

Nurture and education

The twentieth century has inherited three ways of bringing up the young which need to be seen as distinct from education. The oldest of these is *nurture*. This is the idea that children are trained by upbringing, as well as by deliberate instruction, to follow in the footsteps of adults. Muslim children, for example, absorb Islam through their environment in the home as well as receiving it by direct teaching. This is an extremely effective method of influencing the young because it works by immersion within a culture, and by example.

Nurture in some sense is inevitable because children are bound to be influenced by the adults in their environment. Deliberate nurture is generally part of what responsible parents and adults do – that is, those who really care for and delight in their children. In the West, however, because of uncertainty concerning culture, beliefs and values, and also considerable break-up in family and social life, the systematic nurture which used to be the norm is becoming rarer.

The relationship between nurture and education is complex and the two concepts should not be equated. Nurture can be the cradle of education, when it is conducted in a way which enables children as they grow to question and reflect upon how they are being brought up. It can, however, be simply another word for conditioning, having the effect of closing doors and producing tunnel vision. It can leave its recipients at the mercy of tradition, fortunate or unfortunate as this may be, unless accompanied by and extended into education. By building on nurture, education must seek to open up vistas beyond nurture.

Nurture of the right kind is of immense value in promoting education. But what do we mean by 'the right kind?'

We need to be *treated* as people before we can begin to develop our potential as people for ourselves. Teachers and psychologists constantly draw attention to the crucial role played by adults in a child's earliest years. A child deprived of love and security is handicapped for life. Systematic nurture, even of an educationally unenlightened kind, can – and usually does – provide this love and security. The child is the subject of attention from adults who care for it and who wish to pass on what they feel is meaningful and important. The child is therefore brought into living conversation with other people, and has a chance to grow in the ability to make relationships. Casual nurture, however, can be damaging; the child may feel neglected, unloved and unable to trust anyone. Such a child, will not easily develop a proper self-respect, and the journey towards becoming at all educated will be a long and arduous one.

Ideally, nurture should be characterised by another feature, namely an interesting and stimulating environment, in which the child has sufficient space and freedom to explore and to begin to make independent assessments and decisions. This is where much systematic nurture fails: it is too narrow, restricting and adult-bound. The child should be able to turn to loving adults, but should also have the freedom to be alone and enjoy discovering with its growing powers of awareness unfettered.

It would not be true to say that education cannot happen unless this right kind of nurture has prepared the ground. Fortunately, later experiences can remedy much of the deficiency, which is why schooling can be crucial. Even one teacher can make an immense difference. Nevertheless the great advantage or disadvantage to education which nurture can give needs to be underlined. Indeed the two features of good nurture outlined above form part of the educator's role as well (see Chapter 6 pp 63ff). The necessary difference between nurture and education is that in the former the focal-point for the adult is bringing the child up in a particular lifestyle, while in education the focal-point is the child's self-fulfilment as a person – a process which may, and usually does, involve criticism and perhaps abandonment of at least part of the nurtured lifestyle.

A *utilitarian approach and education*

A second pattern for bringing up the young, which should not be confused with education, may be termed the *instrumentalist* or *utilitarian* model. Historically this derives from the school of philosophy founded in the late eighteenth century by Jeremy Bentham, but its most usual modern form is rather different. Today the emphasis is on training young people to take their place in the world of work, and in creating prosperity. Society must be run efficiently and people must fulfil appropriate functions. Schools must be judged by their effectiveness in producing competence and a sound pragmatic attitude to life. Material and scientific performance is stressed, together with values conducive to such ends – which include industry, ingenuity and social responsibility. It is sometimes dubbed a philosophy of instant results.

Such an approach chimes in readily with the needs of our technological society, just as its historical forerunner was a response to the Industrial Revolution. This is not as heartless a model as caricaturists would have us believe; the philosophy behind Utilitarianism rates happiness and harmony as the end product. Without a stable society, life is in fact, as the seventeenth-century philosopher Hobbes said: 'nasty, brutish and short'. J S Mill, a leading Utilitarian thinker, believed in education as a means of improving the quality of human life as a whole – including its personal, cultural and aesthetic dimensions. Modern advocates of the philosophy also maintain that people who know where they are, and who contribute effectively to their society, are in fact happy and fulfilled at a personal level. Incompetence, lack of structure and absence of direction are the fertile soil for deep unhappiness.

As a protest against the perennial danger of academic escapism, the utilitarian approach has something valuable to say. The 'ivory-tower' mentality is proverbial. Many, both in schools and in institutions of higher education, pursue (and teach others to pursue) learning as though on some desert island without much sense of responsibility to the people on whom they depend. It is reasonable to suppose that individuals who benefit from what society gives them should contribute to that society. Often they do not, but go off on a whirl of their own.

At a much more mundane level, the problem of motivating students in schools has forced educationalists into talking about 'relevance'. People learn better if they can see the point of what they are supposed to learn, and a clear, down-to-earth, measurable objective seems to fulfil this condition.

There is a grave danger, however, that the instrumentalist or utilitarian approach may be over-stressed. Indeed, it has always been strong behind the scenes; those concerned with learning for learning's sake have had to wrestle with its presence in schools, colleges and universities ever since the great expansion of educational systems in the nineteenth century.

Many recent statements concerning schools have knowingly or unknowingly conveyed ideas far removed from the main concerns of education. An example is the Department of Education and Science document *Curriculum 5–16* issued in January 1984[1]. Despite an appearance of educationally impeccable aims and objectives, the *real* beliefs advocated in that document may be expressed in quite different terms, harsh as it may seem:

- that economics is the key to life;
- that technology can control the future;
- that people matter chiefly in so far as they work;
- that the arts, humanities and religion are to be seen largely as pleasant extras, to be accommodated if there is time;
- that there is either no spiritual side to life or if there is it is unimportant and secondary;
- that in the end there is only matter, money and the industrial machine.

Such an approach is not education. As Roger Scruton tersely commented in an article in *The Times*: 'Education, unlike prosperity, is an end in itself'. He went on to liken education to friendship:

Friendship is unquestioningly profitable. However, you must never value friendship for the profit that it brings. To treat friendship as a means is to lose the capacity for friendship. Your companion is no longer your friend when you begin to weigh him in the balance of advantage. So it is with education; the profit of education persists only so long as you don't pursue it.[2]

Education should indeed be mindful of the needs of society, and of the individual who must live in that society, and it should seek to accommodate immediate as well as more seemingly remote relevance into its curriculum and structures. An artificial divide between the worlds of learning and everyday life has been, and is, pernicious, depriving the one of realism and the other of vision. The challenge of the utilitarian approach may serve as a corrective, restoring a lost balance. But when the utilitarian motive takes over, education cannot be itself and cannot offer its real gifts to the world of work.

Indoctrination and education

A third model for bringing up the young, which must not be confused with education, is that of indoctrination. The word 'indoctrination' presents some problems. Sometimes it has a neutral connotation, being simply another word for teaching. More often, however, it is used to denote something sinister, namely, the process by which certain beliefs and values are stamped upon the mind in such a way that the person concerned will not question them or reflect upon them consciously and freely with the possibility of ceasing adherence to them (see Figure 3).

Figure 3   The difference between Indoctrination and Education

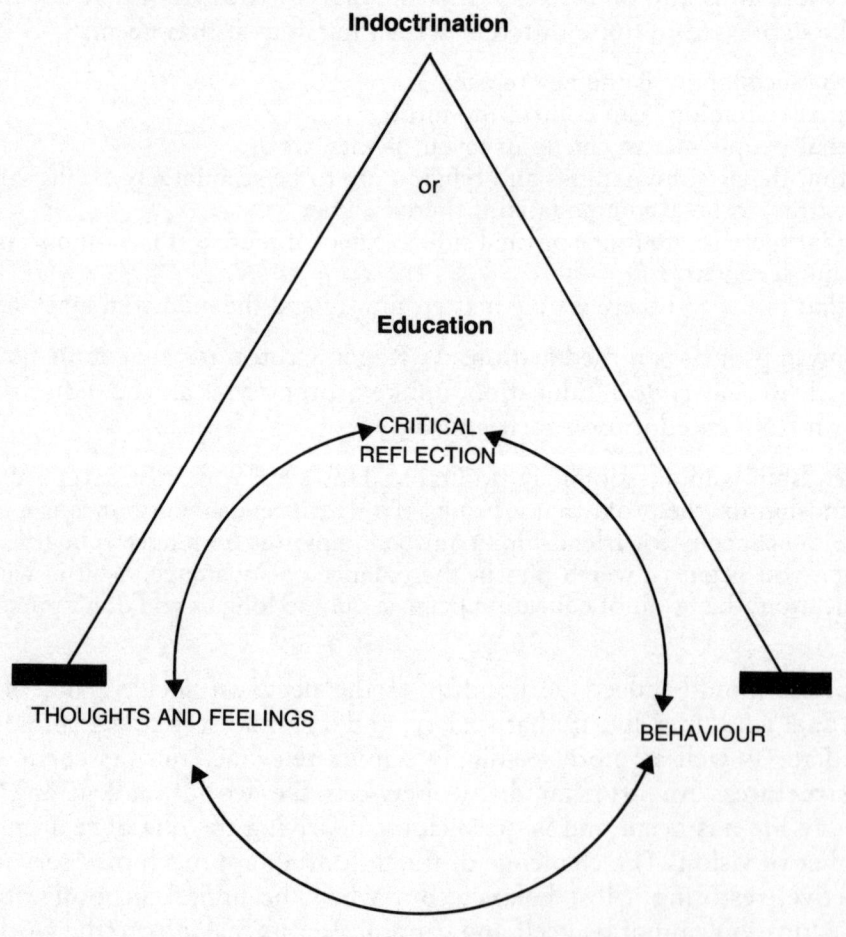

The classic examples of intentional indoctrination in the twentieth century have been in countries dominated by Communism and Nazism, but there has been considerable infiltration of attempted ideological manipulation within other countries too. Concern about this has been voiced, for example, in the recent denunciation of certain developments at the North London Polytechnic, and discussion of the threat behind the whole 'Peace Studies' movement, proponents of which often do not live up to their title in the forcefulness with which they 'push' a particular controversial position.[3]

There is a further difficulty with defining 'indoctrination'. Some people insist that the word implies a deliberate intention to indoctrinate; others see at its centre 'the closed minds and restricted sympathies' which are produced, whether intentionally or not. In this book the word will be used in this latter sense, on the grounds that the undesirable effect is what matters, and if 'indoctrination' were not used to express this idea then another word would have to be invented.

Indoctrination is the opposite of education because, whether deliberately or not, such teaching bypasses the autonomy of the individual. A person is inwardly taken over, and their thought and behaviour programmed according to the particular viewpoints, or ideology, favoured by the communicator. Indoctrination works by sending the mind effectively to sleep, so that what is impressed upon it is soaked up as by blotting paper. As such, it is important to note that even reasons for a given idea can be indoctrinated.

Indoctrination is closely linked to a narrow concept of nurture akin to conditioning, but it relates directly to the beliefs and values conveyed to an individual, whereas conditioning is more indirect. Conditioning is however a powerful way of indoctrinating by omission: reinforcing desired attitudes without encouraging thought about the validity of reasons for those attitudes, and excluding from the environment anything that might provoke thought.

This particular point about indoctrination deserves more prominence than it is usually given. Indoctrination operates most efficiently when there is a failure to draw attention to other ideas and other areas of experience. What is presented therefore tends to be seen as comprehensive and complete in itself without the need to consider other possibilities. The indoctrinated person is completely unaware of the validity of genuine questioning and reflectiveness.

Hence indoctrination is often a by-product even of the right kind of nurture (see above pp 8ff). If nurture is conducted without due regard and sensitivity to the awakening maturity of the child as a person in his or her own right, then it has a claustrophobic effect upon the child's development. Many 'good' parents and teachers, who think that they are doing their best for their children, are perplexed by the fierceness of the rebellion on their hands. This is usually a sign that well-meaning nurture or teaching has become unintentionally and subtly indoctrinatory. As the recipient becomes aware of this, he or she struggles to break free.

Similarly, it is chiefly through omission of other considerations that the utilitarian model can become a form of indoctrination. An almost exclusive concern with the 'nuts and bolts' of existence can so powerfully distract people that they never reflect upon wider issues. Nevertheless it may also be true that behind the appeal to the utilitarian model there lurks a more deliberate threat to education. Mary Warnock, for example, warns that 'the new Philistinism may be seen as an ideology which may appear to regard education as a tool for a particular use just as blatantly as does the 'indoctrination' of Marxists'.[4] Whether this is the case or not, the hallmark of a true educator's approach is to resist making education a tool for anything external to itself – although inevitably it will have consequences, for good or ill.

What is education?

Education, unlike the other three ways of bringing up the young which we have looked at, centres upon enabling the human personality – in freedom – to gain knowledge and enlightenment as something worthwhile in itself. The benefit to society is seen as an off-shoot, which will come about through such individuals being balanced people whose presence and self-chosen involvement will help to create a healthy society.

Education is therefore about helping people to think and act responsibly for themselves, and to find self-fulfilment and a quality of life appropriate to their own particular gifts, opportunities and insights. It is about promoting personhood.

Being a person involves a five-fold attitude of respect: for oneself, for other people, for the environment, for beauty and for truth. Together these form a creative circle. They may be seen as corresponding to the classical ideals of justice, beauty and truth, allied to the ancient maxim 'know thyself'.

Here, the word 'respect' has a basic meaning of 'looking at' or 'paying attention to' something, and a further meaning of 'esteeming, honouring, valuing' something. Respect is the opposite of indifference and contempt. The five-fold nature of this 'respect' draws attention to the need for balance. Thus respect for oneself does not involve ultimate devotion to oneself; such respect would be inordinate because it would exclude other aspects of reality. There needs to be a quality of all-roundedness, whereby over-attention to one aspect is corrected by being mindful of another. Exclusive attention for any one concern can lead to dangerous obsession.

Many people regard respect for a person *as* a person as axiomatic, yet this view can be challenged. The importance of affirming oneself and other people will form the subject of considerable discussion in Chapters 3 and 5.

The question of the justification of values of any kind is raised in Chapter 7 on pp 75ff.[5]

Respect for the environment is not simply a new insight of the 1980s. It relates to the fact that people are part of the world of nature, a world which has its own autonomy, and that they influence one another powerfully through the atmosphere they create.

The word 'beauty' suggests a heightened awareness, and delight in qualities such as shape, proportion and colour which the environment – natural or manufactured – can display. Quite apart from the vexed question as to whether beauty is 'in the eye of the beholder' or whether it has objective reality, the appreciation of beauty has been one of the hallmarks of every civilisation.

Finally respect for truth is fundamental. Without it there can be no respect for the self that one really is, for other people as they are, or for the world which happens to be in existence. Even awareness of beauty is, for most writers, artists and musicians, in a deep sense linked to awareness of how things actually are. Chesterton once expressed it like this:

> I do not think there is anyone who takes quite such a fierce pleasure in things being themselves as I do. The startling wetness of water excites and intoxicates me; the fieriness of fire, the steeliness of steel, the unutterable muddiness of mud . . . [6]

The pursuit of knowledge – understood as the opposite of ignorance, blindness and delusion – is central to education and to being a person. It follows that a lack of emphasis on the search for truth is a serious omission. Yet this has been an unfortunate feature of much educational thinking in recent years, which has concentrated on relevance, meaning and description rather than truth (see Chapter 3 pp 27–29 for a fuller treatment of this issue).

A person who genuinely pursues the five-fold attitude of respect will tend to develop certain traits of personality. There are many ways in which these can be summarised, as any search for shared values will show. In a nutshell, it can perhaps be expressed like this: such a person will have a quality of openness, characterised by delight, perceptiveness, integrity and a concern for fairness for all.

Openness is a tricky concept, which will be discussed at some length in Chapter 4 – particularly the kind of openness which is properly educational. It includes openness to evidence, to further possibilities, and to new areas of experience; it can lead to an attitude of critical affirmation (see Chapter 5). *Integrity* is concerned with developing a self-assurance which is honest and realistic, it enables the individual to see the importance of being someone, as well as of doing things and acting roles. *Fairness* relates to the search for justice, kindness, generosity, and a spirit of cooperation. *Perceptiveness* includes imagination, awareness, the ability to see relationships, appreciation of beauty, and acknowledgement of insights. It should be penetrating, giving a person the capacity to see behind false impressions or deception. *Delight* is of great importance as a major motivating factor in undertaking self-education. It is generated by attentiveness and shows itself in a heightened sense of wonder, and often in a capacity for humour (see Figure 4).

Figure 4 The educated person

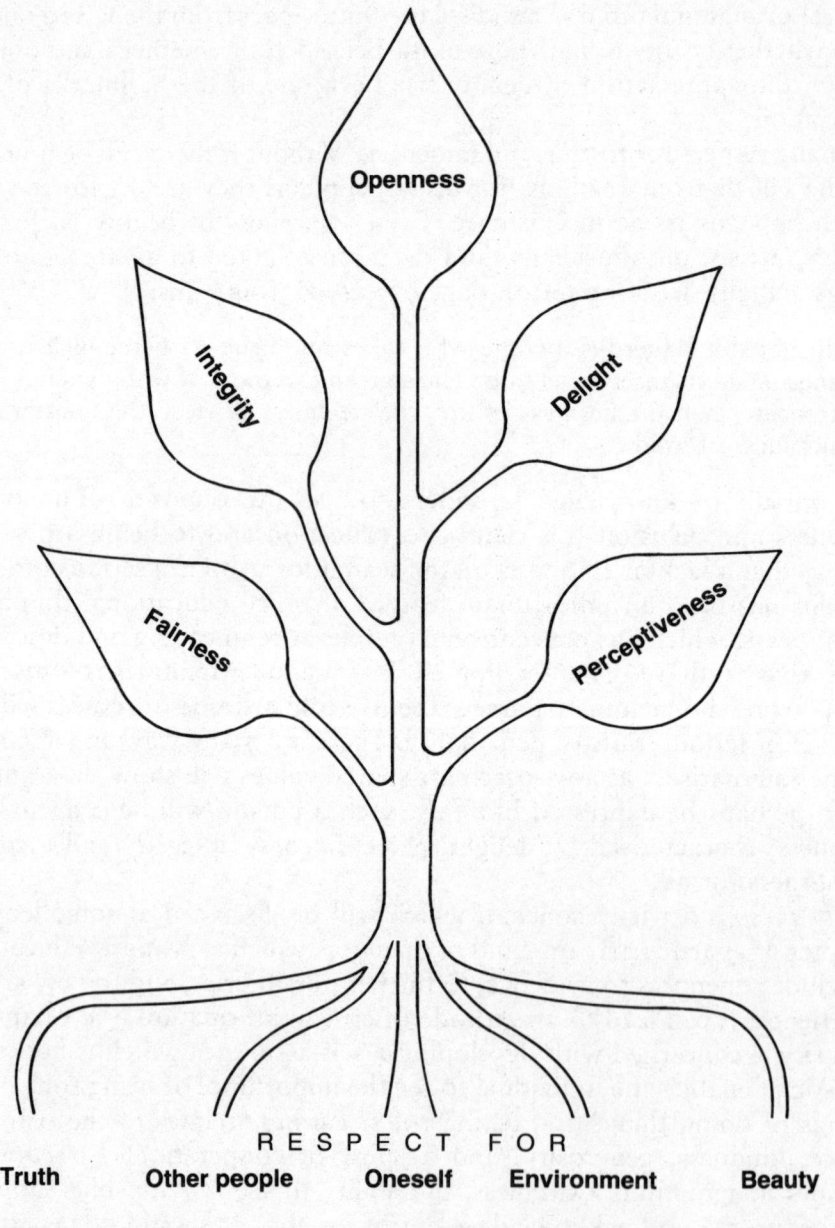

The need for clarity

The understanding of education outlined above needs to be expressed in a positive way which clearly acknowledges the beliefs and values on which it is based. In a half-understood form it can do great damage. So much attempted education fails because those called upon to implement it do not thoroughly appreciate the nature of the educational goal and the appropriate way to it. Education often deteriorates into a vague do-it-yourself approach, where young children and older students seem to be left to their own devices. Such an approach is a gross travesty of the educational ideal. It is also unrealistic. In the vacuum created by such inadequate notions, even though the rhetoric of fully educational aims and objectives may be retained, recourse is often had, in practice, to the other models for bringing up the young.

Our educational institutions reflect a number of attitudes: there is usually some attempt at education, mixed with some nurturing in consciously traditional beliefs and values, with here and there some deliberate indoctrination by enthusiastic individuals – especially in those subjects which most lend themselves to it. But the framework, especially in secondary schools, is largely governed by administrative convenience, over-specialisation, fragmentation, competitiveness, examination-orientation and an impersonal atmosphere. This all serves to impose a largely unintentional form of indoctrination into a utilitarian approach to life – despite noble efforts to overcome the worst effects of these systems in the interests of real education.

'Liberal' education

The term 'liberal' is often applied to the view of education argued for in this chapter. It is usually contrasted with interpretations of the purpose of schooling which can be labelled 'conservative' or 'radical' and which may or may not have political overtones.

Some people look to education to ensure the stability of society in a world of uncertainty and change; they emphasise the importance of maintaining traditional standards. Others see education as an instrument for reforming society in the interests of justice and freedom; they pay great attention to the inadequacies of the *status quo* and the need for courage in working towards change. For others, however, the central consideration is that education is a valid end in itself, quite apart from its possible benefits to society. They hold that the freedom of the individual to be a person who is not manipulated or conditioned by external forces is crucial, and must be safeguarded by the manner in which schooling is conducted.

Although in their extreme form the conservative and radical views are incompatible with the liberal, the distinctions are not as absolute as they are sometimes made out to be. There is much overlap between the positions, as Figure 5 shows. It is often just a question of emphasis. Many of those who argue for initiating the young into a heritage see this as acting through the freedom of the child, and indeed supplying the means by which the child's freedom can be served. They do not want indoctrinated people but people who have real understanding and self-chosen commitment to those values which support liberal education.

Figure 5 Why education?

Three views of the purpose of education

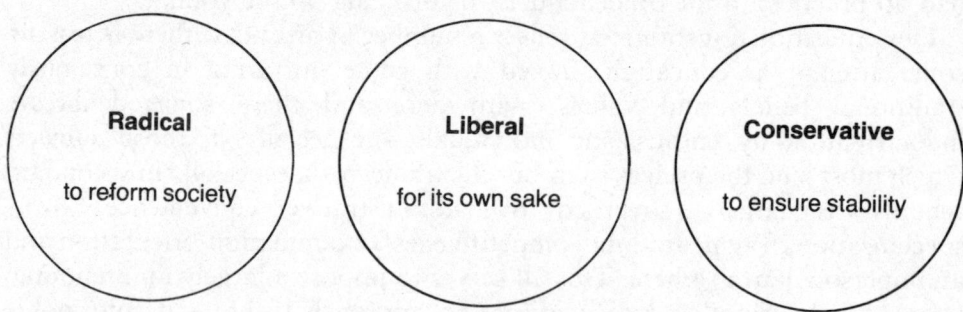

The three views can overlap

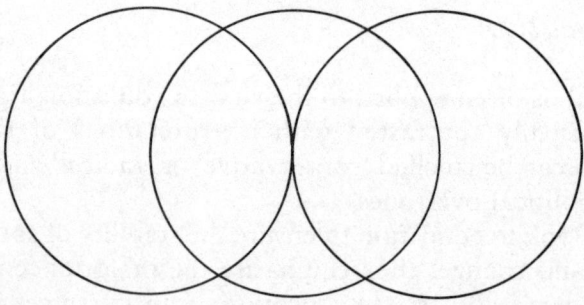

If people truly experience education for its own sake they will be better able to be responsible members of society, to uphold what is positive and challenge what is negative.

Reform of society needs to be organic, building on the best in what is inherited.

Keeping the tradition alive means being prepared to be as creative as were those who formed the tradition.

An example

On what grounds should a child's freedom be curtailed?

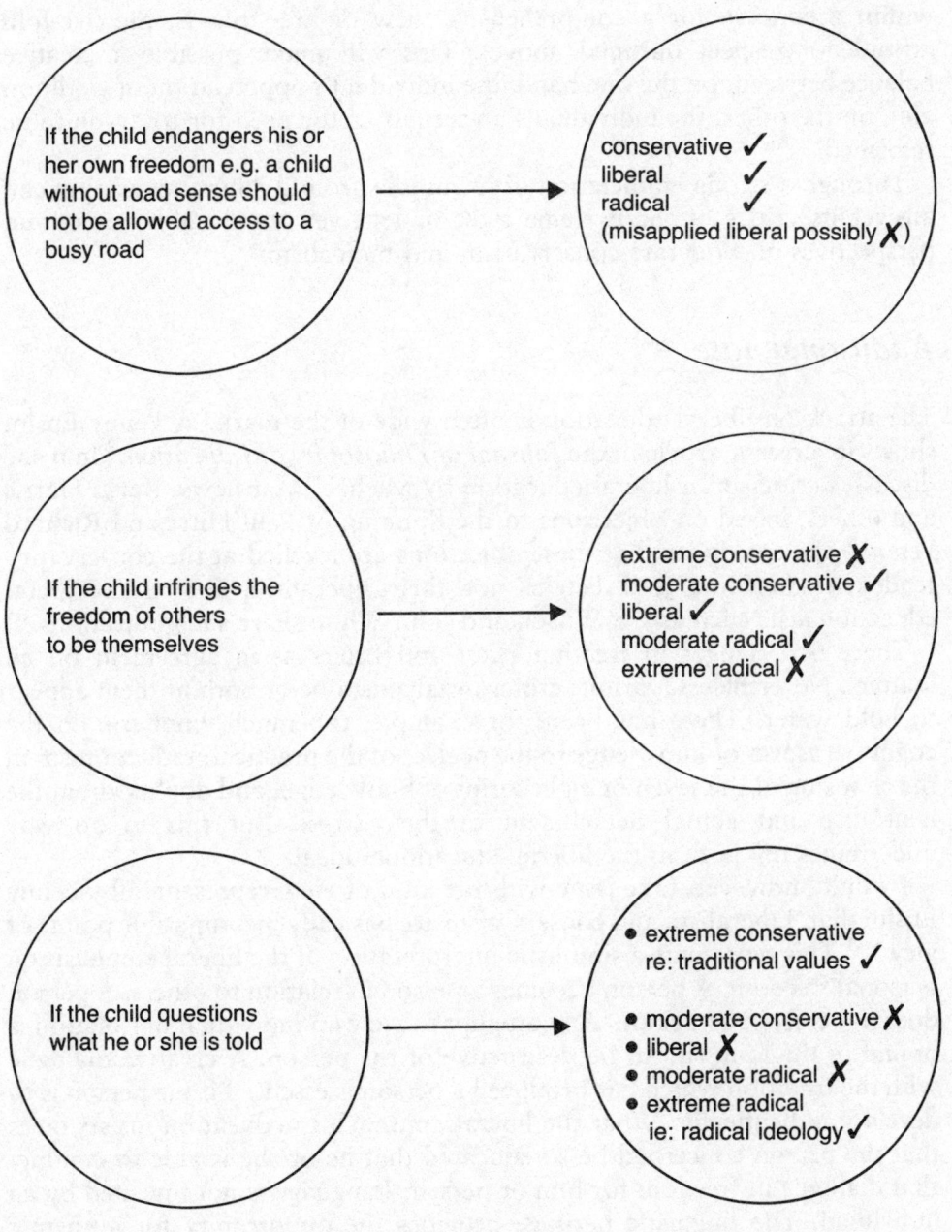

Similarly, those who adopt the radical position are deeply concerned about people's freedom, and seek to eradicate any infringement of this freedom. The radical approach becomes involved in a logical inconsistency if it advocates that any human being should be taken over for an end outside him or herself. It has therefore a professional interest in supporting one of the main tenets of liberal education – the freedom of the child.

My view is that education should stress the freedom of the individual within a concern for a comprehensive view of life (that is, the five-fold attitude of respect outlined above). This will make possible a creative balance between, on the one hand, the individual's appreciation of tradition and, on the other, the individual's awareness of the need for tradition to be reformed.

Through a strong enunciation of its middle ground, liberal education can answer its critics of the extreme right or left, yet remain able to contain perspectives of moderate conservatism and radicalism.[7]

Additional note

The attack on liberal education is often wide of the mark, as Penny Enslin shows in a recent article in the *Journal of Philosophy of Education*.[8] In it she discusses criticism of liberal education by Michael Matthews, Kevin Harris and others, based on objections to the thinking of Paul Hirst and Richard Peters.[9] She concludes that these objections are levelled at the conservative tendencies in Hirst and Peters, not their liberalism, for many liberal educationalists such as P S Wilson and John White share such objections.[10]

There is a danger in treating Hirst and Peters as in agreement on all matters. Nevertheless, various criticisms against one or both of them appear to hold water. There has been, for example, too much emphasis on the cognitive aspect of knowledge to the neglect of the practical; reductionism in the choosing of the seven or eight forms of knowledge; and doubts about the neutrality and actual detachment of their work. But this in no way undermines my faith in the liberal educational ideal.

I would, however, take issue with the kind of view represented by Penny Enslin that 'Liberalism and conservatism are basically incompatible points of view'.[11] This represents a simplistic interpretation of the liberal emphasis on personal freedom. A person becomes a person in relation to others. A person does not exist in a vacuum. Any attempt to view an individual in isolation is bound in the long run to be destructive of the person. A creative dialogue with the tradition which has produced a person is essential if the person is to develop authentically. What the liberal approach to education insists on is that the person concerned be so educated that he or she is able to conduct that dialogue in freedom for him or herself. Language is not invented by an individual. The linguistic heritage provides the opportunity for authentic dialogue and the essential context in which it can take place. I believe that Hirst and Peters did not make this relationship sufficiently clear.

Again, I would want to argue that the relationship between radical and liberal views is not as exclusive as it is often portrayed to be. Radicalism is concerned with freedom. If enthusiasm, anger, or blinkered vision overrides such considerations radicalism is being selective with regard to whose freedom it supports. Logically, it should offer reasons for such discrimination. But these reasons will relate to alleged infringement of freedom experienced by those involved, and so we are back to a central concern of the liberal educationalist.

Change, to be just and enduring, needs to be organically related to what has gone before. Inaction and apathetic non-involvement in the effort towards establishing justice for all represents the absence of liberal education in any real form.

Notes and references

1 *The Organisation of the 5–16 Curriculum, A Note by the Department of Education and Science and Welsh Office* September 1984.
2 Roger Scruton, article in *The Times* 12 June 1985.
3 See, for example, Keith Jacka, Caroline Cox and John Marks *Rape of Reason: The Corruption of the Polytechnic of North London* (Churchill Press, 1975); also Caroline Cox and Roger Scruton *Peace Studies: A Critical Survey* (Institute for European Defence and Strategic Studies, 1984).
4 Mary Warnock, article in the *Times Educational Supplement* 7 June 1985.
5 A close study of the philosophical base for such respect and what it means may be found in *Respect for Persons* by R S Downie and Elizabeth Telfer (Allen and Unwin, 1969). The authors argue that morality characterised in terms of respect for persons must be regarded as objective because of at least three factors: its rationality, moral disagreement and moral seriousness (pp 120–2 especially).
6 I am indebted to Charles Barnham for this quotation.
7 There is a useful article on 'Manipulation in Teaching' by Vance Kasten in *Journal of Philosophy of Education* Vol 14, No 1, 1980.
8 Penny Enslin 'Are Hirst and Peters *Liberal* Philosophers of Education?' *JPE* Vol 19, No 2, 1985, pp 211–22.
9 For example, P Hirst and R S Peters *The Logic of Education* (Routledge and Kegan Paul, 1970); M Matthews *The Marxist Theory of Schooling* (Routledge and Kegan Paul, 1980); K Harris *Education and Knowledge* (Routledge and Kegan Paul, 1979).
10 P S Wilson *Interest and Discipline in Education* (Routledge and Kegan Paul, 1979); J White *Towards a Compulsory Curriculum* (Routledge and Kegan Paul, 1973).
11 Enslin *Op cit* p 219.

3 Assumptions, Valid and Invalid

Confusion as to the purpose of schooling is made more serious by the pervasiveness in our society of certain assumptions which are barely acknowledged and therefore largely unexamined. Many of these assumptions are hostile to education. They operate against the possibility of such an ideal school as was depicted in Chapter 1. In this chapter I will look at some of these assumptions, why they inhibit education and how they can be challenged.

Assumptions and indoctrination

An assumption is 'what is taken for granted', the starting point for discussion. All human beings, in their everyday living, take certain things for granted as the basis for their opinions and their constant and necessary decision-making. It is impossible not to make assumptions.

An assumption may be valid or invalid. It is valid if it happens to correspond to reality or the way things actually are. It is invalid if it does not. If someone, for example, assumes that the world is flat they are mistaken – and any decisions made on the basis of that assumption are misguided.

When an assumption is recognised by other people as being important and worthy of being either supported or rejected it is often summed up in a word ending with '–ism'. Thus when a dominant nation assumes it is superior to others and has the right to dictate what is good for them, the assumption can be called *imperialism*. Or if people assume that other people are inferior to them on the sole ground of their being of another race or the other sex, it is called *racism* or *sexism*, respectively.

Our society is gradually becoming aware of the dangers of these assumptions and of others such as totalitarianism and élitism, and is making a great effort to eradicate them. Other assumptions, however, which in their different ways are just as damaging and untrue, go largely undetected or, even if acknowledged, are not seriously challenged with regard to their validity.

It is with regard to these unacknowledged assumptions that words like indoctrination and conditioning should properly be used. An indoctrinated person is one who just does not consider any other possibility. An educated person, on the other hand, is one who has thought about, and continues from time to time to think about, the assumptions upon which he or she habitually argues and acts. An educated person is prepared to modify or abandon such assumptions if evidence suggests this to be appropriate. An indoctrinated person will not consider as evidence anything which runs counter to his or her indoctrinated convictions and therefore will be unable to change them.

Frequently concealed assumptions

The following example may perhaps serve to help readers identify their own particular assumptions.

Some years ago a housewife in Balham named Rosemary Brown began producing music which she said had been given to her by Liszt and other great composers now dead. She said, and still says, that they appear to her from time to time and dictate compositions. Writing these down is laborious work for her because she is not in any sense a trained musician. She also claims that Einstein, Bertrand Russell and others have communicated statements to her.[1]

The attitude of large numbers of people to this has been one of frank incredulity. Such people dismiss the matter, asserting: 'Of course she must be deluded; things like this cannot happen.' This scepticism, however, is selective. It does not apply to *all* unusual experiences; only to some. If, for example, Rosemary Brown had been the first woman astronaut in space and reported seeing some highly unusual objects, the same people would be more likely to listen carefully to what she had to say. They would be less sceptical because she was engaged on a scientific enterprise and reported experience amenable, to some degree, to scientific testing.

This indicates the nature of bias in the common kind of scepticism practised today. An elaborated version of the initial sceptical comment on Rosemary Brown's experience might run 'What she says goes against common sense and scientific knowledge, therefore she's obviously mistaken.'

This reliance on scientific method relates, in its academic form, to the philosophical attitude known as positivism. According to this view, knowledge which is trustworthy is that reached by logical proof or scientifically acceptable demonstration of evidence. The positivist stance is one of the long-term products of the so-called Age of Enlightenment in the eighteenth century, with its emphasis on the efficacy of reason, coupled as it has been with the tremendous expansion of the sciences since the seventeenth century. Its most explicit expression has been in the positivist school of philosophy which grew up in Vienna in the mid-1930s and made an impact in Britain through the work of A J Ayer and others. Although in its most extreme form it is largely discredited in intellectual circles, in a diluted fashion it is still powerful, and seen as embodying the temper of the times.[2]

The presence of positivist-scepticism has the effect of consigning every-thing which is not capable of being proved in some empirical or scientific way to the realm of subjective opinion. Many people hearing Rosemary Brown's story are inclined to say: 'How interesting; it may be true but of course we cannot know. It's just one person's opinion against another. Such matters lie outside the scope of scientific investigation and therefore all we can be sure of is that they are meaningful to the people concerned.'

According to this view Rosemary Brown's experience is not automatically written off, and the possibility of its being true is not ruled out, but there is no hope that anyone can ever know. The phenomenon is just interesting in itself and the truth-question of 'did it happen?' can be dismissed because there is no way of finding out and no evidence to be taken into account.

Such reasoning is relativist and develops along these lines: saying that I know does not mean that I *do* know. What a person believes is related to the circumstances of his or her upbringing; it is unintentional conditioning. Someone brought up in one milieu may speak about the plight of the proletariat and the ideal Communist society; another may speak about submission to Allah and reverence for the Qur'an because he or she has been brought up in that setting. If the little Muslim had been born and brought up in a Communist family he or she would have been different, and vice versa. Relativism is a way of handling the diversity of views which people hold on matters not amenable to straight scientific investigation, and matters which are therefore beyond demonstration. Everyone has a right to his or her opinion and as no-one can prove they are right, however subjectively certain they feel, all opinions sincerely held by people are of equal validity and deserve an equal hearing. So the relativist sees it.

Some people, while adopting a sceptical attitude towards Rosemary Brown's disclosure, do not just deny it, or regard it as interesting but automatically inconclusive; they re-interpret it. They find alternative ways of describing it with which they can agree, such as 'It's all in the mind. Psychology and a fuller understanding of telepathic phenomena will explain it.'

This attitude can be termed 'reductionist' – it has the effect of 'reducing' accounts of people's experience to just what can be studied in an apparently objective scientific way. Hence it not infrequently leaves out altogether what is at the heart of the experience, without making clear that it is doing so – it pretends to give an adequate explanation when in fact the most important aspect has been ignored or explained away.

Like scepticism, reductionism is selective. It operates in one direction. People, for example, are not usually 'reduced' to the spiritual aspect of their personalities, ignoring the physical; psychic phenomena are not 'reduced' to a supernatural dimension, leaving out of consideration altogether any possible empirical data. A visitor from another culture or time (from, for example, the medieval period in Western civilisation) might well take for granted that a spiritual explanation of Rosemary Brown's experience was adequate and see no need to search for further reasons in the context of this fleeting and ambiguous world. This would be reductionism of an opposite kind.

The responses described so far reflect the prevalence of the four kinds of assumptions which support, and are encouraged by, a particular kind of lifestyle (see Figure 6). The materialist, consumerist, competitive, 'busy' aspects of Western civilisation are more widely acknowledged than the 'intellectualisms', (even though they are not seriously challenged by those caught in their web) and have been highlighted by closer contact with other cultures and ways of life.

There is increasing awareness that such a lifestyle is unsatisfactory and does not develop people's potential as persons. Views such as 'There is more to life than matter', 'Money isn't everything', 'Co-operation is more important than competition' and 'People need time to be still' are beginning to redress the balance, but only slowly, because our society as a whole still gives priority to the assumptions associated with materialism. Daily living along such lines serves to reinforce the intellectual apologia for the lifestyle. If people spend almost all their time and energies on getting money, keeping up with the Joneses and pursuing chores and pleasures, they will tend to think that this is what life is about. Given such assumptions, Rosemary Brown can be no more than an entertaining diversion, irrelevant to the real world.

The damage to education

If thought of in terms of a five-fold attitude of respect – for self, other people, the environment, beauty and truth – education rests on a different set of assumptions altogether. Those commonly accepted today have a claustrophobic and inhibiting effect on the whole educational scene, both as to what is taught and as to how education is organised.

Nevertheless, there *is* something valuable and right in these assumptions. Scepticism draws attention to the place of doubt in thinking; positivism to the achievements of scientific method; relativism to the importance of context in the development of people and the views they hold; and reductionism to the need to isolate factors in order to arrive at factual knowledge. They become harmful only when they join together to offer a complete approach to life.

a) Scepticism
Scepticism is only a part, and often not the most important part, of education in its ideal sense, for 'respect' has as much or more to do with affirmation. In place of scepticism a phrase such as *critical affirmation* would be better (see

Figure 6 Frequently concealed assumptions

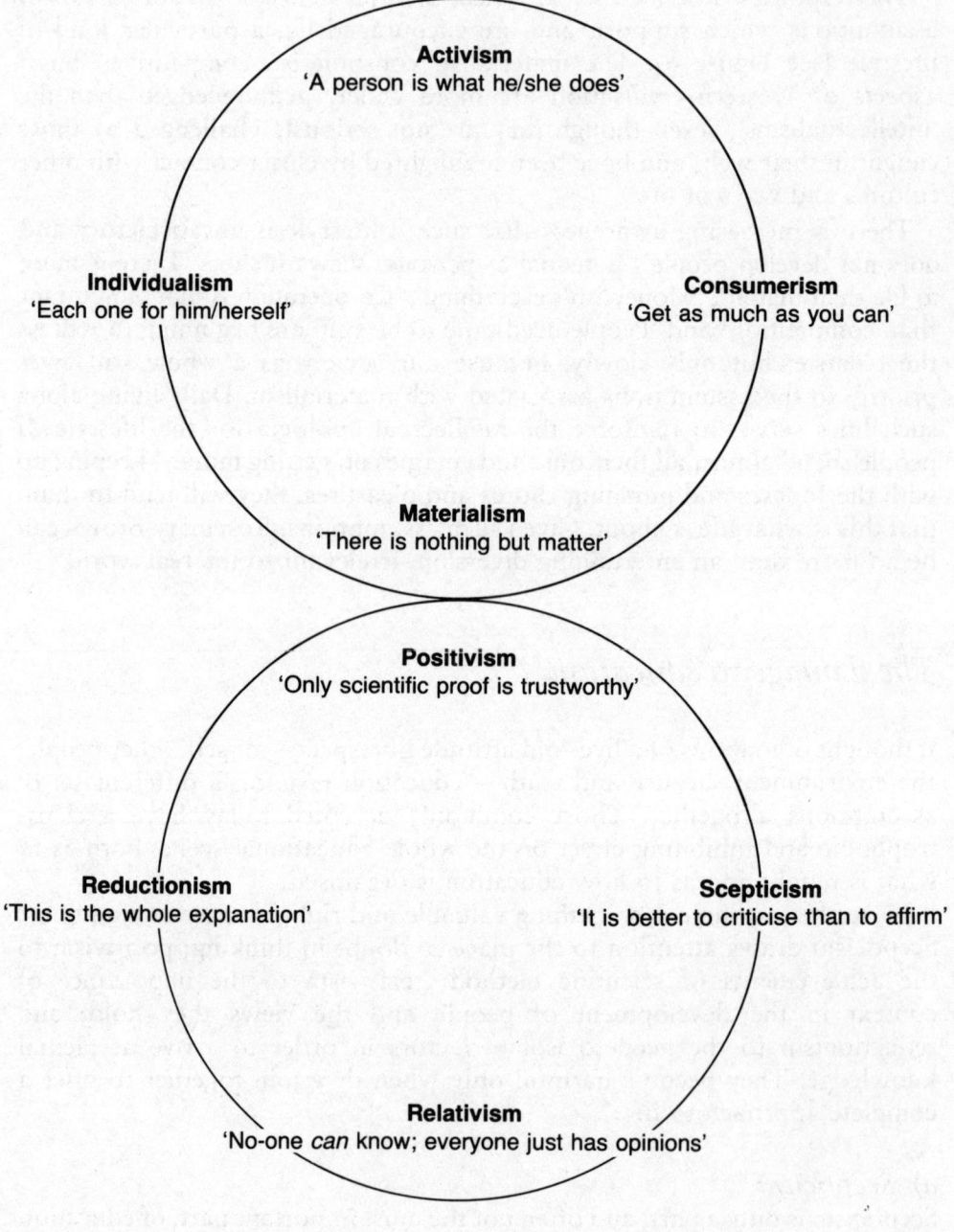

Activism
'A person is what he/she does'

Individualism
'Each one for him/herself'

Consumerism
'Get as much as you can'

Materialism
'There is nothing but matter'

Positivism
'Only scientific proof is trustworthy'

Reductionism
'This is the whole explanation'

Scepticism
'It is better to criticise than to affirm'

Relativism
'No-one *can* know; everyone just has opinions'

Chapter 5). Yet frequently the impression given in schools, colleges and universities is that the ability to doubt is the highest academic achievement. Subjects like history are frequently proclaimed to be a training in doubt. Respect does not preclude criticism, but it cannot survive in an atmosphere of radical doubt.

b) Positivism

Positivism points to part of what is valuable in education. Scientific method and concern for what objectively is, quite apart from any subjective imagining, is important not only in the sciences but in many other areas as well. Yet if this poses as the sole reliable method of arriving at knowledge it is deeply destructive of other ways of knowing. One of the most fundamental assumptions behind education is the importance of people as people. Positivism, however, acts against the possibility of taking people seriously as centres of experience.

Positivism is therefore reductionist with regard to the humanities and arts. It is also hypocritical with regard to sciences, as is being increasingly acknowledged. It is impossible to take out of science a certain subjectivity. Selection of hypotheses and method of experiment, and interpretation of results, are but two of the non-objective factors influencing science. Certainty in mathematics is also debatable. As long ago as 1901 Bertrand Russell made the point that change and revision were needed:

> Macaulay, contrasting the certainty of mathematics with the uncertainty of philosophy, asks in 1840 whoever heard of a reaction against Taylor's theorem? If he had lived now, he himself might have heard of such a reaction, for this is precisely one of the theorems which modern investigations have overthrown.[3]

Modern quantum physics, for example, powerfully reinforces this point.[4] Yet still positivism reigns supreme in much science and mathematics teaching in schools and colleges.

c) Relativism

Relativism underlines the importance of context in the development of people and the views they hold. As such it contains valuable insight. Yet it does so at a price, the price of taking seriously the search for truth. This is another of the fundamental assumptions necessary to proceed with education.

Truth-claims are frequently ignored in education at every level. Attention is constantly drawn to what people say or believe, and quotations are in vogue, but the validity of what is thought is given little attention except where scientific method is appropriate. This is especially serious with regard to controversial isssues, many of which are extremely important in considering all five aspects of the attitude of respect.

In a recent document on how to handle controversial subjects in class, Social Science and History inspectors stated:

> It can be very helpful for pupils to know their teachers' views, providing these are offered as *one among many possible perspectives* on an issue with no more weight or 'truth' than any other.[5]

It is probable that the inspectors wrote this, and underlined the key-phrase, against a background of situations where teachers used their authority in such a way that students would not take account of other divergent views. If, however, *this* kind of context for the advice is forgotten, or not appreciated, their words may easily be interpreted as appealing to the view that no-one *can* know and that degrees of significance need not be attached to statements.

This relativist assumption is extremely pervasive and subtly damaging to education; it inhibits any in-depth discussion of the values necessary to education by assuming from the start that they are subjective and just a matter of consensus.

This point is so important that a longer discussion may he helpful, in the light of the concern expressed in Chapter 1 about the desirability of shared values. Often the attempt to get to grips with the question of what values are educationally valid is vitiated by the relativist assumption. This is well illustrated by reference to the editorial in the first number of *Values* a new journal devoted precisely to the question of values.[6]

The editorial is impeccable in its commitment to educational ideals. It is a plea for clarity, understanding, self-knowledge, and awareness of the power of implicit values and of the difference between what people say and what they do. Attention is drawn to the skills of being able to cope with situations in which values conflict. The undesirability of being programmed into a value-system and the importance of being able to make decisions for oneself is stressed.

There is also an assumption, however, that values are what people cherish, and nothing more. They can have no objective referent. There is no hint that values might be anything other than what a person chooses to choose. Values are just subjective. Because the question of whether what people value is what they *ought* to value never surfaces, the view of reality underlying the approach is one of relativism, assuming that we can only have opinions and not in any sense knowledge. It implies, in other words, that all opinions are of equal value. This is individualism in that what the individual *thinks* matters is all that does matter, and also reductionism in that all statements concerning 'I ought' or 'You ought' can be reduced to the level of psychology (it being decided in advance that any sense of moral imperative is subjective). In essence, therefore, such an approach does not take seriously what any of the great religious or philosophical systems of value have had to say.

The net result of the views put forward in the editorial is that a young hooligan or racist could accept the proposed course of study and from it find grounds to reinforce and more successfully practise his or her own values of selfish aggression, manipulation and debasement of others.

The tenor of articles in the rest of the journal suggests that this is not what the editors had in mind. In fact another assumption is operating, namely, that people can respond properly to 'fairness' through the exercise of reason: 'It is obvious we must be fair to each other because otherwise society will fall apart, and besides other people are like us, people. We matter, so they matter'.

Yet one can imagine a young Hitler undergoing such a course in values education and receiving little to make him think further than this: 'Why do other people matter if I can ensure that their disapproval doesn't damage me? That is, if I am stronger than them? And *why* shouldn't this society fall apart if I can create a better one in which I am boss and do what I like? And if I can set this up by using the weakness, vagueness and illogicality of the 'nice' people in my present society, so be it. Their sense of the importance of being fair to me will be my ladder to the success of my own intentions: and when I've got where I want I can kick them away.'

Discussion or teaching based on relativism is dangerous in its naïvety. Schools must look deeper; they must, in fact, challenge the assumption. If everything is relative, and any opinion is as good as another regardless of considerations of evidence, logical consistency, comprehensiveness, or experience, then the basis for civilisation is destroyed. What will inevitably happen is that the one who shouts loudest and longest will prevail.

Nature abhors a vacuum. Action and lifestyle depend upon underlying values, principles, or convictions, strong or weak, acknowledged or not acknowledged, known or hidden, chosen or conditioned. If people do not think these out properly for themselves, they will be swept along by whatever is most forceful in their environment.

d) Reductionism

Reductionism points to the need to isolate factors in order to arrive at factual knowledge. This is of only temporary use in coming to understand reality. To analyse, clarify and distinguish one thing from another is part of the process of learning to understand. This part should never, however, masquerade as the whole. The links between disciplines are as important as, or more important than, the distinctions, because reality itself is not neatly partitioned-off into separate compartments.

Reductionism is often the unintentional result of enthusiasm channelled in one direction and of specialist knowledge (see p 52 of Chapter 5). It is perpetuated however by the closed mind, which fails to distinguish between different kinds of evidence and 'reduces' them all to one kind. Reductionism in biology, for example, may 'reduce' human beings to the level of molecular machines, ignoring the data associated with consciousness. Reductionism in history may see a historical event as entirely due to economic and political causes, failing to consider, for example, the influence of ideas and of leading personalities, of sociological factors, or of the part played by religion.

A particularly clear example of reductionism is Nietzsche's comment 'Man is what he eats'. As a strong statement of the importance of the physical aspect of life, this may have its place, but when taken as a complete statement it is misleading. It implies that nothing beyond the physical matters or exists. It is helpful to contrast this with the biblical saying 'Man shall not live by bread alone'. This includes the importance of the physical within a much wider framework and is therefore not reductionist. This example relates directly to the prevalence of materialist, consumerist and competitive attitudes in schools, to which Tim Brighouse drew attention (see page 1 of Chapter 1).

Reductionism also shows itself in the compartmentalism of knowledge which is reinforced many·times over by the way in which schooling is organised, especially at secondary and tertiary levels. Specialist teachers, timetabled slots and distinctive examination structures convey very effectively to students that learning does not – and need not – relate across subject areas.

The comprehensiveness of the five-fold attitude of respect is limited by an atmosphere of selectivity and studied refusal to consider other aspects of reality. Education is concerned for truth in its totality, not just in fragmented parts. It therefore acknowledges the complexity of issues and the need for many different approaches to the question of knowledge. It does not arbitrarily decide on the limits of what can be known, and it seeks to give due status to all aspects of human experience.

Adjudication between assumptions

The four '-isms' of scepticism, positivism, reductionism and relativism reinforce each other just as the five objects of respect support and promote each other. Education itself rests on certain assumptions, notably two fundamental ones: that people matter, and that the search for truth matters. But both of these can be challenged.

The assumption that a human being is a person of infinite worth who ought under no circumstances to be treated as a means to an external end has never been universally held. Few would openly admit that people do not matter, but behaviour often suggests a different story. The second assumption, that the search for truth in all areas of life matters, is more open to question. Probably few would disagree if it were expressed in the following way: that people should strive as hard as they can to know and understand and not be the victims of ignorance, blindness, misunderstanding and error. Even the person who says that there is no truth and thus no distinction between truth and falsehood says it out of a conviction that the assertion is true. Nevertheless, many people in our society have questioned the possibility of truth at all, and have assumed that the search for truth as an educational aim is meaningless.

Is it possible to decide fairly between different assumptions? The power of reasoning is rightly acknowledged as of vital importance in the search for truth and appropriate behaviour-patterns. But reasoning itself has to start somewhere. Logical progression of thought begins by accepting premises, and unless these are of a strictly mathematical nature – of the kind 'If X and Y' – those premises are accepted as trustworthy without having been logically proved. A problem therefore presents itself. Even if it is possible to eliminate subjective emotional reactions, allowing reason to work untrammelled, this will not necessarily produce consensus between people whose assumptions are opposed. By itself, reason is powerless to establish assumptions.

Nevertheless, education can and should uncover assumptions so that the real issues can be perceived. Reason can play a very significant role in supporting or discouraging assumptions, even though it cannot by itself supply sufficient grounds for their acceptance or rejection. In the end, that will be a matter of what makes sense to a particular person because of his or her unique experience, insights and intuition.

Adjudication between assumptions such as those inhibiting and those encouraging education should not be regarded as an arbitrary matter like throwing a coin, even though the absolute certainty for which the positivist craves cannot be attained because of the depth of the issues involved. This point can be well brought out in relation to the status accorded to teachers' views in the extract from the Inspectors' document given above (see page 28). It is undoubtedly true that teachers can be mistaken; their opinion is no more right, by virtue of their articulating it, than anyone else's, including the humblest student. On the other hand, in so far as teachers are more experienced than their students, and have given time and effort to studying the topic, their opinion does deserve more weighty consideration. Historians who have studied the reign of King John in depth deserve to have their opinions concerning King John given more weight than those who have hardly given a moment's attention to the historical evidence. The fact that they *may* be deluded is no excuse for putting them on the same level as the ignoramus.

Rosemary Brown re-visited

Possible responses to Rosemary Brown's experience can offer an example of adjudication between conflicting assumptions for those who are concerned about the truth of what she says about her own experience (see Figure 7). Do we assume that she is wrong in the deep convictions with which at the moment we may disagree but by which she lives, unless she can *prove* she is right? Or do we assume that she is right in those convictions and therefore that it is *we* who need to widen our grasp of experience to take her insights on board, unless there is very strong evidence that she is unlikely to be a reliable witness? The relativist's refusal to engage in the truth question at all is discussed on p. 34. (see Figure 7).

Figure 7 Different assumptions   *An example*

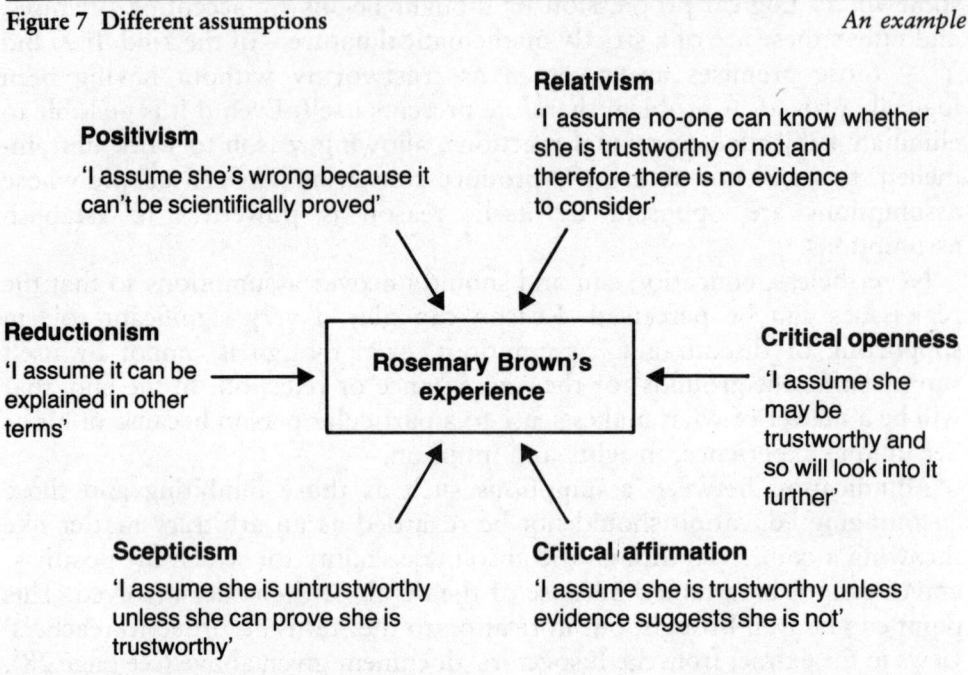

Relativism
'I assume no-one can know whether she is trustworthy or not and therefore there is no evidence to consider'

Positivism
'I assume she's wrong because it can't be scientifically proved'

Reductionism
'I assume it can be explained in other terms'

Rosemary Brown's experience

Critical openness
'I assume she may be trustworthy and so will look into it further'

Scepticism
'I assume she is untrustworthy unless she can prove she is trustworthy'

Critical affirmation
'I assume she is trustworthy unless evidence suggests she is not'

This is a crucial difference in outlook. It is not possible to hold both assumptions at the same time. Neither, however, is it just a matter of personal opinion – which is how a thoroughgoing relativist might see it. For reason can shed some light on the question of how to choose between them. To hold the second assumption that people are right unless shown to be unreliable, promotes a positive and creative approach to what is new, strange and apparently conflicting, an attitude of great respect for the person holding such views, and a desire to empathise with that person and really understand how he or she see things. It enables one to build on such encounters to widen one's own experience and convictions. It sharpens critical powers in the effort to distinguish insights from what is irrelevant or harmful and negative to others, yet it never sinks to the level of imagining that reasoning is all that is needed. It is optimistic yet not naïve.

The first assumption, however, that people are wrong unless proved right, involves an inner contradiction in that one's own convictions, including this assumption, cannot be proved. This contradiction does not affect the second assumption (discussed above) for it does not lay down the condition of proof. Furthermore, the first assumption leads to an attitude of constant sitting-on-the-fence. This is to maintain a viewpoint or position for which again there is no proof as to its truth or wisdom. For if what Rosemary Brown asserts is true, awareness of such knowledge would make a difference to one's attitude to life. The assumption that people are wrong unless they can prove they are right also involves upsetting other people by failing to take their sincere beliefs seriously. Furthermore it subjects to the test of reason what reason alone cannot appreciate.

The incredulity with which so many people react to Rosemary Brown springs from the assumption that because the idea of any form of life after death runs counter to beliefs they already hold, she must be deluded. The working out of these beliefs and of this assumption means that people tend either to pay no more attention to the matter, shrugging their shoulders with a smile if anyone mentions it in conversation, and moving briskly on to the next subject, or to become interested in the phenomenon, but without considering whether there can be any evidence with regard to its truth.

The alternative assumption, that unless there are strong grounds for supposing Mrs Brown to be insane, foolish or ignorant her testimony must stand, produces a very different development. Instead of failing to consider the matter further, one can be open to study the evidence. This may still result in a denial of any truth in Rosemary Brown's story, if such study leads to the concluson that it is, in fact, a hoax. But it may result, as it did in the case of the composer Ian Parrott, in a fundamental acceptance of her insights and veracity.[7] In his book *The Music of Rosemary Brown*, Parrot points to such evidence as the unassuming, down-to-earth, yet confident character of the witness herself, the fact that the innumerable tests to which she has been submitted cannot convict her of psychological abnormality, and the fact that the music she has produced is in the authentic style of the composers to whom she ascribes it. Musicians can vouch for this last point, yet all agree that it would constitute quite a remarkable achievement for an advanced student in composton to produce such pieces in the style of each named composer. Rosemary Brown has never been a music student, her piano playing is mediocre and her grasp of musical theory scarcely above Grade VI standard. It may still be possible that both Rosemary Brown and Ian Parrott are wrong. But it would be reprehensible for someone to assert this who had not examined such evidence.

This example has been discussed in some detail in order to illustrate the potential importance of the assumptions which undergird attitudes. Moreover, it highlights the fact that such assumptions can be subjected to a good deal of rational study without in any way compromising people's integrity or pre-judging the result for other people.

But what of the relativist who assumes that no-one *can* know and who therefore is not concerned about evidence at all? Is the search for truth important, or is it unnecessary and irrelevant? Education in the sense of an attitude of five-fold respect assumes that it *is* important, and so this is a crucial question to discuss.

The reasonableness of the search for truth

Reason can shed light on the assumption that the search for truth matters. People who argue for relativism usually do so with great emphasis, believing that what they say is true and that everyone should acknowledge that this is the case – even though they say that no-one can know. The truth question will not go away. Often the relativist links this with a profession of faith in people. Yet to say 'I am not interested in truth, but only in people' begs the question, for behind the interest in people is a hidden assumption that people matter and that this is the way things are. People matter not just because I think they do, or you think they do or they think they do, but because they happen to be people.

This century has seen horrific examples of the de-personalizing of people, manifestations of a belief that people do not matter, that they are merely fodder for an end outside themselves, whether economic, political, social, scientific or religious. It is peculiarly ironic, therefore, that educationalists do not appreciate the fundamental nature of the truth-claim that people matter, nor acknowledge that it is by no means universally held. Any classroom will show up many examples of children for whom other people only matter in so far as they are 'pieces of furniture' in the child's environment. The arena of politics is strewn with situations in which those making decisions, or those opposing them, regard people as pawns to be moved about at will. Those who call most loudly for tolerance and kindly relationships between people should be in the forefront of education in truth-claims. The harmonious society they desire depends upon people having a deep sense of this truth, if of no other: that people matter.

Many people find talk about truth meaningless or irrelevant because they objectify it; they see it as a supposed object, one among others, which clearly does not exist. Yet truth, in fact, is just a simple way of referring to what would otherwise become a very complicated and roundabout description. Truth refers to the *facticity*, the 'is-ness' of the world and anything that lies beyond the world. It is concerned with the way things *really* are, as compared with the way I or anyone else think they are. Truth is a neat way of describing reality, what actually is the case.

As such, a concern for truth lies behind all sincere questions, including the very simplest. What is the time? When do swallows migrate? How does a glider stay in the air? Was Richard III responsible for the disappearance of the princes in the tower? Why do people become football enthusiasts? Is this picture a worthwhile work of art? Is hooliganism the result of unemployment? What kind of discipline do children need? Does mental capacity diminish with age? Is a sunset more beautiful than a slag-heap? Does this novelist portray characters one can meet in real life? How does home background affect the way a child develops? Do you love me? Is there a God? Does life have meaning? Who am I? If the people asking and trying to answer these questions do not care whether what they say has anything to do with what happens to be the case, then the question is simply flippant.

Education is not a flippant activity. It has purpose and meaning. Education, therefore, cannot ignore the question of truth. There could be no science, or history, or sociology, for example, without taking the truth question very seriously indeed. Students cannot simply make up scientific conclusions or historical or sociological statements and be correct. There are criteria by which such conclusions and statements can be judged; it is part of the educational enterprise to familiarise students with these criteria, so that they can practise them to the level of their ability, needs and interests. The fact that the criteria are the more difficult to apply in an externally-demonstrable way does not mean that there are no such criteria. The *latter* belief does *not* logically follow upon the former; but it rests on what is the fundamental weakness of the relativist assumption behind it, which fails to distinguish between knowing and what is to be known, or between the subjective and the objective in knowing.

The ancient Jain parable of the elephant and the blind man is illuminating. According to this, several blind men feel an elephant. One gets hold of its tail, and says 'Reality is like a rope'; another grasps its leg and says 'Reality is like a tree trunk' and a third feels its trunk and exclaims 'Reality is like a snake'. This bears out the relativist insight that people see reality from their own point of view; the circumstances of each are different and it is foolish to deny or undermine other people's views or say that the other is wrong when you have not stood where he or she stands. But the parable does not support the relativist argument that therefore no-one can know anything – they can only have opinions, none of which has more validity than another. For reality is there. Reality is the elephant and the blind men do in fact apprehend an aspect of reality; they know truly even though only partially.

Analogy may convince where reason fails because analogy awakens our capacity to imagine possibilities, but neither analogy nor reason can compel agreement. What matters is that assumptions *are* debated and that all involved in education, including students of all ages, begin to appreciate the importance, complexity and excitement of the on-going debate.

Notes and references

1 Rosemary Brown *Unfinished Symphonies* (Souvenir Press, 1971); *The Rosemary Brown Piano Album* (Novello, 1974); Rosemary Brown *Immortals at my Elbow* (Bechman and Turner, 1974).

2 For example, A J Ayer *Language, Truth and Logic* (London, 1936) and *The Foundations of Empirical Knowledge* (London, 1940). Ayer himself in his *Philosophy in the Twentieth Century* (Unwin Paperbacks, 1984) concedes that 'few of the principal theses of the Vienna Circle survive intact. Metaphysics is no longer a term of opprobrium . . . ' although he considers that 'the spirit of Viennese positivism survives . . . in its re-accommodation of philosophy with science, its logical techniques, its insistence on clarity . . . ' p 140f.

3 Bertrand Russell 'Mathematics and the metaphysicians' (1901) in *Mysticism and Logic*, (Allen and Unwin, 1917) p 73.

4 The philosophical implications of quantum physics are complex and far from conclusive. As a short introduction see P E Hodgson *The Implications of Quantum Physics*, Science and Theology Seminar Paper No 1 published by The Farmington Institute, Oxford 1986.

5 *History and Social Sciences at Secondary Level*, Part III (Inner London Education Authority, 1983) p 48.

6 *Values* January 1986. Published by RMEP in co-operation with the Moral Education Centre, St. Martin's College, Lancaster, and the Centre for Social and Moral Education, University of Leicester.

7 Ian Parrott: *The Music of Rosemary Brown* (Regency Press, 1978).

4 Coping in the Classroom with Controversial Issues

Controversy is part of life. The shared values which a school needs must have the power to contain a proper expression of controversial views on important matters without disrupting the community, or causing it to collapse into anarchy. Education must therefore cope with controversy creatively. Failure to do so can make education seem anaemic, vague and redundant. Seriously insufficient attention has been given to this area, and this provides a third major reason why many people have lost faith in education.

With regard to schools, those concerned with one of the alternative ways of bringing up children and young people – nurture, utilitarian motives or indoctrination – will tend to bypass the need to help people cope with controversy. A single view on controversial issues can be conveyed so much more easily and effectively than when we muddy the waters by introducing question-marks. However, for those whose primary concern is a genuinely educational one, a serious problem is presented by the way in which so much thinking today has capitulated to a relativist view of controversy, as has been discussed in the last chapter.

This has resulted in an avoidance of real involvement with important issues both in the school as a whole and in the classroom. Much teaching has succumbed to superficiality by being robbed of the controversial elements in education – elements which enable students to gain real understanding because they are a vital part of the subject-matter.

Certain recent developments are beginning to stir people to see the dangers in this evasive attitude. The anti-racist movement, for example, expects teachers to take a strong line to persuade, and, if necessary to enforce, anti-racism. Such persuasiveness and enforcement on the part of those in positions of authority can itself threaten education, and yet education which fails to take seriously such issues as racism is already denying itself. Those who believe in the five-fold attitude of respect which I have argued is the basis of education (see pp. 14–16) realise only too vividly that there are many ways in which respect does not operate in our schools and in our society. Failure to point this out may, perhaps legitimately, be seen as connivance at their perpetuation. The need for reform, for trying to correct injustice and so forth, is important. Constant evasion of discussing controver-

classroom and of arousing any sense of responsibility with regard to these issues is not conducive to real education.

Educationalists have so far been unable to provide clear and adequate answers to the very real problems involved in dealing with controversial issues in a classroom situation. How can teachers help children and students to become discerning without over-influencing them? How can they ensure that experience in school demonstrates and promotes fairness to all people (including those who are uncongenial); impartiality to all views (including those they dislike); and a balanced perspective in evaluating complex questions and data?

Should teachers aim at neutrality?

The concept of procedural neutrality has been frequently invoked in the legitimate and necessary search for a means to guard against indoctrination.[1] Clearly, there is a real danger where a person with a strong commitment is in a teaching position. It is easy for the mis-directing enthusiast or the bigot who has authority to control young minds in a way which restricts them and obliges them to conform.

To require teachers to be neutral does not, however, solve this problem. The arguments against the neutral position are numerous. First, there are, of course, situations in which it is helpful for teachers to withhold or hide what they personally think, for example, with children or young people who betray a 'follow-the-teacher' mentality or dislike the trouble of thinking for themselves. However, the stance of neutrality is often, perhaps mostly, professionally inappropriate. In a recent article, R F Dearden noted that the expression of 'ignorant alternatives or mere indisciplined assertiveness' will not improve understanding. Furthermore 'the teacher may confront such massive prejudice that he or she is the only source of possible "divergence", that is, acknowledging that other views are possible. In such situations teachers are professionally obliged to contribute their own views.'[2]

Second, the attempt to suppress one's own convictions has a highly constraining effect on the quality of teaching. It is not educationally desirable for the teacher or lecturer to suppress all facial expression, humour or signs of interest in the subject – such teaching suffers from a fatal flaw: it is boring. Yet the slightest nuance can betray one's real standpoint. The following comment was made by someone who has spent over 20 years advising and inspecting schools:

> If there be such a thing as neutral teaching, which I greatly doubt, it is quite marvellously dull. We shall not interest pupils or students through attempts at neutrality of approach. What is required of us is indeed that we display our assumptions, that we make the implicit explicit, but that we are fair and have professional integrity in our work.[3]

This brings us to a third point about neutrality, namely that it is impossible. Attempted neutrality is bogus because selection of material, manner of presentation, the handling of questions and discussion and what is omitted – deliberately or otherwise – all reflect a viewpoint. It is dishonest and damaging educationally to pretend that this is not so; the neutral stance itself rests on assumptions and convictions which, if not expressed and openly acknowledged, may contribute to indoctrination.

One's personal convictions affect one's views on everything else. This was brought home to the writer with great force by a visiting speaker on the School Council Humanities Curriculum Project at a college seminar. The discussion with students moved from Roundheads and Cavaliers to whether people believe in God and how they picture God. The speaker effectively acted the part of a neutral chairman, giving the impression that historical evidence counts for nothing and that questions of the existence of God are just a foible of certain human beings. But when asked how she would respond to a boy who insisted that Jews did great harm to society and that Hitler was right to try to exterminate them, she changed her tune: 'You cannot be tolerant of intolerance', she said. Yet what about the intolerance which caused the Civil War, and the intolerance on both sides of the divide between religion and non-religion? In fact the speaker was indirectly revealing her own subjective attitudes: she was *not* a historian, she *was* an agnostic. Yet she was seeking to teach and exemplify respect for persons, tolerance and openness without drawing attention to this philosophy except, significantly, when she found herself drawn outside the barrier of her supposed neutrality.

This example draws attention to an odd trick about the nature of commitment. The illusion that we can maintain neutrality has been so effective partly because of a simple mistake, that of defining commitment in a narrow sense: as that which is made outwardly obvious by adherence to a set of propositions 'I believe in the Bible. . . or Chairman Mao' or whatever; or which is demonstrated by special behaviour such as saluting the flag or entering a church, when believers stand up and allow themselves to be counted. Such commitment is seen, by those who do not share it, as a kind of package-deal – little differentiation is allowed, and wide generalisations are in vogue; there is a tendency to classify people and put them in compartments. Rarely is the situation so simple: on examination many distinctions need to be made.

A more insidious danger, however, is that this obsession with obviously explicit forms of commitment easily hides the less obvious: the minute, mildly-fluctuating, and hardly realised examples of commitment which *everyone*, without exception, has. One of the most important duties of education is to seek to lay bare, clarify and evaluate precisely these numerous convictions which affect how we live but which may be obscure to us unless critically examined.

Is openness possible?

As a method of guarding against indoctrination the concept of neutrality does not work. As far back as 1955 M V C Jeffreys, in his book *Beyond neutrality*, summed up what was needed: 'The guarantee of freedom is not the teacher's neutrality but his or her respect for the integrity of the pupil's personality.' He considered it to be most important for teachers to give examples of 'how the possession of well-thought out ideas and convictions gives depth to personality'. Teachers must always remember, however, that 'it is more important that our pupils should think for themselves than that they should think as we do'.[4]

Such an attitude on the part of the teacher requires a quality of openness. This is a word constantly in use today. It denotes an attitude in which people are not closed and restricted in their sympathies but instead are prepared to consider, without hasty judgment, many different and new possibilities.

By itself, however, openness can be a misused concept, referring to the practice of non-reflectiveness whereby a person refuses to think about anything, but simply receives – like blotting paper – any and every notion that comes along. Such a state of permanent openness would be one of indoctrination because the person concerned would accept the judgements of other people without reflecting upon them. Furthermore, evaluation and choosing are unavoidable when contradictions appear and when matters of great importance are discussed.

This 'pseudo openness' has become a stance in itself, but it suffers from the same handicap as procedural neutrality: it is impossible in practice. Nor is it desirable. Always to be an outsider, describing or finding out what other people think without participating in the conversation, trivialises the subject and inhibits the person. So, for example, a person is not being open to Humanism or to Islam, if he or she is not prepared to consider the possibility of becoming a Humanist or a Muslim. A permanently detached position is no more open than that of the Humanist or Muslim who knows where he or she stands and looks on everything else from the perspective of Humanism or Islam.

For this reason, therefore, the word 'critical' has in the last few years frequently been added to 'openness'. This suggests that the openness advocated should be a meeting in which what is met is carefully considered and reflected upon. The openness ceases to be an openness to every influence, idea or whim but instead becomes openness informed by analysis and rational judgment.

Is the phrase 'critical openness' adequate?

The question can be posed, however, whether this phrase is adequate. Does it express what the educationalist needs to express in a way which is not counter-productive?

'Critical Openness' does not include the necessity for conviction

Often 'critical openness' has been used to mean the opposite of a committed approach. It has been paraded as superior to the attitude of someone who has deep convictions – especially a strong religious or political affiliation – as though such people cannot, by definition, be critically open. This is much to be regretted. Not only is it offensive to people; it actually fails to demonstrate the openness talked about by pre-judging these people as 'uncritically closed'. It is also foolish, because there is no logical reason why critical openness should not be turned upon itself, so that commitment to it may be upset. The mistake here is in imagining that there is nothing more to the journey than trying to find out where to go and being open to various possibilities. Yet the time comes for actually going, and the looking stage must become part of a bigger operation.

Critical openness is appropriate at one stage but not at another. There *is* a time to be critically open – that is, when one has the chance or the necessity to consider something new and different. But there is also a time for conviction and decision-making and saying 'therefore this and not that'. One cannot be permanently open all the time, or permanently critical. One can only be critically open on the basis of being decided on certain matters and accepting them. The criticism and openness is in the past with regard to *these* matters, but not to new aspects as these occur.

Arthur Rowe puts this clearly:

> Criticism is the passing of judgments and judgments can be passed only from a position which is taking certain things for granted. In this respect critical openness is not a position in itself over against other positions but rather a tool which people of different positions use in relation to their own and other people's beliefs and views . . .
>
> . . . The actual exercise of judgment, like any communication, is in fact a network of inter-related assumptions, convictions, ideas, and so on, about which the critic is more or less certain. While the less certain parts can themselves be subjected to criticism if one's basic convictions are overthrown a conversion occurs and one becomes a new person. What one cannot do is to question everything all at the same time, because on that basis one would never begin to say anything at all. In practice then openness is limited at any one time.[5]

The danger here is that if too much emphasis is placed on critical openness it will tend to be seen as the only tool all the time. We should make clear that it is vital to maintain a balance between this and the issue in question. It is helpful perhaps to distinguish four elements needed in coming to terms with new ideas (see Figure 8).

Figure 8 Coming to terms with new ideas and experiences

There are four important elements in this process

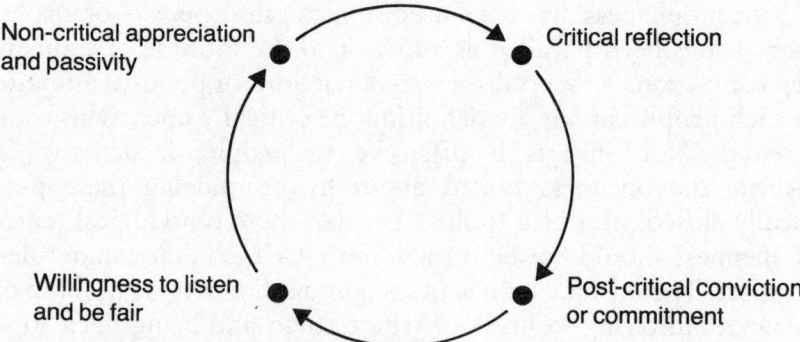

If the conviction or commitment reached is exclusive and rules out the possibility of anyone else having any insight or of there being any other insights to learn, then a dead end is reached. This is the *dogmatic* stance.

If people, while being sure of their own carefully arrived-at convictions, are also aware that there is so much more to be known, they will be willing to go on listening and being fair to other people, and so the creative circle will continue.

Critical openness does not refer to education *per se*, but to the way in which people may be encouraged to take seriously beliefs and ideas and ways of life which are very different from their own – perhaps strange, certainly new, and possibly contradictory to their own – *before* they arrive at their own conclusion about them. It is necessary in order to prevent the automatic switch-off.

Critical openness tends to imply an over-emphasis on reason
In our Western society 'critical' tends to have destructive overtones. Hidden in the use of critical is often a reductionist acceptance of reason as a sufficient guide in itself. Yet outside mathematics and logic this is not true. There are many other ways of knowing. It is, for example, impossible to prove to someone who is tone deaf that a particular series of vibrations in the ear is, in fact, great music. How can one prove the glory of a sunset or a piece of coral seen under a microscope? Can anyone reason their way to love?

Critical openness may suggest to many that only what can be judged by the standards of purely rational criticism is trustworthy. Yet reason needs to be balanced by other ways of knowing. A poem does not yield its secret through a simple analysis of its grammar. Charles Barnham, whose comment on the ideal school closed Chapter 1, gave me a particularly clear example:

> At a course for teachers of English an hour was spent studying a poem in which the poet discovers their newly born baby is handicapped. The structure of the poem was dismantled, and I recall feeling outraged at this misuse of the poem as a vehicle of 'structure'.

Appreciation of such a poem rests on intuitive understanding which has sources other than just reason or empirical investigation. It requires insight which operates not by dissection and scepticism but by seeing-things-whole and creative appreciation, which gets on the same wavelength as the subject under study.

Critical openness is difficult to learn

A third reason for suggesting that the phrase 'critical openness' is not adequate is that the capacity of people to think clearly varies greatly. It is indeed one of the aims of education to develop skills in this as in many other areas, but it needs to be remembered that teachers are dealing with immature minds. Great care must be taken to ensure that children and students do not 'get hold of the wrong end of the stick'. It is easy to sow doubts without giving people the skills and capacity to think through them and gain a more secure footing.

Teachers and lecturers often spend much time on controversial points at the periphery of a subject. To teach questioning before establishing a firm grasp of what is more assured, which gives meaning to the questioning, is to risk exposing children and young people to situations which they are not equipped to handle. A remark of Nietzsche is apposite: 'If a man has a strong faith he can indulge in the luxury of scepticism.'[6]

The impact of 'critical openness' as a method of dealing with controversial matters in the classroom may give an appearance of fairness, objectivity and balance when what has actually been received by students is a negative over-throwing of what other people, their parents, or perhaps they themselves, believe. Their own convictions and those around which their home-life revolves may be undermined without anything positive being put in their place; students may not have the psychological or intellectual maturity to cope with this. Teachers have a great responsibility in this respect. Sometimes one hears someone announcing joyfully how they have succeeded in asking their students to question everything they or their parents stood for. They have enjoyed 'stirring them up'. But what really counts is how they have helped to build people up, how they have developed in students the insight and the maturity to look in a really fair, impartial and balanced way at their own and other people's traditions and convictions.

It is easy to pull down, and then to fill the vacuum with one's own persuasions, that is, to indoctrinate. It is tempting to say that anyone can do it. But it demands great skill and perceptiveness to build up in a way which does not do violence to the integrity of another person.

The value of a four-fold openness

Despite these problems, openness is still a helpful term to use provided it is seen as an approach or attitude of mind, and not in any way as a dogmatic stance. Openness, properly understood, has, I believe, four components. These correspond in part to the five attitudes of respect outlined in Chapter 2 (see Figure 9).

1 Openness to fresh evidence as it presents itself with regard to the question of truth. The opposite of this is a closed mind which refuses to take seriously the possibility of further data and more perceptive interpretation.
2 Openness to the experience of others, seeking to affirm their insights and so arrive at an ever more comprehensive interpretation of life. Lack of interest in what others believe and value, and a failure to weigh these carefully in a positive way, is the mark of an immature, selfish and rigid attitude to life which imagines that 'what I know is all I need to know'.
3 Openness to appreciating the real needs and situations of other people, for example, their sensibilities, their level of understanding, their need for self-affirmation, all of which cannot be met by any form of dogmatic approach which diminishes the other as a person.
4 Openness to critical assessment of the ease with which people, including oneself, can be self-deluded. This constitutes the safeguard *par excellence* against practising the wrong kind of openness.

Such openness is not easy to practise, but it 'opens' the way to a far richer and deeper mode of living. With regard especially to the second and third components it has been observed:

It requires from us more courage than we have at times; more detachment also than we have at times. More courage because to look deeply at a person, or a group of people, in order to see whatever may appear – or to listen so intently as to hear whatever may reach us – requires courage because we do not know what we will see or hear. We do not know how we will be challenged. And we know only too well that if we accept the risk, and see and hear, we will be involved once and for all. We will never be able to escape this first moment of vision or of hearing, even if we do not meet this person, or this group of people ever again; they will remain with us, and we will never be able to escape what we have seen.
A French writer once said: 'Suffering passes, but to have suffered never passes'. It remains with us. Not to meet a person is a problem because we

Figure 9

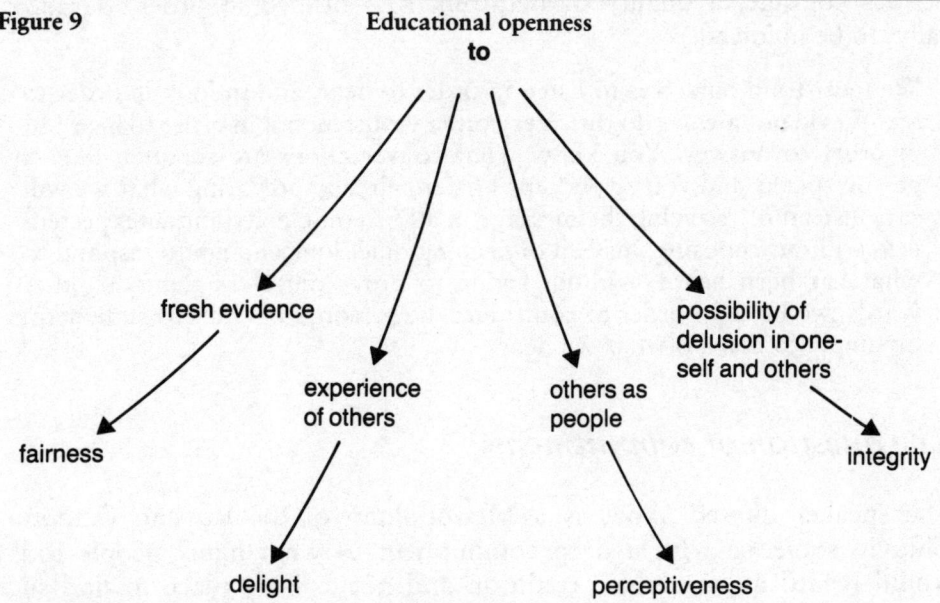

Educational openness
to

fresh evidence

experience
of others

others as
people

possibility of
delusion in one-
self and others

fairness

integrity

delight

perceptiveness

The educated person is open and characterised by

- fairness to evidence,
- delight in the otherness of people,
- perceptiveness as to their real gifts and needs,
- and integrity which can see through deception.

have no right to be cowardly and escape meeting the person who is in front of us. But when we have met a person, even if we run away afterwards, we take this person with us. This requires a determination, courage and openness that must be acquired, because we do not always posses them.

The same speaker goes on to note how selectively the ideal of openness is so often applied. People do not usually try

. . . to the same degree with regard to people whom we like and people whom we dislike, for instance, or with regard to people who are alien to us in one way or another. It may be language, it may be faith, it may be all sorts of things; but we are selectively open and selectively closed, and must learn to be open without this kind of selection. Of course we will inevitably be more perceptive in one direction or another. We have within ourselves a limited number of strings, as it were, that are capable of sounding in response to other strings. But we mut be prepared to allow all the strings within us to resound, and to acquire new ones at times, so as to be able to respond to what is new in other people or groups.

Besides courage, a quality of detachment is needed in order, paradoxically, to be involved.

> We must train ourselves to listen in order to hear, and to look in order to see. We do not always do this. Very often we listen, not in order to hear but in order to answer. You know what conversations are so often like: a person speaks and you or perhaps I listen, already preparing what we will say, instead of receiving the message in all its complexity and unexpectedness without choosing, instead of keeping quiet long enough to respond to what has been heard, without trying to prove ourselves right. In other words, we listen in order to contradict the person, to better his statement, or simply to dismiss what we hear.[7]

The question of commitment

The speaker quoted above is a Metropolitan of the Russian Orthodox Church, someone with a deep commitment to what many people today would regard as an archaic tradition and not a likely place to find such advocacy of openness. To Metropolitan Anthony of Sourozh such awareness of the importance of openness has come to him as a result of his Christian commitment, and his efforts in living it are sustained by that commitment. His own very strong convictions are in no way inimical to his pursuing the vision of openness; what is inimical is the difficulty inherent in human nature which lacks the security and the selflessness to attain the vision in practice.

Consideration of commitment is an aspect of education which has been much neglected, owing to the very proper and real fear of indoctrination. The word 'commitment' here is a convenient way of describing the pattern of convictions, assumptions or prejudices from which a person operates, and which informs the way in which he or she lives (as already discussed on page 39). This is no idle academic matter: as a person thinks, so is he or she, and the real commitments which people have may be ascertained from how they habitually act and react.[8]

It is important to note the distinction between what people may say, or imply by not saying, and what they really think. A car-driver may indicate right, but it is only by watching the vehicle that another motorist can be sure, and act accordingly.

In recent years Edward Hulmes has powerfully advocated the case for 'the Education of Commitment'.[9] He speaks of commitment as

> a comprehensively descriptive term which can be applied to levels of disbelief as well as of belief . . . The difference between two people, teachers for example, may not be that one is 'committed' (having already decided on a particular issue, and thus being incapable of an appropriate level of critical detachment), and the other 'uncommitted' (having reserved judgement, and thus being in a better position to exercise judicial balance).

Both individuals are *committed*, in the sense that their decisions to believe or not to believe, to act or not to act, are based on conscious reflection or unexamined assumptions. The difference between them is one of different commitments.

He goes on to say

What people with different commitments have in common in our society is the freedom to consider the evidence for many different kinds of personal conviction. There are few signs that this freedom is often used for this purpose, but that may be because so little guidance is provided.

He argues that schools must take seriously the challenge of a society which is developing to a point of cultural, ideological and religious diversity and 'attempt to grapple with the needs of a generation faced with making choices as perhaps never before.' He considers:

This calls for more than a description, however full and accurate, of the various options from which the individual may choose. It involves teachers and pupils alike in questions about *how* such choices are made, about *how* different types of evidence are to be distinguished, and about *how* it may be possible to affirm the beliefs and experience of others, whilst holding firmly to one's own.

He adds that 'pupils can be taught to recognise their own convictions, prejudices and assumptions, for what they are.' On the question of pupils learning to assess these he urges teachers to take up the task:

. . . of enabling students to consider what counts as evidence, and to think for themselves what significance it may have for them, now or at some future time. This is not a task which can ever be completed, but it can be started, and continued in ways that are demonstrably appropriate to the developing needs of teachers as well as their pupils . . . Schools may not be places where individuals are told *what* to think, but rather *how* to think.

Teaching students *how* to think involves introducing them to the twin principles of respect for any seriously-held opinion and a consideration of evidence supporting the opinion. In classroom terms, the teacher needs to show an interest in what even the very young child authentically thinks, to allow the natural multiplicity of views (which will emerge in a situation where people are not conscripted or over-inhibited) to surface, and constantly to ask the question '*why* do you think this?' The teacher should also share his or her own viewpoints and the reasons for them, thus giving an example of how a responsible person copes creatively with the challenge of pluralism and the possibility of doubt. The dangers of a young child's simply accepting 'what teacher says' need to be guarded against not by a studied neutrality or non-involvement, or a refusal to enter into the vulnerability of expressing opinions which can be questioned, but by a clear and genuine interest in helping children to think for themselves, treating their opinions with respect and helping them to make them stronger and more comprehensive.

The importance of education in commitment

Many people today are afraid of strong commitments. They are seen as fertile soil for intolerance, fanaticism and bigotry. A *New York Times* editorial on a speech by Solzhenitsyn, for example, commented

> He believes himself to be in possession of The Truth and so sees error wherever he looks.[10]

Whether true of Solzhenitsyn or not, an extract from a seventh century writer puts the question of conviction in an entirely different light:

> Someone who has actually tasted truth is not contentious for truth. Someone who is considered among men to be zealous for truth has not yet learnt what truth is really like: once he has truly learnt it, he will cease from zealousness on its behalf.[11]

Indeed I would consider that the more a person is sustained by a certainty in convictions, the more he or she is capable of seeing truth wherever he or she looks. The reasons for this will be developed in Chapter 5. True openness is paradoxically only possible on the basis of firm convictions. The opposite of firm commitment is not no commitment but a confusion of weakly-held or conditioned commitments, mostly unarticulated and imprecise. Free choice is crucial, but life does not wait for ever. Decisions have to be made on one basis or another. Not to choose is in fact to choose in a weak and unintended form, just as failing to answer a letter is itself answering it.

The only protection against being indoctrinated lies in people developing their capacity for choice in such matters. Either one has chosen beliefs and values which have been thought about or one succumbs, through inertia and naivety, to the pressures of conditioning and indoctrination. As Wittgenstein noted 'The game of doubting itself presupposes certainty',[12] so that permanent indecisiveness and scepticism concerning every view is ruled out. Non-commitment on this matter always rests upon commitment in another, whether acknowledged or not.

The impression however should never be given that arriving at opinions which are true and valid is easy. Indeed the teacher needs constantly to draw attention to the complexity of the task, that in a sense it is a lifetime's occupation searching for that about which one can be legitimately certain.

One of the most urgent educational needs today is to engage students, from the infant years upwards, and including those in higher education, in a creative search for the beliefs and values by which to live. In this search, sincerely-held convictions must not be trivialised. Study in depth is required and a slow year-by-year development of understanding and skill in the handling of ideas, paralleled, for example, in the development of language skills. The controversial element must be central, and the beliefs and values of those responsible for teaching must be made available to those taught for scrutiny and criticism. In this living way education in commitment can take place constructively.

The education of commitment is not therefore a kind of optional luxury to be slipped into the curriculum if there happens to be time. It is the key which can render a nurture approach educational, give vision to a utilitarian framework and guard against indoctrination. It can free institutions from the inhibition of so-called neutral attitudes and permit positive teaching without betraying professional integrity. It will also challenge schools to work out the shared set of principles which alone can make an institution into a flourishing community.

Notes and references

1 See *The Humanities Project: an Introduction* published for the Schools Council by Heinemann 1970. Page 1 sets out the idea of the teacher as a neutral chairman. Lawrence Stenhouse was the Director of the Project

2 R F Dearden: 'Controversial Value Issues in the Curriculum' *Journal of Curriculum Studies* Vol 13, No 1, 1981

3 Roy Wake, in the address to the SCDC Seminar referred to on page 2

4 M V C Jeffreys: *Beyond Neutrality* (Pitman, 1955), p. 9f

5 Arthur Rowe: 'Critical Openness and Religious Education' *British Journal of Religious Education*, Vol 8, No 2, Spring 1986, p 63

6 Nietzsche: *The Twilight of the Idols: Things the Germans Lack,* 12

7 Metropolitan Anthony of Sourozh, speaking at a conference at Effingham 1985. Reported in *Sourozh* February 1986, page 24f

8 This is close to a quotation from G B Shaw 'What a man believes may be ascertained, not from his creed, but from the assumptions on which he habitually acts' *Man and Superman*, 1903, page 235

9 See especially Edward Hulmes: *Commitment and Neutrality in Religious Education* (Geoffrey Chapman 1979); The quotations which follow are taken from Farmington Institute Occasional Paper No 20 on 'Openness and Commitment', 1986

10 *New York Times* June 9, 1978

11 St Isaac of Nineveh quoted by Sebastian Brock in 'Isaac of Nineveh: some newly discovered works' *Sobornost* Vol 8, No 1, 1986, page 30

12 Wittgenstein: *On Certainty* 115

5 Critical Affirmation

Education is about meeting. It can only flourish in a situation where meeting is allowed to happen, indeed where it is encouraged. Chapters 1–4 examined three of the ways in which education has 'gone wrong'. A fourth is that young children and students and staff have so often not been meeting each other as people. The first ingredient – essential to all the others – which a child needs in order to learn, is the security of being loved and taken seriously as a person. It remains the prime underlying factor in motivation for students and staff. If this security is not present people tend to be incapable of relating for long to anything or anybody outside themselves.

This deprivation is most marked in the young child as all infant teachers know well. With older people it shows itself in a variety of ways: a need to dominate conversation and a corresponding inability to listen; being unable to attend to anything long enough to gain real understanding; a need to play a role all the time and hide behind various fixed ideas; boredom and failure to get on the wavelength of what is outside their own immediate experience; disruptive behaviour of all kinds; obvious selfishness and possessiveness, ruthless ambition and so forth.

This kind of behaviour indicates the absence of real meeting between people, for that requires an atmosphere of mutual respect. Such respect involves an attitude towards people not only of openness (critical or otherwise) but a desire to understand, appreciate and 'take on board' their insights. This chapter will discuss how such respect can add depth to relationships; it will, in so doing, also relate closely to the theme of Chapter 4, that of coping with controversial issues.

What is insight?

Insight is a valuable word; it is used in a variety of circumstances, non-academic as well as academic, to point to knowledge felt to be self-authenticating, sure and related to experience. Insight denotes something very precious to a person. The accumulation of insights is, in fact, what makes a person tick. People cannot deny their insights with integrity, and they react strongly on the defensive if other people try to attack those insights.

'To have an insight' is one of the most significant ways in which the verb 'to know' can be used, whether it means 'to know how', 'to know that' or 'to know a person.' It means to experience in a totally self-evident way an understanding of reality; that is, perceiving what actually is, or what reality is. In its simple form this is a very common experience. Insight is behind such expressions as the 'the penny drops', 'the light dawns', 'now I see' and so on.

One of the most famous examples of the receiving of insight was when Archimedes suddenly discovered, while in his bath, his law about the displacement of water – at which he is reported to have run naked down the street shouting 'Eureka'. Usually, however, the process of acquiring insights is unobtrusive, slow, unnoticed by subject or observer, as when children accumulate the insights which enable them to read. This is why people sometimes say 'I feel as though I've known it all along.'

Some people show a greater capacity for the attainment of insight than others. As Lonergan in his important book on *Insight* notes, such people are

> marked by a greater readiness in catching on, in getting the point, in seeing the issue, in grasping implications, in acquiring know-how . . . For insight is ever the same, and even its most modest achievements are rendered conspicuous by the contrasting, if reassuring, occurrences of examples of obtuseness and stupidity.[1]

Although insight is thus related to intelligence, it is important to note that insight is in no way the prerogative of so-called intellectually able people. Anyone, including any child who lives a fully human life, is capable of insights, however small.

Insights evoke commitment, because the understanding gained is not just cerebral but involves feeling and will. Insights give stability and conviction to the person concerned and attach to themselves that sense of absolute certainty which human beings need if they are to become mature persons. People have a right to trust their insights, that is, what they have come to understand through direct experience and genuine reflectiveness.

The discernment of insight is not a straightforward, rule-of-thumb matter. People may, for example, imagine that they have seen a ghost, which turns out, on further inspection, to be a horse seen in certain atmospheric conditions.[2] This is initial misinterpretation of a single experience. What is interesting, however, is that the conviction that it was a misinterpretation is itself an insight which can be trusted, and must be trusted if the people concerned are to continue to be rational beings. This example draws attention to the way in which certainty regarding insights is cumulative and must take account of all possible factors – including the possibility of misinterpretation, that is of calling by the name of insight what is in fact illusion. Leontes in *A Winters Tale* believed he had insight concerning his wife's behaviour when in fact his whole vision had become warped by a demonic frenzy of jealousy. The Delphic oracle was able to convey to him insight regarding his real condition, and this insight saved him. Trusting it implicitly he was sustained through 16 years of penitence for his wrong-doing. Thus, although discerning insights is no rule-of-thumb matter, it remains true that only through insight can misinterpretation or oversight be appreciated. The safeguard *par excellence* against misconstruing insights is that four-fold quality of openness already discussed in Chapter 4, together with a deep appreciation of the danger of ignoring or denying the insights of others. A genuine desire for a comprehensive view which takes in all aspects protects an individual from any severe self-deception.

Verbalisation of insights and its problems

Just as people should be on their guard against such misinterpretation of their experience whilst trusting their capacity for ongoing accumulation of insight, so they should be aware of the pitfalls in verbalising insights.

There is an important distinction between insight itself, derived from experience, and the conscious presentation of it to oneself and to others. Without entering into the enormous philosophical problems surrounding any attempt to define 'knowing',[3] I believe it is necessary to appreciate the difference between what may be called 'inner knowing' which is often only semi-self-conscious, and 'verbalised knowing' − knowing which is clothed with words − which seeks to express for oneself as well as for others what is known inwardly.

This second kind of knowing has to wrestle with a host of hazards connected with language, intelligence, motivation, and so forth. They include the following.

1) *Emotional involvement* can tend to bestow on an experience a quality of completeness and absoluteness which does not properly belong to it. Each insight is by itself partial: it is wholly true but not the whole truth; it is valid but not comprehensive. Yet it is easy to fall into the trap of seeing such an insight as the only thing that matters. This is because it is not possible to concentrate on, or be excited about, more than one thing at a time. We cannot listen fully to Mozart and Stravinsky at the same moment! People in love, for example, often feel that everyone else is incredibly boring by comparison. The centre of the stage is so filled with this experience of being in love that by comparison there is nothing else.

2 *Dependence upon the vocabulary and thought-forms available* to people exercises a highly constraining influence on the way they try to express an insight. People can only use the concepts they have come across. Translation-work constantly draws attention to this problem. Some people go so far as to say that fluency in other languages causes people to think differently in each of them. Awareness of this permits us to acknowledge that if something

appears to be contradictory, it may be that we have misunderstood, or that the language in which the thought is expressed is inadequate for its message. People are dependent on their cultural setting, and seemingly conflicting truth-claims can easily arise, especially between civilisations long separated or isolated.

3 Words enshrine the accumulated experience of centuries of human endeavour and are often misunderstood so that they become *jargon and clichés*. Such secondhand thinking presents a major obstacle to discerning the presence of genuine insights. The language is either dead language, or expresses a conditioned response which a person has not in any sense freely chosen. Often in the cut-and-thrust of conversation people use such programmed phrases when they are not really 'present' in what they are saying.

4 A related problem is the snare of *misreading how words are being used*. Wittgenstein's analysis of language-games is illuminating in this respect.[4] Care in recognising figurative use of language needs to be especially noted. It is easy for figurative language to be misunderstood outside the area of common discourse in which it arose. 'He was out for a duck' may make no sense at all to someone who knows nothing of cricket but there are many uses of metaphors which can be taken literally by those 'not in the know'. If someone speaks of a wet weekend, most people unacquainted with fairly recent colloquialisms in English would assume the speaker meant it was raining, when in fact it may have indicated a miserable and unfriendly time. When, for example, one of the journalists talking to the crowd who had been waiting all night on the streets to see the royal wedding procession (July 23, 1986) asked 'What was the atmosphere like?' one woman said 'Oh it was *so* cold – I was glad of my coat' when the journalist really had in mind 'Were people friendly etc?'

In areas of experience like religion which use figurative and symbolic language a great deal, the misunderstanding can be very serious indeed.

5 *The overtones acquired by words* constitute a barrier to communication. A subjective element is always involved in the understanding of all but the most obviously empirical language; overtones can change meanings. For example the word 'discipline' may be perfectly innocuous to one, but act like a red rag to a bull for another. Words like 'democracy' are similarly 'loaded' with a number of overtones.

This question of the subtly different meanings given to the same words is important, because apparent contradictions often turn out on inspection to be logically compatible differences of opinion.

6 Overtones relate closely to *the context in which words are spoken or heard*. Context gives meaning to a statement. Abstract the statement from that context and it is likely not only to be misunderstood but to be an

incorrect rendering of a person's insight because that insight depended on a polarity: it took for granted much in the context, and perhaps opposed an aspect in that context which was found wanting. By itself, the assertion could be said to be wrong, but within that context it would be right.

7 A knowledge of context is particularly essential with regard to the use of *overstatement* in order to make a point more effectively. Doubtless this is often needed on the rostrum or in the pulpit. Emotive exaggeration can be likened to an extra big wave which carries a swimmer over a barrier. It must be recognised as such, however, otherwise it becomes itself a barrier in the path of those soberly trying to discover the nature of other people's insights.

8 Insights are often *inexpressible in words.* As T S Eliot put it,

> "Words after speech, reach
> Into the silence."
> "Words strain,
> Crack and sometimes break, under the burden,
> Under the tension, slip, slide, perish,
> Decay with imprecision, will not stay in place,
> Will not stay still."[5]

There is bound to be a considerable gulf between the original intuition and the reflection and eventual expression of it in words or action. To describe a bus-journey may be easy, but an appreciation of a poem is not. Although we should have certainty in our experience, we should not be so sure of the verbalised form in which we declare that experience. We should be aware that we may have been misled, and that we may be misleading others, by the words we use. It is said of Beethoven that he would 'hear' a whole symphony in some ecstatic moment and would then have to undertake months of agonising hard work trying to get it right on paper.

This distinction between the trustworthiness of insights and the problems associated with expressing them in words, that is, the distinction between 'inner knowing' and 'verbalised knowing', means that great skill in discerning insight needs to be developed.

Critical affirmation

Learning such skill is part of the respect due to people and to oneself. It involves more than the openness discussed in the last chapter and is better denoted by a term such as 'critical affirmation.'

The word 'affirmation' is a warmer word than openness. Its primary meaning is to make firm, strengthen, support, confirm. It has an essentially positive ring about it. In logic it is used as the opposite of 'negative.' It is a strong word which chimes in with concepts such as conviction, commitment, certainty. There is nothing vague about it, yet it is a welcoming word. Affirmation of people means acknowledging that they exist as living centres of reality, being willing to relate to them and appreciate all that is worthwhile about them, and confirming them in their status as persons.

Affirmation does not, however, involve being a rubber-stamp, saying yes to everything and losing one's own integrity. Just as openness involves at least four components, so affirmation must reflect a similarly comprehensive view and be directed not just to this person or that, but to all people in principle, to oneself, and to truth so far as it is discerned.

The apparent conflicts which such a comprehensive vision raises call for the exercise of discernment. The word 'critical' attached to affirmation underlines this. Critical is used in the sense of 'involving or exercising careful judgement or observation' (*Shorter Oxford English Dictionary*). By being attached to affirmation it loses the fault-finding, censorious, negative over-tones which it so often has (as discussed in Chapter 4).

Affirmation and criticism in this sense are not opposed. We can, for example, show respect for and affirm people as people precisely by taking them and their opinions seriously enough to disagree with them. To be critical of someone can in fact be one of the highest compliments we can pay, because it shows we are in active conversation, bringing our own personalities and insights into the meeting. Jane Austen, for example, in *Sense and Sensibility* (chapter 36) writes that Elinor Dashwood agreed to all the foolish Robert Ferrars had to say because 'she did not think he deserved the compliment of rational opposition'.

An attitude of critical affirmation gives us the capacity to deal creatively with controversy. It does this because it takes seriously the experience of other people, and the insights arising out of that experience, and seeks to affirm them whilst also affirming other experiences and insights including one's own. Critical affirmation helps to build up a person by encouraging the search for trustworthy convictions which can give depth to personality. Indeed we are trifling with people unless we do have very great concern both for our own and other people's integrity.

In sum, critical affirmation covers at least five intentions;

- the desire to find insight;
- the expectation that probably insights are there to be found;
- the determination to try to uncover them;
- the rigorous use of critical faculties in so doing, but not for the sake of destruction, as though scepticism were the be-all and end-all, but for the purpose of creating a larger grasp of understanding and commitment both for oneself and for others;
- the desire to make other people's insights one's own.

An immediate objection might be that convictions as divergent as Marxism and Hinduism, Humanism and Islam cannot be reconciled in this way. Anyone trying to affirm them all would be likely to become torn apart. There are, however, two considerations which suggest a way through this dilemma. The first is the distinction between insight on the one hand and oversight, blindness, hypocrisy, deception and ignorance on the other hand. The insights which it is desirable that another person should affirm must be searched for. A person is likely to present a precious insight embedded in phrases and patterns of behaviour which are not necessary to the insight. This is not just clutter, it may actually be destructive of, or negative towards, the insights held by other people or indeed other insights which the person concerned holds. This packing must be discarded and not affirmed.

A second consideration is that insights as such are complementary. Often it seems as though insights conflict. This gives rise to controversy which can have extremely far-reaching repercussions. Yet the conflict is apparent only because an insight which really is an insight can cohere with other insights. If it does not it is because the unpacking just referred to has not been done properly. The insight has become confused with its expression in words which may, for any of the eight reasons already listed (pp 52–54) amongst others, be an inadequate vehicle for it (see Figure 10).

It is important to note that insights may be different without being contradictory. This relates to the philosophical principle of complementarity of disciplines whereby the same thing can receive many different descriptions which are nevertheless entirely accurate within their separate frames of reference. The analogy is often used of the many plans, views and schedules which describe the construction of a building, each accurate, each expressing only a part of the truth, each complementary to others; the analogy may be extended to point out that all the plans are simultaneously necessary for portraying the building truthfully in every respect.

If the blind men in the parable given at the end of Chapter 3 had understood this principle of complementarity it might have saved them from jumping to conclusions too quickly. The experience of each gave him insight into the nature of reality, in that each was actually in contact with the elephant. The mistake each made was in identifying a part with the whole.

In order to avoid making such a mistake, and in order to arrive at a more complete knowledge, it is essential – not just optional – to try to appreciate and make others' insights one's own. This procedure not only affirms the insights but affirms the people who hold the insights.

Suppose there are four blind men: A, B, C and D. A decides to walk around. He talks to and stands with B, C and D in turn, feeling what they feel. His understanding of the elephant will be greater because more comprehensive than that of the blind men who stand still. If he tells the others what he has come to experience they may say he is wrong: 'This is what reality is and it is no other'. But A can reply 'Yes reality is as you say, but it is also as C and D and as I have experienced it. We must widen our

Figure 10 Discerning insights

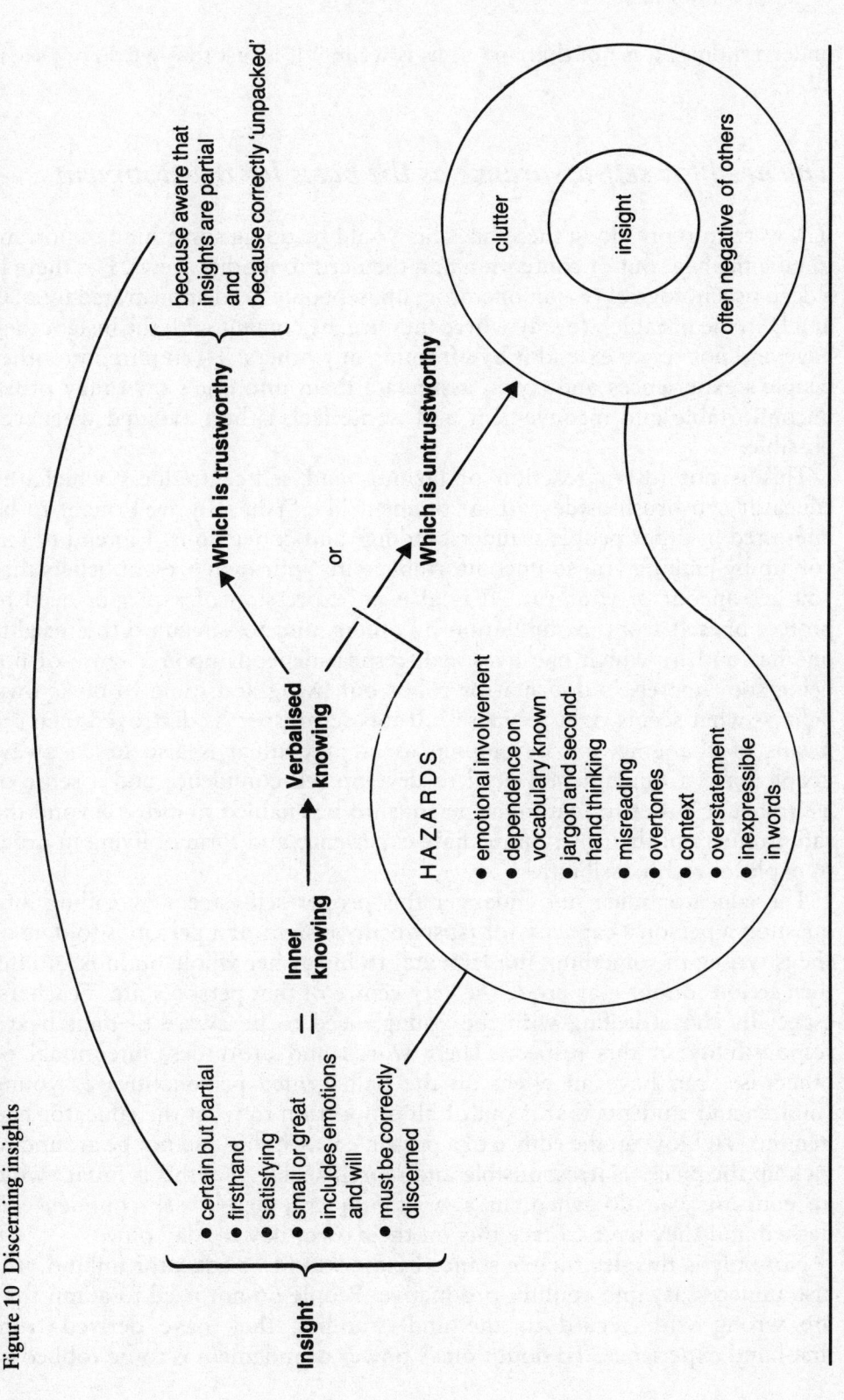

understanding. It is not that any of us is wrong. It is just that we do not see it all.'

The need for self-assurance as the basis for development

If A were to reply along these lines he would be doing something important to take the heat out of contention and the need to modify views. For there is a deep psychological reason operating upon people (as demonstrated by B, C and D in the parable), to stay where they are, be content with the insight they have and not try to extend it by affirming any others. To enquire into other people's experiences and try to assimilate them into one's own may prove uncomfortable and inconvenient and, some feel, is best avoided whenever possible.

This is not just a reaction of laziness and self-centredness which the educator can brush aside with a comment like 'You jolly well ought to be interested in other people's understandings and convictions. I intend to stir you up by making you so uncomfortable with your own present beliefs that you get up out of your rut.' It is also an expression of a proper need to protect oneself from manipulation by others, and to safeguard the insights one has and by which one lives. Self-respect depends upon a sense of not being someone else's doormat or robot but living according to one's own lights – what seems right to oneself. If this self-respect is destroyed then the means of changing and developing as an individual is also taken away. People have a fundamental need to develop self-confidence and a sense of assurance in order to mature as persons, to be enabled to move beyond the safe frontiers of their own immediate experience and form of living in order to explore fresh possibilities.

The educator must not endanger this proper self-esteem by calling into question a person's capacity for trustworthy insight. If a person is told he or she is wrong in something fundamental to his or her whole outlook on life, then serious doubt may erode the very centre of that person's life. Teachers, especially those dealing with the young, need to be aware of their heavy responsibility in this respect. Their words and attitutdes, intentional or otherwise, can have an effect on the half-formed personalities of young children and students that is out of all proportion to what the educator had in mind. To blow up the edifice of a person's way of life and not be around to pick up the pieces is irresponsible and reprehensible. Yet this is in fact what an educator can do when, in a brief moment, pupils' self-confidence is dashed and they have to face this on their own, day in, day out.

Not only is this destructive stance by the would-be-educator unkind, it is also unnecessary and counter-productive. People do not need to admit they are wrong with regard to the understanding they have derived from first-hand experience. To doubt one's power of judgment is to be robbed of the capacity for enlightenment, even where this involves what to the outer world may be called conversion. All real development, cognitive and emotional, must be organically based on what is already deeply known. This ensures that necessary stability of character which can promote the greatest spirit of adventure into the world of others.

Pascal wrestled with this whole question in the seventeenth century as the following quotation from the *Pensées* shows:

> If we would reprove with advantage, and show another his fault we must see from what side he looks at the matter, for usually the thing is true from that point of view, and we must admit this truth, but show him the side on which it is not true. That satisfies him, for he sees that he was not wrong, and that he merely failed to see all sides of the question. Now people are not vexed at failure to see everything. But they do not like to be mistaken, and perhaps this comes from the fact that naturally man cannot see everything, and that by nature he cannot be wrong from his point of view, since what we apprehend with our senses is always true.[6]

I think that in the last sentence Pascal is not referring to the reliability of empirical evidence but rather to the way in which first-hand experience gives certainty to the person who has had the experience, bearing in mind the necessary degree of caution concerning self-deception already discussed on page 51f.

This is an approach to educating others which really works; it is based on a recognition that everyone is limited in experience and understanding: knowing this and not that, feeling this and not that, doing this and not that. Such limitation is an unavoidable aspect of being human and therefore it is not belittling to oneself to acknowledge the need for further enlightenment.

The nineteenth century thinker F D Maurice agonised over a highly controversial issue, that of the unity of the Church. While ardently supporting this he managed to avoid any bitterness towards sectarians by exemplifying powers of discrimination along these lines. His son wrote of him that he came:

> more and more to hold that there was something to be learnt from everything 'positive', as he came to call it, in each one's faith, and that the mischief lay in the 'negative', that is, in the denunciation of imperfectly understood truths held by others.[7]

I believe that in this approach lies an answer to the destructive side of controversy.

Additional note

Behind this idea that people are right in what they affirm from their own experience and wrong only if they deny that of others lie at least two considerations. The first is that a person's experience is a fact which enables one to apply to it the analogy of light. Absence of experience can in this sense be likened to darkness. Absence of experience is the weakest kind of evidence, for it can never answer the charge of possible blindness, only ignore it. By itself, therefore, the absence of evidence is unreliable. In Chapter 3 the experience of Rosemary Brown was referred to. Her critics have not had her experience and therefore they have poor grounds for dismissing her interpretation of it unless other evidence is forthcoming which calls her trustworthiness into question.

Secondly, criticism and opposition are often based on a lack of understanding of what is being criticised and opposed. One frequently notices how in arguments one group does not actually attack what the other group is defending, this fact being obscure to the contestants. In any discussion about the desirability of democracy, it may be that by democracy the contestants mean something so different that each could say 'If that is how you understand "democracy" then I agree with your statement.'

Discussion about the existence of God often reveals serious differences of opinion with regard to the 'God' who is supposed to exist or not. If one person, for example, considers that God's existence ought to be provable, a theist could reply 'If that is how you understand "God" then I agree God does not exist, but when I say that God exists I mean by "God" something very different. For me God is infinite and cannot be subjected to scientific proof.' The invitation is thus given to the other person to extend the range of his or her experience, by taking on board the insights of the other person. Such an approach can turn controversy which might otherwise be bitter into something creative. It can overcome the dilemma, which often seems to face people, between easy-going tolerance on the one hand and firmly standing-up-for-the truth on the other.

The solution calls for a positive tolerance which is very different from that motivated either by indifference to the truth, or by a search for convictions by those who think they have none. It gives the lie to the view that strong convictions and an open attitude towards others cannot belong together; in fact, the reverse may be true, for a person with strong convictions may be better able to appreciate those of others and accord them the careful respect they deserve. Moreover the attitude of affirmation can lead to a great strengthening of mutually realised convictions. The seeker after truth can never stand still; everyone is limited in experience and understanding.

Metropolitan Anthony, quoted in the last chapter, puts it like this,

> Listen to other people, and whenever you discern something which sounds true, which is a revelation of harmony and beauty, emphasize it and help it to flower. Strengthen it and encourage it to live. This requires from us a great deal.[8]

This approach to controversial issues is possible but not easy. It requires great courage and a spirit of detachment when it involves, as it often does, affirming others who do not return the compliment, that is, affirming them in the face of being ignored, slighted or rejected. But the extraordinary thing is that one finds, in the end, that in affirming others one also affirms oneself. Many people find it difficult to like themselves – when they are honest they admit that they are highly critical of themselves without affirming themselves in equal measure. Paradoxically, genuine affirmation of others for *their* sake carries with it, as a corollary or unlooked-for offshoot the capacity to affirm oneself. This is probably because if one learns to look for the good in others one can also see it in oneself.

It may be that readers consider this attitude of critical affirmation to be unrealistic. I commend it, however, as an approach which I have found to work with regard to the meeting of beliefs as widely divergent as Marxism and Hinduism, Humanism and Islam. I believe it does so, because it takes seriously both concern for truth and concern for people, realising that people live by their insights but that oversights, blindness, hypocrisy, deception and ignorance degrade the person who perpetrates them as well as his or her victims. On the other hand, interest in others, the desire to know more and to widen one's horizons, and willingness to modify previous convictions so that they can become part of a larger and more comprehensive understanding, build people up as authentic persons.

In this way education *can* happen.

Notes and references

1 Bernard Lonergan *Insight* (Longman, 1957) p 173
2 I acknowledge discussion with Dora Ainsworth on this point in which she referred to such an experience
3 Ever since Plato raised the question 'What is knowledge?' in the *Theaetetus* it has continued to fascinate philosophers. See, for example, a very short article by Michael Welbourne 'What is Knowledge?' in *Cogito* January 1987 published by the Department of Philosophy, University of Bristol, pp 12–14. The philosophical problems involved are well set out in the Open University Press book entitled *Knowledge* prepared by Tom Sorell (1981)
4 Wittgenstein *Philosophical Investigations* 7, 23 *et al*
5 T S Eliot *The Four Quartets: Burnt Norton* V
6 Pascal *Pensées* (Les Editions Brunschvig, 1905) p 684
7 *The Life of F D Maurice* Vol I, ed Frederick Maurice, p 127. He was remarkable for the catholicity of his mind as shown, for example, in the two volumes of his *Moral and Metaphysical Philosophy*
8 Metropolitan Anthony of Sourozh *op cit* p 24

6 The Role of the Teacher

The last four chapters have looked at underlying causes of our failure to produce schools which are places of real education. Such causes surface as mistaken emphases in organisation and teaching. A huge number of factors operate to make any inroad on the working of the administrative machine difficult. All the problems associated with money, time, staffing, promotion prospects, numbers of students, geographical location, building, fair involvement of all who have an interest in the running of the school, claims of examination-procedures, and so forth suggest that substantial changes of outlook in society as a whole are required before much progress can be made in this direction. This does not mean, however, that nothing can be done to improve the situation in ways which can quietly be quite dramatic.

The role of the teacher is crucial. The most consistently identified factor in situations where education is seen to be effective is the personality and commitment of the teacher concerned. It is quite astonishing what a difference one person can make. In one school music can flourish, while in an adjacent school, it is boxing: the same catchment area can produce distinctive excellences according to the enthusiasm and professional skill of two outstanding teachers.

It is often remarked that the tone of a school is set by the head. What this actually means is that the degree of influence a person has corresponds to the amount of scope, or power, they have. In British schools the head does have tremendous sway, notwithstanding increasing moves towards staff democracy and active participation by governors and parents. The humblest teacher, however, does have scope for far-reaching influence in every single contact he or she makes: the opportunity is sufficient, if used to the full, to absorb the energies of the fittest and most gifted. The extent of the influence will depend on the quality of commitment to education which the teacher brings. As Roy Niblett wrote:

> It is a mistake to imagine that the members of a school staff are even approximately equal in their influence upon their pupils. One teacher who passionately cares for his subject or for his children will have far more influence than five or six who are merely professionals.[1]

He went on to identify one of the 'the great secrets of teaching' as intensity. There needs to be an energy, an involvement, a brightness about the way the teacher relates to his or her students. This can only come from a conviction that the task in which the teacher is engaged has real significance.

Teachers are among the most important sector of the community and it is sad indeed when this is not adequately acknowledged by the public at large. It is even more unfortunate when teachers themselves have a low self-image and lack of vision, for teaching is a profession which only yields a sense of fulfilment if entered into wholeheartedly.

It has not been easy for teachers to adjust to the changing nature of society in Britain. An increasing instability and lack of direction and consensus on values has been reflected in schools. Furthermore, the immense amount of research and reflection upon educational theory in recent decades, much of it seriously challenging traditional patterns, has imposed a strain on teachers. The theorists have themselves often not been consistent, responding to current trends as they do, and many teachers have had but a superficial understanding of the changes which they have been expected to implement at the chalk-face. Ill-digested methods of teaching frequently jostle with ill-assimilated information in the classroom, so that students are caught in the cross-fire between the old and the new. Teachers need to be especially clear about their role in order to educate in situations which are in many areas uncongenial to education. Much has already been said, by implication, in earlier chapters about what the teacher's role is. The purpose of this chapter is to draw together the threads.

The teacher as exemplar

An old maxim runs: 'Education is not filling a bucket but lighting a fire'. The implications of this for teachers are considerable.

Integrity

Teaching is about sharing what one is oneself just as one flame kindles another. Attitudes such as the five respects listed earlier (on pp 14–16), and qualities of character which they promote, are 'caught, not taught'. They are imparted through the teacher's own integrity, genuine interest and diligence. It is useless to talk about openness, for example, without demonstrating it oneself. As the Zulu proverb puts it: 'I cannot hear a word you are saying because what you *are* shouts so loudly in my ears.' Even the most apathetic or recalcitrant of students, of any age, can pick up an impression of the teacher's real attitude and character, both of which embody his or her beliefs, for, in the phrase made famous by Marshall McLuhan 'The medium is the message.' It is perhaps true to say that the younger the student the less hypocrisy a teacher can get away with.

Integrity is certainly another of the great secrets of teaching. By this, I mean a concern that people develop a true individuality which, because it is not a role or mask behind which someone hides, is capable of real relationship with other persons. Yet the question Roy Niblett asked over 30 years ago is just as pertinent today,

> Is it not true that some of our teaching is more successful at getting people to act at being instead of really being – to act at being knowledgeable, to act at being citizens even to act at enjoying themselves?[2]

Such acting is encouraged by so much in modern life, but it can lead to deep crises of identity and a lack of self-esteem. It is fundamentally superficial, like the veneer on a painting. The good teacher is more concerned about helping students to create the painting which they each have within them, rather than diverting their energies to the veneer. To do this teachers must themselves be real people, prepared to have real relationships, indeed not tolerating false ones if at all possible.

Commitment as a primary resource

The question of the teacher's commitment – that is, the complex of convictions and attitudes which constitute his or her own philosophy of life – is central. Commitment, as Edward Hulmes has argued, is the teacher's 'primary resource'.[3] It can be made to work for the purposes of education and not of indoctrination provided that certain safeguards are observed. Figure 11 offers a five-point check-list.

Teacher-profile: animating not dominating

Psychological factors are very important in communication. Too high a teacher-profile will impede education for many students as seriously as too low a profile. This is not just because over-enthusiasm builds up resistance, but because of the claustrophobic effect of a dominating personality on students' powers of self-involvement – upon which education depends. Many teachers do not perceive how by their excitement or conscientiousness they actually take away from their students the capacity to respond. Cardinal Hume at his inauguration in 1976 said that his role was 'not to dominate but to animate'[4] and this could be sound advice for teachers. It again reinforces the importance of example, for example animates without dominating.

The process of conveying something to someone else often carries with it an implication of superiority on the part of the communicator and this must be guarded against. As Pope intuited:

> 'Men must be taught as if you taught them not,
> And things unknown proposed as things forgot'.[5]

What this means in practice is that the teacher needs to balance the various attributes (listed in Figure 12 as Low profile and High profile) and give

Figure 11 How to make commitment an educational asset

1 Acknowledge the controversial nature of issues and their complexity and be aware of the ease with which bias and distortion can creep in to all opinion

2 Declare one's own commitment and invite discussion, accepting vulnerability

3 Encourage students to think for themselves and probably to disagree with one's own view. Do *not* try to get consensus or assume students' agreement, but stand back and give space to them

4 Help students to learn skills of discernment and decision-making. Teach them the nature of evidence and its importance in supporting or discrediting opinions, and enable them to be aware of the tricks of crooked thinking (See Figure 18 on page 130)

5 Discuss the educational problems with students so that they are are alerted against such dangers as indoctrination, from whatever source it may come

careful attention to teaching methods appropriate for the personalities of all involved, including him or herself.

Patience and poise

Teaching by example, however, should not be over self-conscious, or overbearing. Communication is about what is received by people, not what is consciously given. There is a need for qualities which may be summed up as patience and poise. Patience is needed because it is so easy to imagine that if one talks long enough, or has sufficiently interesting means of presentation, communication will be achieved. Yet everything said and done is interpreted by recipients according to their own particular understanding and attention. Often the undertones or overtones which words and actions have for the person trying to communicate are quite different from the undertones or overtones present for each of those on the receiving end. Understanding indeed comes from within and awaits the right time. And the right time is related to the unique experience, capacity and motivation of

---

Figure 12 Paradox and the requirements of teaching

Low profile	High profile
Cool approach	Warm approach
Critical	Affirming
Personally distanced	Involved and committed
Stressing objectivity	Stressing subjectivity
Intellectual	Emotional
Non-dogmatic	Definite
Asking questions	Giving answers
Learning with others	Teaching others
Acknowledging limitations	Confident
Non-interference	Taking initiative
Listening	Talking
Non-authoritarian	Exercising the authority of a teacher
Awareness of complexity	Clarity and simplicity
Reticence	Self-assurance
Patience	Persistence
Not concerned with response	Expecting much
Take-it-or-leave-it attitude	Strong desire to help
Turning a blind eye	Disciplining
Concern for skills	Concern for content
Voicing doubt and controversy	Voicing certainties and convictions
Stressing relevance to students	Stressing heritage of the past
Teacher subservient to routine	Teacher-controlled novelty
Acceptance of external norms	Inventive, creative approach to assessment
Stressing student experience	Stressing presentation by the teacher

This list is offered as a talking-point. The pairs are paradoxes not contradictions. The qualities listed under both profiles are needed in the same person for really effective teaching.

Readers may like to arrange the items differently so that they correspond to old and new emphases in educational theory. It may be interesting to note that in some ways the new requires a higher profile for the teacher than the old, despite the apparently authoritative nature of the old and the non-authoritative ideal of the new. Thus, for example, the authoritarian teacher claimed to be teaching both objectively and with warmth and concern for emotional involvement. Similarly, adherence to a syllabus can be regarded as either demoting the position of the teacher to simply that of a mediator or as enhancing the teacher's place as the mediator of something objective – it depends on how it is seen. Often too, the newer approach is as reliant as the old on, for example, acceptance of external norms, stressing the importance of exposition and so forth.

each individual. 'Never answer a question until it is asked' is a safe rule for effective communication.

Attempting communication before the time is right is not only unsuccessful but can actually prevent understanding later on. Patience and willingness to be responsive to the needs and interests of students is essential. This is often difficult because it seems to run contrary to the enthusiasm and emotional drive to communicate which must also be present. It involves really listening and taking seriously the personalities of those taught, and of affirming their capacities as people.

The poise required of the teacher draws attention to the delicate balance needed between the high and low profiles outlined above. Patience, especially if it has had to be worked at, must not turn into escapism or failure to be a strong, clear-headed and warm-hearted personality oneself. There is a time for action, for decisiveness, for taking the initiative. The word 'poise' suggests that that time is understood. Opportunities are not missed. The teacher is ready. A most striking example of such poise is given in the anecdote concerning Einstein which closes this chapter (see page 71f).

It may help to contrast the good teacher with the opposite. This is someone who does not realise opportunities but breaks in abruptly, unaware of other peoples' experience and only concerned with his or her own objective. Roy Niblett gives an example of a 'class absorbed in The Passing of Arthur, intensely disciplined in imagination by their actual experiencing of what is being read'. The insensitive 'may suddenly break off reading and say "Jones, sit up straight . . . yes, *all* of you attend to the onomatopoeia in line 86 . . ."' Such a teacher is indulging in superficial propaganda for self-interested purposes'[6] – even if he or she is unaware of it.

Practice of such poise does not diminish the teacher's role as an initiator of learning. It may be helpful to see this as a fourfold role, as summarised in Figure 13.

Teacher assessment

There has been much discussion of teacher-assessment in recent years, and it may be something which, as Mary Warnock advocated in her BBC broadcast in 1985,[7] needs to be taken more seriously by the profession as a whole, in order that the teacher's image in society at large may be improved or preserved, and in order that better and fairer career structures can be worked out for teachers.

Yet it remains true that the teacher must learn to live without a sense of obvious achievement because one can never know the true effects of teaching. Education, like understanding, comes from within and cannot be programmed in a demonstrably certain way, nor objectively evaluated. The reverence accorded in our society to examinations and other assessment

Figure 13   The role of the teacher

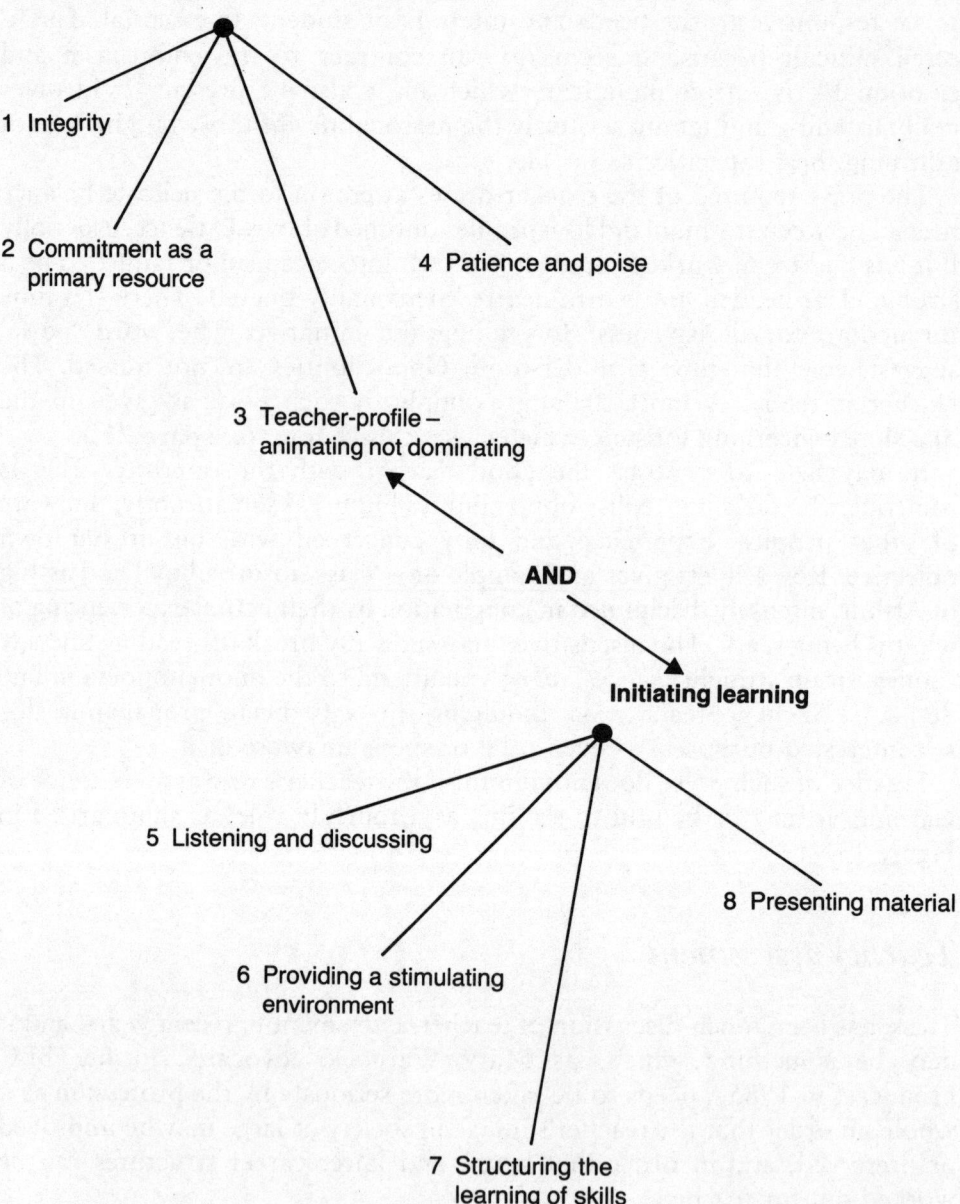

Being an example

1 Integrity

2 Commitment as a
   primary resource

4 Patience and poise

3 Teacher-profile –
   animating not dominating

AND

Initiating learning

5 Listening and discussing

8 Presenting material

6 Providing a stimulating
   environment

7 Structuring the
   learning of skills

Role-play, dance, drama, art-work, music, visiting speakers, educational visits, field-work, and all manner of audio-visual and computer aids can be used in relation to 6, 7 and 8, as well as basic talk-and-chalk, worksheets and/or textbooks.

techniques denotes how people do not realise this. Despite increasing awareness of the inadequacy of all evaluation procedures, and recognition that the spirit of the thing is lost in so-called 'factual' work or performance of technical skills which is all that can be assessed with scrupulous fairness, people go on according it very high priority.

Students' education cannot be truly measured by objective testing, and no more can teachers' success in educating. Teachers must trust that what they do will bear good fruit later, even though these results will almost certainly be unknown to them.

The public, also, must learn to trust teachers just as teachers trust students, for then teachers will rise to the level of that trust. Otherwise their self-image will be low and morale will decline still further than in recent years.

With regard to the effectiveness of one's teaching there is satisfaction in increasing self-awareness and appreciation of the nature of one's own personality, gifts and attitudes and how they can best be of use in helping others towards education. The list in Figure 12 already referred to may be a help in such self-assessment.

Yet perhaps T S Eliot was right when he wrote in the *Four Quartets*:

'For us, there is only the trying. The rest is not our business'.[8]

New technology and the role of the teacher

Many people are afraid that the computer revolution may make such inroads into education that the role of the teacher will be seriously diminished; they fear that computers may in some sense replace teachers.

If teachers see themselves as primarily purveyors of information or trainers in specific, clearly-analysable skills then this may be so. It is possible to envisage computer programming of a high enough order to do both as effectively, or more effectively, than teachers. The above discussion of teaching method, however, sees teachers as primarily educators who use information and skills-training in order to develop in students the capacity for life-long self-education.[9]

Two of the most serious drawbacks for teachers attempting this wider and more responsible role have been the numbers of students with whom they have had to relate, and the lack of time and energy which conscientious, hard-pressed teachers face. Both these factors operate at their worst in secondary schools but they make a significant impact at primary school level as well. The arrival of large-scale computer-teaching would alleviate both these drawbacks in a way beneficial to education. By relieving teachers of much of the chores and donkey-work of finding information and of interesting large numbers of students, it could liberate them to be educators in reality as well as in intention.

The lengthy anecdote about Einstein with which this chapter closes may seem remote from the world of computer-technology. But it encapsulates what education is about. It also draws attention to how unrealistic the educational ideal is in the present school set-up. Yet it is significant that in several ways the presence of computers could free the teacher to be able to act as Einstein did in his encounter with the young journalist, Jerome Weidman (see Figure 14).

Figure 14 Computers and the teacher

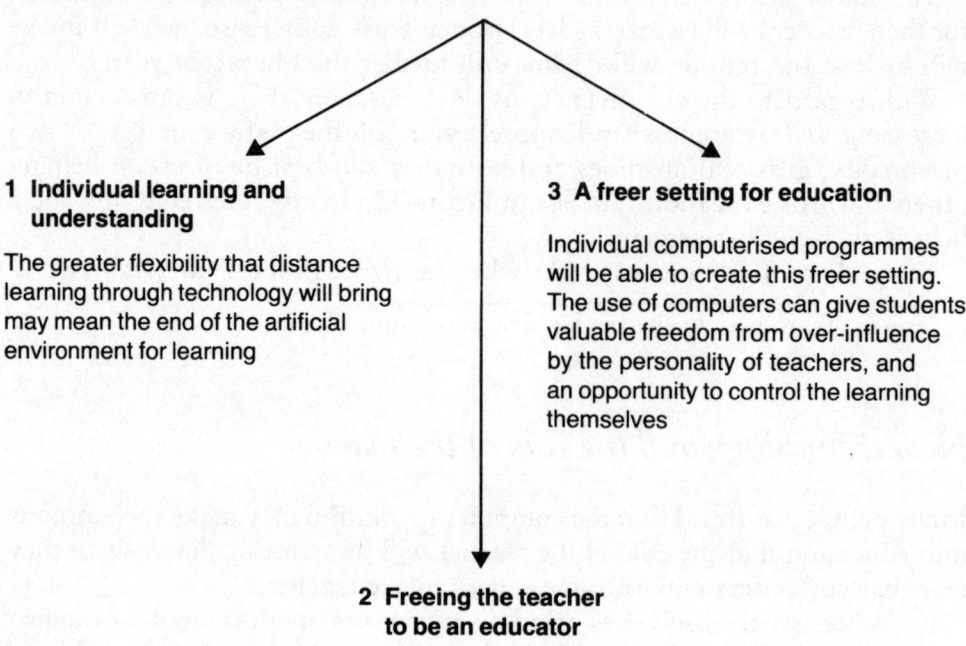

**1 Individual learning and
    understanding**

The greater flexibility that distance learning through technology will bring may mean the end of the artificial environment for learning

3 A freer setting for education

Individual computerised programmes will be able to create this freer setting. The use of computers can give students valuable freedom from over-influence by the personality of teachers, and an opportunity to control the learning themselves

**2 Freeing the teacher
    to be an educator**

Computers will never replace personal contact despite the development of interaction computers. Only a person can help another to be a person. Yet by reducing the need for large class teaching and supervision, and for preparation of presentation-material and need for marking factual understanding, computers can play an invaluable part.

'Opening up yet another fragment of the frontier of beauty'

In an article entitled *The Night I Met Einstein*[10] Jerome Weidman relates how as a very young man he was invited to dine at the home of a distinguished philanthropist and found himself unwillingly 'in for an evening of chamber music', 'in for' because he was almost tone deaf and to him serious music was no more than an arrangement of noises. It chanced, however, that he was sitting next to Einstein who at the end of the first piece turned to him and said 'You are fond of Bach?' A casual question in the interests of politeness prompting a casual reply? 'No,' Weidman wrote 'I could see from the look in my neighbour's extraordinary eyes that regardless of what value I placed on my part in the verbal exchange, to this man his part in it mattered very much.' Here was a man 'to whom you did not tell a lie, however small'. He admitted he did not know anything about Bach. I will go on in Weidman's words:

A look of astonishment washed across Einstein's mobile face. 'You have never heard Bach?' He made it sound as though I had said I'd never had a bath. 'It isn't that I don't want to like Bach', I replied hastily, 'It's just that I'm almost tone deaf, and I've never really heard anybody's music.' A look of concern came into the old man's face. 'Please' he said, 'You will come with me?'

He stood up and took my arm. A rising murmur of puzzled speculation in that crowded room followed us out into the hall. Einstein paid no attention to it. Resolutely he led me upstairs. He obviously knew the house well. On the floor above he opened the door to a book-lined study, drew me in and shut the door . . . 'Tell me, please', he said, 'Is there any kind of music that you do like?'

'Well', I answered, 'I like some that have words, and the kind of music where I can follow the tune.' He smiled and nodded, obviously pleased, 'You can give me an example, perhaps?' When I ventured, 'almost anything by Bing Crosby', he went to a corner of the room, opened a gramophone and started pulling out records. At last he beamed, 'Ah', he said.

He put the record on and in a moment the study was filled with the relaxed, lilting strains of Bing Crosby's *Where the Blue of the Night Meets the Gold of the Day*. Einstein beamed at me and kept time with the stem of his pipe. After three or four phrases he stopped the gramophone. 'Now', he said, 'Will you tell me, please, what you have just heard?'

The simplest answer seemed to be to sing the lines, I did just that, trying desperately to keep in tune and prevent my voice from cracking. The expression of Einstein's face was like the sunrise.

'You see' he cried with delight. 'You do have an ear!' I mumbled something about this being one of my favourite songs, something I had heard hundreds of times, so that it didn't really prove anything.

'Nonsense', said Einstein, 'It proves everything. Do you remember your first arithmetic lesson in school? Suppose at your first contact with numbers your teacher had ordered you to work out a problem in, say, long division or fractions, you would have reacted in panic, it is possible that throughout life you would be denied the beauty of long division and fractions.'

'So it is with music,' Einstein picked up the Bing Crosby record. 'This simple, charming little song is like simple addition or subtraction. You have mastered it. Now we go on to something more complicated.' He found another record and set it going. The golden voice of John McCormack singing *The Trumpeter* filled the room. After a few lines Einstein stopped the record. 'So', he said. 'You will sing that back to me, please?' I did – with a good deal of self-consciousness but with, for me, a quite surprising degree of accuracy. 'Excellent', Einstein remarked, 'Wonderful. Now this.' 'This' proved to be Caruso in what was to me a completely unrecognizable fragment from *Cavalleria Rusticana*. Nevertheless, I managed to reproduce an approximation of the sounds. Einstein beamed his approval.

Caruso was followed by at least a dozen others. I could not shake off my feeling of awe over the way this great man, into whose company I had been thrown by chance, was completely pre-occupied by what we were doing, as though I were his sole concern.

We came last to recordings of music without words, which I was instructed to reproduce by humming. When I reached for a high note, Einstein's mouth opened and his head went back as if to help me to attain what seemed unattainable. Evidently I came close enough, for he turned off the gramophone. 'Now, young man,' he said, putting his arm through mine, 'We are ready for Bach!'

As we returned to our seats in the drawing room, the players were tuning up for a new selection. That night for the first time in my life I heard Bach's *Sheep May Safely Graze* and when the concert ended I added my own genuine applause to that of the others. Suddenly our hostess confronted us. 'I'm so sorry, Dr. Einstein', she said, with an icy glare at me, 'that you missed so much of the performance.' Einstein and I hastily came to our feet. 'I am sorry too', he said. 'My young friend here and I, however, were engaged in the greatest activity of which man is capable.' She looked puzzled. 'Really?' she said, 'And what is that?' Einstein smiled and put his arm across my shoulders. And he uttered ten words that – for at least one person who is in his endless debt – are his epitaph:
'Opening up yet another fragment of the frontier of beauty.'

This anecdote suggests at least five points concerning the role of the teacher.

1 *The immense value of personal relationships* People learn best when they are with someone who cares to communicate with them, and shows delight at their progress, someone who believes in them and treats them as a friend and equal partner in the business of education, someone who is enthusiastic about something and can inspire other people to give 100% attention to it by demonstrating such attention. By entering into the 'orbit' of another person, people are enabled to leave the confines of their limited experience and make that person's experience their own.

2 *The importance of utterly honest conversation* This needs to be conversation which really relates to the other person and in which people actively listen to each other. It must be conducted in straightforward language in which people are not trying to impress, or hiding behind clichés, but struggling to say what they genuinely think.

3 *The need to start where a person really is* It is vital to go back to the very root of misunderstanding and work up gradually – by easy stages and missing none out – from the known to the unknown. In this way education can develop an authentic inner response, putting the responsibility for development on the person being educated, not keeping him or her dependent on the authority of another.

4 *The value of a certain casualness in learning* Over-structure kills. Most education necessarily takes place in odd moments, mainly out of school – through the chance conversation or in a particular setting. People need freedom in order to learn, and also inspiration, from beautiful surroundings or challenging circumstances, quietness or a dynamic bustle of activity . . .

5 *The importance of a coherent philosophy of life* The teacher needs this in order to make the most of the opportunities for education which are presented. Precise help can then be given out of a vast storehouse of experience, reflection and understanding. This philosphy of life needs to be coherent and assured, broad in concept and challenging, committed to the insights it has attained and yet open and welcoming to those of others.[11]

Notes and references

1 Roy Niblett *Education and the Modern Mind* (Faber, 1954), p 84
2 Niblett *ibid* p 85
3 Edward Hulmes *Commitment and Neutrality in Religious Education* (Geoffrey Chapman, 1979) p 32
4 Basil Hume reported in *The Times* 13 March 1986
5 Alexander Pope *Essay on Criticism* 574f
6 Niblett *ibid* p 85
7 Mary Warnock 'Teacher teach thyself' 1985 Richard Dimbleby Lecture published in *The Listener* 28 March 1985
8 T S Eliot *Four Quartets: East Coker V*
9 There are many books available on the uses of the new technology – see, for example, Alan Maddison *Microcomputers in the Classroom* (Hodder and Stoughton, 1982) – but very little literature discussing how this may influence the teacher's understanding of his/her role
10 Jerome Weidman 'The Night I Met Einstein' *Readers' Digest* March 1979, pp 99–102
11 A potentially very important project, raising issues concerned with the role of the teacher and organisation of the curriculum and suggesting a positive way forward in secondary schools, is that on *Flexible Learning in small Fifth and Sixth Forms* run by the National Extension College in conjunction with Hertfordshire LEA (1982–1984) under the coordination of Pamela Harding. The Final Report (NEC Trust Limited, 1985) has disturbing things to say. For example, most teachers 'acknowledged that they were only just beginning to think about how students learn' (page 6) and 'The majority of sixth form students have had no previous experience of individualised learning . . . As a consequence, almost none of them has the skills necessary to organise either their study or themselves' (page 7). It would be very hard to find a more damning indictment of the effect of eleven years' official schooling! See also 'Learning and Belief' by Andrew Davis in *JPE*, Vol 20, No 1, 1986

7 Education in Beliefs and Values

The first part of this book has drawn attention to the paramount need for education in beliefs and values. For a school to be truly educational there must be awareness of the fundamental convictions inspiring the educational ideal. Furthermore, this awareness should permeate the whole life of the school so that everyone, including the youngest child, is encouraged to become more and more perceptive about it.

Acceptance of controversy

The problems presented by the fact that people have controversial views have been considered in some depth. The way forward would seem necessarily to begin with acknowledging that people do think differently on many crucial issues because they start from different assumptions. To pretend there is agreement where there is not, or to try to impose it, is deceitful and damaging to any attempt to educate. Furthermore it fails to capitalise on the enormous amount of interest and involvement which people of all ages are prepared to devote to such issues if they are given a chance. Often controversy concerns matters of great moment; often, too, it is fascinating in itself. Why deprive people of the pleasure it can give in coming to terms with it?

This point can be heavily underlined by the fact that failure to equip students to cope with controversy may have long-term and explosive repercussions. If people cannot learn to handle differences of opinion within a relatively controlled situation, they will be at sea in the wider world.

Acknowledging that people think differently is more difficult than it might appear. Unless strong representations of other views are presented, one tends to take for granted the truth of one's own view and the assumptions behind it, and not see it as a subject for debate.

Yet the fact of controversy can only be realistically accepted within a framework of something which is agreed. Any community must have a common purpose in order to exist, otherwise it is simply a disharmony, a collection of people thrown together by chance. This common mind should itself be kept under review – all concerned should acknowledge that they can question it and disagree with it. The common mind, however, should be broad enough in its base to command a consensus of the vast majority – including the students, who do not have the option open to adults to leave the community if they disagree with its assumptions.

Concern for achieving such a common mind will involve both displaying value-assumptions and questioning why these particular values are held. It may be helpful at this point to take a stage further the brief discussion of values taken up in Chapter 1.

The grounds for holding a value

Attention was drawn there to certain qualities of universalism and 'oughtness' which the word 'value' implies. Strictly speaking, values do not change. It is people's perception which changes, and in this people may be nearer or further away from a proper understanding of the value. The value behind anti-racism, for example, is not new. It has never been right nor ever will be right, so it seems to me, that people be regarded as inferior on grounds of their race or colour. We in the twentieth century may be more aware of this, but people *should* always have seen it. I have just used two words which frequently are not much to the fore in discussions about values in education: *right* and *should*. I believe that until they are more common, discussion will tend to be superficial, because people will be *assuming* that values are simply subjective.

A particular example of the way in which such subjectivism is often just assumed and not discussed is when people bring in to a conversation about truth-claims words such as 'better' or 'superior'. I recall a meeting a few months ago in which I expressed my opinion about something that I believed to be true and was met with the retort 'So you think your view is superior to that of other people?' When I pointed out that my view was right or wrong, not superior or inferior, the reply came 'Even so, you think yourself a superior judge as to what is right or wrong'.

This kind of arguing is dishonest on two scores. First, it introduces a red herring, and an uncharitable one at that, by directing attention away from the content of what is said to the personality of its speaker. Second, it is irrelevant to the argument to bring in the competitive factor at all. If I say 'the time is now 9.50 am' and someone else says 'It is 9.45 am', there is no point in saying that one view is better than, or superior to, the other. One is right and the other wrong, or both are wrong. Even though questions of value and belief do not admit of straightforward empirical verification, so that we can quite properly say of something which cannot be scientifically proved or adequately put into words that one view is nearer the truth than another, or has greater insight, it is still inappropriate to say a view is superior to that of another. Insights, if they really are insights, that is, perceptions of what actually is the case, cannot be in competition or conflict; only oversights can be that.

Use of such language as 'superior' where it clearly does not belong shows how strongly competitive values feature in our society. Yet it could not get a hold at all without the prior assumption that no-one *can* know; and that therefore all discussion of beliefs and values is basically of sociological, psychological or pragmatic interest. Those who are concerned for education and not indoctrination must object to such a view being assumed and not opened up for discussion.

In addition this assumption runs into difficulty when the question 'Why support this value rather than that?' is pursued. Values are presumably the result of enlightened self-interest, authority, consensus or reaction to something we dislike. All these positions, however, would seem to be indefensible and involved in contradiction. Let us take, for example, 'people matter' or 'respect for others'. If I say people matter because otherwise I or my group will have an uncomfortable life, I am treating people as simply a means to my, or our, own convenience, and not as people in their own right. People matter even if authority decrees they do not, as in Nazi Germany; people matter if there is no consensus, even if there are many people who do not think they do; and people matter notwithstanding that there are situations in which people are treated as though they did not matter.

This latter point raises the question of whether a polarity of good and bad is needed with regard to values. Underlying the question is a confusion between *ontology*, or what is, and *epistemology*, or what is known or understood. A most important distinction needs to be made here. It is true that we often learn about health by becoming aware of disease, but that does not mean to say that fundamentally health cannot exist without disease. Hatred, for example, is not required in order that there can be love, even though experience of hatred may help people to become aware of what love is.

Values, understood in the ontological sense, relate to truth. They are self-authenticating, derived from insight, and in line with reason provided the latter is honestly used. As such, values are inescapable: we do not choose values; they choose us, for they come to us and claim us. They involve a sense of inner obligation.

Value and belief

What people value concerns the question of what people know and understand. In this epistemological sense of the word, values are closely linked with what people believe. Values are determined by what we believe, deep-down, about the nature of the world, of reality, of existence. Valuing kindness, generosity, love, reflects an underlying conviction that people matter and are centres of reality which must not be manipulated as means to some other end. Valuing aggression, force and tyranny is the obverse side of faith in competitive self- or group-assertiveness: the conviction that I or we matter in a way that other people do not. The stronger the belief the more emphatic the value. If people are convinced of the truth of life-after-death as are, for example, the Afghan guerillas fighting their *jihād* against the Soviets in Afghanistan, the value they place on continued existence in this world is slight by comparison with that of the hedonist who believes that this world is all there is and so we might as well 'eat, drink, be merry, for tomorrow we die'.

Put in another way we can say that values are beliefs couched in the form of: 'I believe that ———— is important or what life is about.' A value is a statement about how the person who holds the value sees the world. If I believe (*i*) that reality is such that people of my race are superior to others, this leads on to a racist scale of values. If, on the other hand, I believe (*ii*) that reality is such that all human beings deserve intrinsic respect, regardless of colour, creed or sex, this leads on to values such as openness, fairness and toleration of people as persons. Again, if I think (*iii*) that reality is such that economics is the key to life, this will lead me to a utilitarian approach to education. But if I think (*iv*) that reality is such that spirituality is the key to life, this will lead me to emphasise spiritual values as the most significant aspect of education. In the profile of the ideal school I have pictured in Chapter 1 it is obvious that I do not hold the first and third beliefs but that I do support the second and fourth.

The link between values and beliefs is very clear when the beliefs are well-articulated, as in the case of ideologies and religions. It tends to be overlooked when no attention is ever drawn to these beliefs in the form of 'This is what I believe'; it is easy to imagine that therefore there is no belief behind the value, simply because the belief is taken for granted, perhaps unconscious and purely conditioned. Normally, indeed it is *not* the case that people say 'I believe this, and so I will hold this value, say justice or toleration or whatever.' What people value has a direct, though probably unperceived, link with the fundamental belief-structure or underlying framework they have for thinking about the way things are. This framework is picked up, at least in part, from the society to which they belong, the way they have been brought up, the people they happen to meet, the books they read, and so forth.

The social and cultural element here is important. People are in orbit around certain ideas. In Muslim states, for example, the concepts of the Qur'ān permeate people's whole way of life. In this country Judeo-Christian beliefs have permeated society, although in the last two or three centuries a competitor has taken over to some extent (as discussed extensively in Chapter 3 and summarised in Figure 6 on page 26).

The role of reason

In a time such as ours of questioning and inter-mingling of belief-systems, achieving a system of shared values and approaching controversial issues constructively can best be done through an attitude of what I have called *critical affirmation*. Such an attitude goes beyond the advocacy of reason *per se*. It acknowledges the crucial role of clear thinking in both analysis and evaluation but it does not fall into the trap of imagining that reason alone can cure all ills. As already argued in Chapter 3 reason has to accept starting-points which are outside its scope to establish; these may be arbitrarily-chosen like the rules for playing a particular game, or they may be grounded in intuitions concerning the nature of the world which cannot be demonstrated in such a way that any rational person must be obliged to accept them. Reason by itself, therefore, cannot be a final arbiter in matters of beliefs and values.

The notion of affirmation allied to the word 'critical' draws attention to the need for a more imaginative and comprehensive quality of mind and character. In metaphorical terms reason can be likened to walking whilst critical affirmation, with its emphasis upon insight, is like flying. The two should be proceeding in the same direction. If, however, they go off at a tangent from one another, then both modes of propulsion need to be scrutinised, not just one by the other: insight should be tested by reason, but also reason by insight. Another metaphor which might be used is that of human vision and the laser-beam, reason being likened to the former, critical affirmation to the latter, which is able to penetrate solid surfaces which defeat human sight.

Critical affirmation has, however, a rigour parallel to that of reason. It in no way rides roughshod over the importance of testing presumed insight against a reasonable view of all evidence available and of guarding against the dangers of rationalisation. It involves distinguishing between what is positive in people's beliefs and behaviour, and what is negative of others or of oneself. The grounds for this are that derision, denunciation and dismissal of people's deeply-held convictions are usually based on oversight, misunderstanding or ignorance – except where those convictions are themselves negative of others and thus based on oversight, misunderstanding or ignorance.

It has been maintained that education properly understood is critically affirming in this way. It embraces attitudes of tolerance and openness as well as concern for what is true and the evidence supporting it. A school built up on such principles will both demonstrate such attitudes and help all involved to be articulate about them. Within such a broad consensus education will be able to concern itself not with telling people what to think but teaching them *how* to think, leaving responsibility firmly in the court of each individual. It will be education in responsibility.

Summary of the need for education in beliefs and values

1 Education in beliefs and values focuses on what is basic to the whole educational enterprise. So much of what is done in schools plunges people in, as it were, half-way; the children and students for whom schools exist miss out on any discussion of the fundamental reasons for education. It is not surprising that many come to see schooling as largely irrelevant, boring and a waste of time once the child's initial interst in everything and compliance with the wishes of adults can no longer make it seem important, acceptable or pleasant.

Education in beliefs and values would seek to share with everyone the rationale behind education as a goal and the school as an institutional means towards that end. It would help everyone to evaluate the desirability of the values underlying what is done in school, the possible need for change, the way these values are or are not implemented in practice and so forth. Education in beliefs and values would mean vulnerability for dogmatic views and attitudes whether of a traditional or a progressive complexion, but it would help to ensure high motivation on the part of everyone, staff and students alike, in seeking to make the school a living community.

2 Education in beliefs and values would enable the principle of the autonomy of the child to be taken seriously.[1] Indeed one might express this more emphatically and say that without education in beliefs and values the autonomy of the child is seriously threatened. The pressures both within the school and in the outer world to encourage a person to conform to this or that outlook are so great, especially in these days of sophisticated communication techniques, that to fail to alert even young children to the dangers of their being 'taken over', and to fail to equip them with necessary skills of perceptiveness and evaluation, is to betray them educationally, no matter how high-sounding our aims and objectives may be. We owe it to children to develop their capacities both for honest reflection upon the convictions presented to them, and also for their own genuine search for convictions by which to live.

What constitutes clear thinking needs to be within the grasp of every citizen of a democratic society, as does the ability to detect dishonest thinking and arguing. If this understanding is lacking, the capacity of an individual to be independent is inevitably impaired; so often when someone thinks he or she is being independent, someone else can identify the thought or behaviour as a reflex-action of a group. To be truly independent a person must be able to look at issues on their own merits, not coloured by other people's or his or her own emotional reactions. On the basis of this appraisal individuals can form their own authentic commitments which harness emotion and will-power as well as mind.

3 Education in beliefs and values would help to create an atmosphere in which people develop not just autonomously but responsibly. Much of the disquiet felt by some people at the concept of the autonomy of the child has its source in the awareness that by itself this is an inadequate principle to guide education; it must be balanced by the notion of responsibility. No civilised society can allow its members literally to do what they like, unless what they freely choose to do happens to cohere with the common good. This radical freedom was what St Augustine had in mind when he coined the aphorism 'Love God and do what you like'. He believed that if someone genuinely loved God as He is, then they would want to do what was pleasing to God, and this would ensure that the purpose of legal and moral codes would be attained directly without infringement of personal freedom.

Such an aphorism is not, however, helpful as a principle to guide education, not just because belief in God is itself controversial and not held by everyone, but also because the levels of possible misunderstanding and self-deception in fulfilling so apparently simple a precept are unimaginably complex. A secular version, in the form of, for example, 'Develop the five-fold attitude of respect for oneself, other people, the environment, beauty and truth, and do what you like' would not fare any better; the more that one appreciates what such respect involves, in attitude, intention and behaviour, the less confidence one is likely to have in people's capacity to pursue such a goal with a degree of understanding and purity which would also enable them to do what they liked. Schools have to be concerned with education in responsibility; schools need to take on what Basil Mitchell calls an 'architectonic' role. He takes this word from Plato

> who distinguished between the many and various *technai* (crafts or sciences) which aim at some particular good, and the *architektonike techne* which aims at the form of the good itself, which both explains the character of the world and constitutes the end of human life.[2]

Basil Mitchell goes on to note that this role includes handing on the values by which society lives, or has lived, or thinks it ought to live, as well as helping individuals to find a faith by which to live.

Developmental moral education

A formidable objection to the whole idea of there being any content to be passed on may be offered by the developmentalists whom Derek Wright regards as providing today 'the prevailing perspective among the experts' in Moral Education in schools. They tend to assume that process is everything, so that if one allows discussion and democratic procedures in school then truth and responsibility will automatically ensue. Behind this lies, as Derek Wright puts it, the image of self-directed, open-minded, rational people, guided by flexible moral principles, and particularly that of justice, as sources or originators of moral judgment, and able to meet fresh moral problems in an enlightened way.[3]

A number of difficulties may be encountered with such an approach. First, it fails to take cognisance of the dark side of human nature which all the great ideologies and religions of the world have noted. This dark side quickly becomes apparent whenever, and to the extent that, individuals do have freedom literally to do what they like.[4]

Second, in practice, discussions based upon such a premise are soon felt to be unsatisfactory. Both staff and students weary of an endless recital of simply personal opinions, and much of what goes on in schools unfortunately merits the gibe 'discussion is the mutual exchange of ignorance'.

Third, does not such an approach to Moral Education *assume* that morality is either innate or invented, originating in the mind and feelings of the person making moral decisions? Why then use words like 'justice' or 'enlightened'? To assume in the classroon that there are objective moral norms like justice, to which human attitudes and behaviour ought to conform and concerning which people ought to become enlightened would be regarded as impermissible by many 'developmentalists'. Yet to assume that there are no such norms is equally inadmissible, because equally controversial. Indeed I would argue that the latter is *less* supportable by reason than the former! Yet that statement is itself debatable; it must be the subject of debate, and not be assumed.

Of course the question arises: how can one go on questioning *every* assumption? One must stop somewhere and say 'this is where we're starting and we're having no further argument about it.' But when people within a school situation say this kind of thing, they are being indoctrinatory (however much they may deny it). Attention should constantly be drawn to the fact that, for pragmatic reasons, such a stance is being adopted. Then of course it becomes possible for children and students to question it. I see, therefore, no escape from the necessity to bring assumptions, *all* of them so far as it is possible, under constant scrutiny.

Of the three possible views:

   i   traditional didactic Moral Education;

   ii more recent developmental Moral Education;

   iii Moral Education which applies the process principle of *ii* to the content concern of *i* in a way which draws attention to the assumptions underlining both *i* and *ii*;

it seems to me clear that only *iii* is educationally acceptable, with regard to the indoctrination issue.

Furthermore, it is perhaps the only view which is acceptable with regard to acquisition or development of moral insight and integrity which both *i* and *ii* have as their goal, for it is methodologically the approach most likely to get children and students really involved in learning. Moreover, it does not down-grade what is unique about the moral domain of knowledge, namely the element of 'ought'. Indeed, it focuses attention precisely on the nature of that 'ought'. Does it come from some awareness of absolute standards, or is it a wholly psychological or sociological phenomenon?

Such an approach to Moral Education allows one to agree wholeheartedly with the emphasis on exploratory, discussion techniques and rational study of the developmentalists, without succumbing to the reductionism of much moral philosophy. Such reductionism is evident, for example, in Derek Wright's assertion in another paper[5] that 'theoretical morality forms the basis of our social, political and religious ideologies'. This is to assume that such ideologies do not arise from, nor need to consider, factors other than that of morality. In fact the contrary position, that our social, political and religious ideologies govern our theoretical morality, would seem to be more easily defensible. For it is how we see the nature of reality in all the dimensions including social, political and religious, which provides us with our sense of 'oughtness'.

It is interesting to note that Derek Wright's own views on religion may be seen as influencing his enthusiasm for the developmental approach to morality. His down-grading of any element of doctrine in favour of an understanding of religion in terms of the experience of being transcended would appear to give rise to, as much as reflect, a non-absolutist, largely implicit form of morality.

Derek Wright himself hints at a need to balance developmentalism with the more traditional approach. In the editorial quoted earlier he writes

> Those who think that education should promote certain virtues and eradicate certain vices, and who think the content of morality is more important than its form, have a defensible case. I would like to see that case put as persuasively as possible so that some dialogue can develop with those who take the more child-centred and developmental approach.

What would seem to be beyond dispute is that there *is* a discipline of content and rigour to be mastered concerning beliefs and values in order to know whether or not one should accept or reject them, and for what reasons. To wrestle with this in the context of a real search for truth is fundamental to that attitude of responsibility in thinking, feeling, choice and action which, along with autonomy, marks out the educated person.

Practical implications

On such grounds I would argue for an impressive commitment in schools to education in beliefs and values. This needs to take place in three ways: first, in the whole ethos of the school and how it is organised; second in the way each subject-area is taught; and third by directing a substantial amount of time, the equivalent of something like four hours a week, to a precise consideration of the content of values and beliefs themselves.

Why do I need to argue for this time-commitment in spite of the importance of such education in beliefs and values spanning the total curriculum? Let us take the example of the Sciences. It is very important that Science should not be taught as though it and it alone can arrive at factual knowledge. The subjective elements present in scientific enquiry should be referred to sufficiently frequently for students not to regard scientific method as entirely different from rational discussion of evidence appropriate to every other area of knowledge. It is especially important, for example, that scientific understanding should not be divorced from moral awareness. Yet moral questions and other issues which lie behind the pursuit of Science such as what constitutes evidence, what matters, why it matters and how this affects other areas of experience, cannot be properly attended to simply in Science lessons. This is because they involve so much more than scientific insight and content, and because the proper focus of Science is scientific and not moral or philosphical.

The need for time

When teaching history I was deeply aware of this dilemma. I used, for example, in teaching about ancient Greece, to have long discussions on the validity of slavery or of democracy but there was not the time to do it properly and I was conscious that I was not directly developing students' historical sensitivity. Similarly, when teaching for an 'A' level paper on the Russian Revolution, I spent six weeks discussing Marxism and associated political and economic issues, without even a reference to Russia, because the students were fascinated and wanted to debate them. But it was a risk – they could have failed their examination.

Many people may, however, be inclined to argue that education in values and beliefs can be done under Humanities in one of its forms. Yet an insidious form of indoctrination can enter in very easily when values and beliefs are discussed primarily within Social Sciences, Personal and Social Education (PSE) or a similar area of curriculum. This is because the proper focus of Social Studies is on how people behave in social groups, and of PSE on the adjustment of the individual to society. It can easily happen, therefore, that beliefs and values are treated just as part of the social data or the options open to an individual, without being treated in their own right as serious claims to truth. In other words, the subjectivity of values and beliefs can be assumed without attention ever being directed to that fact and how controversial it is. This is to indoctrinate it.

There needs therefore to be time – and a lot of time – in which the focus is on learning how to think deeply and thoughtfully, how to decide for oneself on the basis of evidence and understanding, and how to sort out commitments.

The concepts to be grasped, such as 'freedom', 'authority', 'justice', 'love', and the complexity to be appreciated, are at least as important and difficult as, for example, the concept of number. To ask for as large an allowance of time, resources, and teacher-preparation for education in beliefs and values as in, for example, Mathematics, is therefore only realistic and not in any way pleading for generosity. Without this kind of commitment to education in beliefs and values many schools will, in my opinion, continue to lurch forward uncertainly into the tough world of tomorrow. If, on the other hand, they were prepared to be courageous enough to invest real thought into the development of this area, it is possible that the whole of school-life could be transformed.

Religious education as an example

Having discussed what education is, the difficulties in attaining it and what is required of schools in order to overcome them, I want to turn in the rest of the book to examining one particular area of the curriculum. It is so easy to talk in generalities. Focusing on one area – looked at in some depth, but also fairly compehensively as regards its scope – can illuminate the arguments for education being put forward. It would, of course, have been possible to take a series of detailed examples from a number of subjects, but these could have been highly selective instances not typical of the subject as a whole. It is the total impact of the subject which needs to be considered as a paradigm for proper educational practice, because education itself is concerned with such all-roundedness.

My choice of Religious Education may need to be argued for, because many people today see this area as highly problematic, irrelevant and unimportant – an area of dubious content, taught for much of the time by teachers who have had little or no initial or in-service preparation for the task and who therefore teach sometimes in an unashamedly dogmatic manner, or, where more enlightened educational practice is evident, in a way which makes the subject largely indistinguishable from Humanities in general. This is a serious indictment indeed. Why not therefore consign Religious Education to the scrap-heap, rather than elevating it to a status deemed worthy of an exemplar function as regards what is truly educational?

I have nevertheless chosen this subject for a number of reasons:

1 It has this kind of image, but need not have. The fact that it is controversial to its very roots and capable of arousing strong emotions presents a challenge to be met, interesting for myself and I hope, therefore,

for the reader. The question is simply: can Religious Education serve the cause of education, and if so what can it uniquely offer? Can its contribution be worthwhile?

2 It has a special role to play in the education of beliefs and values because religious beliefs and derived values have been, and still are, among the most powerful and enduring of convictions. They relate to a distinctive area of human experience which at least raises questions of truth and value.

3 Built in to the idea of religion, whether one agrees with it or not, is the concept of wholeness and breadth of vision. In a close way therefore it is capable of paralleling, and raising questions concerning education. A religious perspective or dimension can indeed deepen and enrich the concept of a person which is so essential to an understanding of education.

4 Religion is capable of offering a penetrating critique of those assumptions discussed in chapter 3 which discourage education from happening in today's world. In this sense Religious Education can provide an excellent training-ground for clear and perceptive thinking.

5 In its long struggle to find educational acceptability, Religious Education has had to find ways of dealing with controversial issues. This is of general educational value, for controversial questions occur in almost all subject-areas. The techniques evolved in Religious Education may therefore be of wider benefit and transferable across the whole curriculum. They may provide an impressive safeguard against indoctrination and conditioning without succumbing to the temptation of escapism and evasion of issues.

6 Religion is a subject which can easily get people deeply involved in discussion. In my own experience, and talking with teachers over the years, I have found that there is never any shortage of interest in the classroom if religion and truth-claims can be discussed in an open way that genuinely welcomes students' expressing their real opinions and also considers the evidence without assuming that everyone must agree.

7 Historically there have been in Britain extremely close links between education and certain forms of religious belief, and between Moral Education and Religious Education.

This last point touches on very contentious matters. I will therefore develop the argument further.

Religious faith and the development of education

Historically, religion has supplied a fundamental theoretical justification or underpinning for the development of education as understood in its western, liberal sense. This concept of education appeared on the scene comparatively recently, in the period when the Enlightenment had challenged the authoritative status of the Church, but nevertheless the basic principles and outlook to which modern educationalists draw attention were produced by the Judeo-Christian tradition. The autonomy of the child is a principle which assumes a *high* concept of what constitutes a person; this is a central feature within Judaism and Christianity, and has also been slowly hammered out in Western societies over the past millenium and more under the aegis of such religious convictions. It is noticeable that people immersed in cultures other than those of the West often perceive more clearly than westerners the way in which our society leans upon religious assumptions derived especially from Christianity.

There may be many readers who would wish to play down this Judeo-Christian element, arguing that just because liberal education arose in a setting imbued with such ideals it does not follow that they were the *necessary* causes; they may have been accidental. Without entering upon a complete history of the world, such an argument cannot be ruled out. What is indisputable, however, it that the inherent beliefs of both Judaism and Christianity can be seen as cohering completely with liberal education.

Even here it may be that many readers would disagree strongly. Orthodox Judaism, no less than ecclesiastical Christianity, has practised forms of conditioning and indoctrination hostile to education *per se*. Only in the light of the great push from secular sources, or those on the fringe of institutional religion and in some sense rebels against it, have many Jews and Christians begun seriously to take on board the principles behind liberal education.

This objection raises, in a cogent and justified fashion, the crucial matter of criteria for discernment as to what constitutes the heart of an ideology or religion. This is further discussed in Chapters 10 and 18 along with the need to establish a yardstick against which the views and behaviour of individuals, groups and institutions should be measured. This means acknowledging that there *is* a distinction between, for example, Marxist philosophy and the Marxism practised in official Soviet circles, or between the central teaching of Christ and the performance of the established churches over the centuries. Crude arguments of the kind 'Marxism=Soviet Russia' or 'Churches =Christianity' will not do. The truth or falsity of Marxism and Christianity are, in a profound sense, independent of the ignorance, blindness, hypocrisy, superstition and manipulation of their followers.

What this means in terms of the Judeo-Christian matrix of liberal education is that those adherents to the tradition who indoctrinate and condition, and fail to practise the qualities of infinite respect and love for every human being towards which both the Torah and the Christian Gospel direct attention, are to be found wanting in the very principles which they say they are supporting. Jews and Christians stand condemned by their own beliefs if they ride roughshod over the fragile uniqueness of any child, and fail to treat that child with the infinite compassion of the God whom they call loving Father of all.

This discussion also relates in an interesting way to another aspect of the historical link between religion and education, namely, the question of the relationship between Moral Education and Religious Education. Traditionally in Britain these have been much confused. Probably a majority of people outside academic and professional educational circles still see them as somehow linked, even if not quite the same. To argue that this is simply an example of historical conditioning and intellectual confusion is inadmissible for at least two reasons: it ignores the high moral awareness associated with all the major world religions, and it dismisses the controversial possibility that morality ultimately rests upon the fact of the Divine and such revelations of the Divine in Torah, Dharma, Tao, Qur'an, Gospel and so forth as have been given to humanity. If this latter possibility is not opened up for discussion, it is unlikely that justice can be done either to religion *per se* or to the depth of the moral imperative.[6]

An agnostic viewpoint

Reluctance to engage in the task of helping students to understand a vital element in the tradition of the society of which they are a part can be deplored by agnostics as much as by religious people.

This is how an agnostic headteacher expresses it in a discussion paper he drew up for his staff:

Nor can we avoid the fact that our values are rooted in Judaism/ Christianity, just as those of a Muslim society are pervaded by the Koran. Given this truism we are remarkably perverse in our approach to intoducing our young people to the Christian base of their value system . . .

. . . and its multivarious schisms can take some blame for this, given the fact that a high percentage of older pupils and teachers react against Christian indoctrination or subliminal evangelism. This may be an unpalatable fact for the faithful but it's a reality to be addressed. Our young people do need to understand the Judaic-Christian ethic and history in depth, plus the nature and teachings of the Old and the New Testament. How else can they make sense of their birthright or make valid value assessments including their own belief systems? . .

. . . It's somewhat farcical that a young man or woman can know more about Islam or Buddhism or Hinduism than Christianity. That's not to imply that they should not have an understanding of other faiths and belief structures but what's sauce for the goose is also sauce for the gander. This raises a fundamental question – can a sense of Christian heritage be activated by an agnostic? I suggest it can. . .

. . . It's not beyond a self-analytical, non-doctrinal, teacher to explore with young people the concepts of God, beliefs and the history of Christianity in a sensitive, tolerant way, which allows young people to reflect and understand. . .

. . . We *owe* our children a Christian *understanding* but we don't owe them indoctrination – the ultimate decision to live out a Christian life-style, and Christian values, is theirs. But the teacher who dogmatically states 'I don't believe in God' risks cutting off the young from its own conclusions as to the meaning of life and creation and cosmology and space ethics! I write from an agnostic position, with a sense that sometimes committed Christians are their own worst enemies![7]

Religious Education labours under great difficulties. It has many suspicions to allay and explanations to give. It has to do this in an atmosphere which is often, perhaps usually, uncongenial – if not actually hostile to it. The subject-matter, the concepts it deals with, and the skills it requires are far from easy. Despite its apparently privileged position as the one subject required by law to be taught in schools it is, in fact as opposed to theory, one of the lowest priorities in almost all schools with regard to the amount of time allowed it, the qualifications and competence of the staff expected to teach it, the help given in resourcing it, and the status accorded to it.

What is astonishing is that despite all these massive drawbacks the subject has shown itself resilient and capable of far-reaching development. There has been much excellent teaching and, although the need for major overall improvement is abundandtly clear, a creative start has been made which needs to be much more publicised than it has been. The image of Religious Education in its outmoded form, or in one of its more eccentric 'modern' forms, needs to be refined and developed into an image which is thoroughly educational.

Religious Education, theory and practice: layout of the rest of the book

It is the purpose of the rest of this book to try to convey such an 'educational' image of Religious Education. It is hoped that this discussion will be of interest to the general reader as well as to those professionally concerned with teaching Religious Education. It purports to show how education works with regard to one area of the curriculum. Furthermore, because this area deals precisely with beliefs and values it is ideally suited to developing people's capacity to think clearly and responsibly on such matters, provided it is taught in a way which really is educational. It will be for the reader to judge whether the presentation of Religious Education in this book does attain that level.

Part B On Religious Education

Part B examines general questions, beginning with a discussion of why we should have the subject at all and moving on to consider what Religious Education should properly be about. Clarity here is needed to dispel the vagueness which so often surrounds the subject.

The following chapters will consider the implications, as regards general approach, content and skills.

Religious Education has acted as a touchstone with regard to the general issue of children's cognitive development, and so this receives a chapter to itself. So also does the role of a syllabus (Chapter 13), because Religious Education has made significant use of this method of finding a *modus vivendi* for divergent opinions, a method which may or may not prove exportable with regard to other controversial areas such as political education.

Historically, the vexed question of school assembly has been closely yoked to Religious Education. Chapter 14 therefore examines in detail what can or ought to be the educational advantage of exposing a captive audience to the opportunity for worship.

Part C In the classroom

The final four chapters of the book seek to place this understanding of Religious Education within the context of primary and secondary schools respectively. Those readers whose prime interest is in middle schools will find relevant material in all the chapters.

Notes and references

1 For discussion of the question of the autonomy of the child, three articles could be helpful: K Ward 'Personal and Social development: a reply to Pring' *Cambridge Journal of Education* Vol 12, No 1 (1982) pp 15–18); R Young: 'The value of autonomy' *Philosophical Quarterly* Vol 23 (1982) p 35f; and J Shortt 'Autonomy' *Spectrum* Vol 18, No 2 (1986).

2 Basil Mitchell 'Religious Education' *Oxford Review for Education* Vol 6, No 2 (1980), p 134.

3 Derek Wright 'Some Thoughts on Moral Education' *Journal for Moral Education* Vol 6, No 1, p 2.

4 Novelists such as William Golding in *Lord of the Flies* and Iris Murdoch in *The Sovereignty of the Good* draw attention constantly to this dark side of human nature.

5 Derek Wright 'Religious Education from the perspective of Moral Education' *Journal of Moral Education* Vol 12, No 2 (1983) p 112.

6 Derek Wright, for example, notes in the article quoted above that, having acknowledged that religion and morality are distinct, and that morality can stand apart from religion, the religious claims need at least to be examined (*Ibid* page 3f.) A classic from a religious point of view is *Religion and Morality* by William Barclay.

7 A Storey, headmaster of Hayfield School, Doncaster, in a discussion paper he drew up for his staff in November 1986.

B ON RELIGIOUS EDUCATION

8 The Educational Case for Religious Education

This chapter is intended as a discussion document, and has been set out in such a way as to facilitate this use.

The case against Religious Education is formidable. People argue against its inclusion in the curriculum of schools in Britain today on a number of grounds. Eight such objections are given below (for convenience, these have been subdivided) followed, in each case, by a response. Finally, I offer independent grounds for the constructive role of Religious Education.

Arguments based on the nature of society in Britain today

Those who hold this view maintain that schools should both reflect the society they serve and promote the kind of society which circumstances require.

Objection 1: Religion is irrelevant

i Schools must prepare people for a techonlogical society. Obvious priorities are increased science and mathematics, computer studies, health education, personal, moral and social development, enviromental studies and so forth, all of which are clearly relevant and for which at the moment there is not enough time. The relevance of Religious Education is not clear in this context.

ii Most people lead the whole of their lives successfully without any religious faith at all, and without reference to religion in either an institutional or a personal form. In fact, religion is largely redundant.

iii Many teachers already find it difficult to teach about religion in a way which their pupils can see as interesting and relevant.

iv For those who do want to find out about religion, churches, synagogues and other religious organisations are available.

Response to objection 1

i Lack of time when there seem to be so many priorities is a serious problem but, as mentioned in Chapter 6, it may be that technology will be able to relieve this by permitting individual choice of what is most relevant and interesting to each person. It is worth recalling the words of the Utilitarian thinker J S Mill: 'If the truth of religion is established, its relevance follows as a matter of course'.[1] Religion is only irrelevant if it is not true. But whether it is or not needs to be discussed, not assumed. Otherwise schools will be guilty of secularist indoctrination.

The view, however, that religion is neither true nor relevant is itself controversial. Religious believers in fact see religion as the *most* relevant factor in the contemporary world as in other times.

ii The large numbers of people who live without religion may in fact be leading impoverished lives, even though they are unaware of it, just as people without education or good health or pleasant surroundings are impoverished, whether they realise it or not.

iii The difficulty which many teachers have in teaching about religion is largely due to inadequate training, to the low status under which the subject normally labours and to the materialistic conditioning of the times. There are also many teachers who find that students are fascinated by religion and are enthusiastic about sorting out their own views on it.

iv If the schools fail to give Religious Education many people who grow up in religionless homes will never have any connection whatever with a religious institution. Schools should seek to make good the deficiencies of home backgrounds, not reinforce them.

Objection 2: Moral not Religious Education is what is needed

i The argument often put forward in favour of Religious Education, namely, that the majority of parents still want it, is not valid. Such people mostly want Moral Education, not Religious Education; they have already voted with their feet against religion as numbers attending churches show. The interest they have in religion is simply a concern that their children should grow up to be decent, good-living members of society. Because they themselves were brought up to think that morality is a matter of religion the confusion continues.

ii People *can* be and are moral without holding any religious beliefs, and there are plenty of examples of religious people acting immorally.

Response to objection 2

i There is indeed much confusion as to what Religious Education is and many do confuse it with morality. This is partly because of poor or non-existent Religious Education and thus the remedy lies in properly thought-out Religious Education.

ii The assumption that religion has only an accidental connection with moral standards needs to be questioned. It is possible that moral standards are in fact based on religion. Historically this is so in Western civilisation and it may be that a religionless generation is living on the reserves of previous generations and is basically parasitical. This could have serious implications for the future. Can morality permanently go on living off a dead host? The Humanist assumption that the basis of morality is in right reasoning needs to be opened up for questioning in the same way as a religious assumption.

All the great religions of the world teach very high moral principles; anyone who takes a religious commitment within them seriously has to endeavour to live up to those high standards. Much of the ritual, discipline and social structure of the various religions is concerned precisely with encouraging people to live according to their ideals. The mismatch referred to, in that some religious people act immorally, is no monopoly of religion. It occurs everywhere and in every commitment, whether political, social, educational or moral.

Objection 3: Religion is controversial

i   Britain is now a pluralist society representing a wide range of commitments, including many which are non-religious. There is no consensus on religion, and many people have grave reservations about the truth of any religious position. The content of much religious belief is frankly incredible. The claim that there *is* objective truth in religious statements cannot be upheld. There is such diversity of views that it is impossible to say that we know anything with certainty. Lacking any kind of objective criteria for assessment of truth-claims religious beliefs cannot in a pluralist society provide the framework for values which they can in a mono-religious society.

ii The values which schools in such a society should put forward are not those of a particular religion but general ones such as tolerance, openness, fairness and co-operation. To subject all children to the claims of religion is not justified, and may even work against these other values.

Response to objection 3

i   It is true that religion is controversial and that there is no consensus in our society about it. This does not mean that there can be no knowledge or certainty. In other areas of knowledge, opinions can be nearer or further away from the truth, and much investigation, experience and reflection is needed to understand and weigh carefully the evidence put forward. The same process is necessary for religion, even though religion deals with matters which, if true, are less amenable to straight demonstration than other areas of knowledge such as science and history. Many religious people display an assurance which is not just verbal but lived, an assurance which can often sustain them in times of incredible difficulty and for which they are prepared even to die. To assume that they are deluded is to beg the question, for it could be that others are simply unaware and inexperienced, as discussed in Chapter 5.

The assumption therefore that religion is just a matter of opinion and not of knowledge is one which should itself form part of the basic content of Religious Education: is religion just a matter of opinion or is it true? The fact that people think differently about it does not mean that none of them knows, for some or most or all of them could be right or wrong. It is important to remember that whilst everyone has a right to an opinion, not every opinion is right.

ii The fact that religious ideas can give rise to intolerance, injustice and hatred through hypocrisy, ignorance, personal immaturity, conditioning and many other factors is itself a powerful reason for the inclusion of Religious Education, in order to promote greater understanding and integrity.

Objection 4: The privileged legal status of Religious Education is unfair

i In such a pluralist society the privileged position of Religious Education as the only subject legally required to be taught in schools is an anomaly. It gives religion an unfair advantage over other subjects and other approaches to life.

ii Its privileged position may once have been justified because society in Britain was more than nominally Christian, despite the presence in it of groups who were not Christian. Since 1944, however, great changes have taken place with the increase in secularism and the arrival of many more immigrants who practise religions other than Christianity. It is likely indeed that, without an Act of Parliament protecting the subject, these changes would have ensured the disappearance of Religious Education in most schools.

Response to objection 4

i The case for Religious Education must rest on educational arguments not on an Act of Parliament reflecting a particular situation decades past. The apparently privileged position of Religious Education has frequently worked against its status, in that many schools have fulfilled the legal provisions in a minimal and perfunctory manner, or have ignored them. Good Religious Education has happened not by virtue of an Act of Parliament but through the educational commitment of teachers. Such commitment cannot be guaranteed by even the most enlightened legislation. In fact Religious Education has been accorded a cinderella status in most schools, given less time, less resources, fewer specialist teachers, poorer career prospects and less significance in the school's order of priorities, than almost any other subject.

ii The difference between British society in 1944 and today ought not to be over-emphasised. There has been increasing secularisation, partly as a result of an educational system which has in fact (as compared with the theory) been largely secularised. It is overstating the case to imply that Britain is now only nominally Christian, that it is post-Christian. Many people well-acquainted with other cultures which have not been impregnated with Christianity notice how 'Christian' Western society still is. Furthermore the popularity, for example, of the BBC series *'What Use is the Church?'* broadcast in Lent 1986, suggests that there is more than a residual interest in religion among the population at large.

It can indeed be argued that Christianity has provided, and still helps to provide, the basis for the development of a more pluralist society, one in which other cultures and religions are accorded tolerance.

Arguments which are more directly educational

Objection 5: The problem of the commitment of the teacher

i Religion is extremely controversial and this places a special responsibility upon teachers to play fair in the classroom. Teachers ought not to use their privileged position of authority with a captive audience of young and relatively inexperienced people to inculcate their own particular views, to influence their students to be favourably disposed to this and not that controversial point.

It follows from this that it is indoctrinatory to put across either a sympathetic or a non-sympathetic view of religion in the classroom. Yet the subject cannot be taught at all without some form of commitment in the teachers towards the subject-matter. Neutrality is impossible, as many leading thinkers in the Religious Education world have shown. By manner of presentation, selection of content, or response to questions or comments, a teacher betrays a particular perspective and is therefore in danger of influencing students in that direction. Furthermore, enthusiasm is essential for good teaching and this inevitably involves emotion and personal involvement in the teacher which is inappropriate for a neutral pose. The contradictions here make the subject an impossible one to teach.

ii The attempt to find an escape from this dilemma by requiring teachers to put forward a variety of views fairly, especially views which conflict with their personal position, does not hold water. The placing of these views and the form of words and expression in which the different views are presented (especially those which are critical of the teacher's own) will always tend to convey the teacher's viewpoint. Lack of time will also effectively ensure that not all views are presented.

Response to objection 5

i   Problems of teacher commitment and the danger of indoctrination are particularly acute when dealing with religion, even though they are present in every subject taught and in every aspect of the curriculum. Yet there is not necessarily a causal connection between religion and propaganda. Underlying the onslaught on religion as indoctrinatory has often been the assumption that religion is not true. The same people often do not object to indoctrination in mathematics, because that is commonly regarded as beyond dispute. Yet the essence of indoctrination lies not in content communicated but in the manner of its communication, as discussed in Chapter 2.

A false polarity has been set up in the objection between neutrality as desirable but impossible, and propaganda. If *this were* so, no education – regardless of the subject-matter – would be possible. Fairness to a captive audience requires not detachment but impartiality. It is possible to hold strong convictions without exercising undue pressure on others to adopt them; this is shown in all walks of life and not just in religion.

ii   Impartiality involves being fair to different viewpoints, especially to those one disagrees with, which one should not misrepresent. This raises the question in any subject of the misleading nature of so many generalisations. Furthermore, selection of material and views to be considered is unavoidable, and will happen whether the teacher consciously exercises it or not. It is in fact extremely difficult, as the objection notes, to be scrupulously fair. This point itself therefore has to be part of what is taught and discussed.

It is essential that in Religious Education teachers share with students the dangers and difficulties they encounter. Alerting people to the possibility of their being indoctrinated, or of getting only a partial view and mistaking it for a comprehensive view, lessens the dangers very considerably. To fail to deal with controversial matters at all would be to deny students the opportunity to develop the much-needed and vitally important skills of how to cope with the controversial issues of life.

Objection 6: Indoctrinatory practice

i   People who argue on behalf of Religious Education always do have a 'hidden agenda'. Often the teaching is frankly indoctrinatory: the passing-on of a belief-system. Religious assemblies illustrate this well:

'Let us pray', 'Let us sing this hymn' leave the students in no doubt as to the assumptions being made about them. It is expected that they either have a religious outlook on life or that they should learn to have one.

ii It is particularly worth noting that the teaching of world religions does not avoid the dilemma. Teachers usually adopt subtle or not-so-subtle ways of presenting religions other than their own as inferior; they are not taken seriously in their own right.

iii Even those who advocate a modern, liberal approach and say they want to be open, fair and comprehensive are still subtly indoctrinating. They are really hoping that the Religious Education they offer will result in commitment to their own brand of religion. Someone who does not share their views can easily detect this bias. They may be educationally well-intentioned, but still their teaching contains hidden values and beliefs which they are hoping to instil or inculcate.

iv The Agreed Syllabus structure does not alleviate the problem of indoctrination because of the number of vested interests represented in the drawing-up of the syllabuses, interests which often have only a minimal commitment to education *per se*. Furthermore, however fair the Agreed Syllabus may be, there is no way of controlling the teacher's interpretation of it. This can still be indoctrinatory.

Response to objection 6

i In the past, much more than now, there has been attempted indoctrination by some Religious Education teachers. It is true that in assuming a religious faith religious assemblies have often, intentionally or not, had a claustrophic effect on teachers and students alike. I believe a radically different educational approach to such assemblies is called for. (This idea is developed in Chapter 14.)

ii In the teaching of world religions, an assertion by the teacher of complete impartiality is to be distrusted. The pitfalls in such teaching are notorious and numerous but they can be made to serve the cause of education provided their possibility is discussed with students at all stages. Chapter 11 includes a development of this approach.

iii To require a teacher of any subject not to entertain any hopes that students will come to appreciate and accept what is meaningful and important to the teacher would be to delete from the equation the desire to try to teach at all. Such hopes only constitute a dishonest 'hidden agenda' if they are allowed to override the basic educational commitment to respect the integrity of the students, however young they are.

iv The Agreed Syllabus is certainly no guarantee against indoctrination, and it can itself be indoctrinatory if seen in a dogmatic light. It is possible however, for syllabuses to promote real education (see Chapter 12).

In light of the constant criticism of schools as remote from the 'real world outside', it would seem desirable to encourage more general participation in what is to be taught and why. There is therefore a bonus in involving interested parties outside the school system in the drawing up of the Agreed Syllabus. This has hardly been attempted at all in areas such as politics where divisions are equally deep.

Objection 7: Religious Education should not be a separate subject

i The descriptive approach to Religious Education is the only way of avoiding indoctrination and is widely accepted by Religious Education teachers and lecturers. The teacher must teach not religion but *about* religion. It is safe to learn about what religious people think and do and how they behave and how they use language, and so forth. But this does not need separate Religious Education teaching. Most modern Religious Education teachers and thinkers are so vague about what they mean by religion that the term is in any case redundant or misplaced. Much, if not most, of what happens in modern Religious Education can better be done as an intrinsic part of multi-cultural studies, social studies, history, geography, humanities, according to how a school organises this aspect of the curriculum.

In fact it is safer to do this, because separate Religious Education tends to wear the complexion of the teacher and his or her parochial beliefs, while if undertaken as part of multi-cultural or social studies, for example, it can be done with fairness. Furthermore the isolation of Religious Education has been bemoaned by many Religious Education teachers and thinkers. This is completely avoided if Religious Education becomes part of other subjects and is not taught by a specialist.

ii The argument that Religious Education deserves a special place because it raises ultimate questions of meaning and of the purpose of life and brings together the rest of the curriculum is not valid. All subjects are capable of raising such questions and being integrative in approach. Often they *are* taught in such a way and when they are not, a wider and deeper approach should be encouraged. There is no necessity for a separate slot on the timetable. Indeed this would mean isolating such far-reaching and all-embracing questions from the rest of what students are learning.

iii A particular form of generalising of religion so that Religious Education is virtually indistinguishable from education *per se* is the 'implicit' form of Religious Education advocated in all the Agreed Syllabuses. Normally, what is meant by 'implicit' Religious Education is general moral, personal and social development. Why not call it this?

It has the merit of being honest and open, and is clearly something which all teachers can engage in without qualms of conscience or loss of integrity. If, however, 'implicit' Religious Education has a hidden agenda, namely the assumption that all children are or should be innately religious, this is a view which is not universally held in our society and therefore should not be presumed to be the case.

Response to objection 7

Objections *i* and *ii* seem to be valid ones unless Religious Education is understood and practised in a much deeper way than is implied. Much, indeed perhaps most, of what goes on under separate Religious Education at the moment in schools *could* better be done across the whole range of curriculum subjects. But that is not to say that it *would* be done. The demands on curriculum time, the distractions of other interests, and limitations in resources, teacher expertise and so forth mean that, without a separate slot, information about religion and the opportunity for serious reflection about ultimate questions would probably not be given, in the present climate of opinion. Religious Education therefore, even when it does no more than is implied in this objection, may be seen as holding the fort in a beleaguered situation until other subjects are enabled to take over the responsibility which is properly theirs, and for which they should be as competent or more competent than a Religious Education specialist.

This would still leave the need for separate Religious Education to fulfil what is distinctively religious. Religion is about what people *believe* and *why* they act as they do; only incidentally is it about what they *do* and the fact *that* they believe something. Everyone acts from beliefs, as discussed in Chapter 4. To understand beliefs it is necessary to pay them the compliment of taking them seriously and weighing their truth claims. This is the proper subject-matter of Religious Education and it requires resources of time and skill seldom allowed it. Chapter 9 includes detailed discussion of what Religious Education should be about.

iii The validity of an 'implicit' form of Religious Education cannot be justified, educationally, for the reasons given in this objection. The idea arose from an effort to meet other objections against Religious Education, including the agnostic and atheistic charge of indoctrination and the view that religion is beyond children's intellectual capacity to understand. Such objections are, however, met on other grounds. The understanding of Religious Education presented later in this chapter is not based on such a view.

Objection 8: Religious concepts are too difficult for children

   i Those who argue that Religious Education needs to be a separate subject because it deals with special and distinctive concepts, run into the problem of the difficulty of such concepts for children. Such concepts as God, prayer, Nirvana, are mostly outside and quite foreign to children's experience. In teaching mathematics it is possible to point to everyday experience and to structure other experience to help children grasp the meaning of mathematical terms. No such obvious route is available with regard to religious concepts. Piaget and Goldman have shown that children are not capable of appreciating religious language below the age of about 13. This would automatically exclude Religious Education from primary and middle schools.

  ii In secondary schools, poor time allowance and low motivation among students make it difficult to teach religion seriously. The simplifications and half-truths usually paraded in the classroom are a travesty of what it is about. Unless a quite unrealistic amount of time and training are to be devoted to it, the subject cannot be taught properly.

Response to objection 8

   i The research on which this objection is based has been challenged.[2] The contrary view, that children are capable of developing an understanding of religious concepts in the same way as they can grasp those related to other areas of knowledge, provided they are given the opportunity, is argued for in Chapter 12. If no-one mentions such concepts to children – if they hear of God, for example, only as a swear-word – their cognitive development with regard to such concepts is likely to remain non-existent. Most children, for example, need to be introduced to algebraic equations, otherwise they do not develop the ability to handle them.

  ii This objection rightly points to the complexity of religious concepts and the fact that much time and training is needed if they are to be properly developed. To assume, however, that it is unrealistic to extend the minimal 35 minutes per week is to assume that religion is a very low priority. But it can be questioned whether it ought to be. (See the response to 1 (i) on page 93f.)

I hope sufficient has been said on these objections to indicate why they do not stand if Religious Education is properly undersood. Nevertheless they are indeed valuable in alerting the teacher to the way in which Religious Education ought to be conducted.

Is there, however, a positive case for Religious Education? Otherwise, in view of the difficulties to which these objections draw attention, it might be argued that it is not worth all the trouble.

The positive case for religious education

I would argue strongly the need for Religious Education for *all* children, whatever their parents' religious or non-religious commitment. It is an essential component of education, without which the student can be said to be seriously deprived. The grounds for arguing this include those outlined below.

Religion is an important aspect of life and makes a fascinating study

Education is concerned with acquiring understanding and knowledge in as broad and comprehensive a way as possible. An educated person is not one who knows little about anything beyond pigs or drainpipes, mathematical equations or social studies, or whatever specialist interest it may be. An educated person is rather someone who has some grasp of the range of human experience and who can show an appreciation and critical awareness of its many different facets. These include, for example, scientific, historical, sociological, artistic and literary perspectives on life, and also the religious approach. Religion is an aspect of life which is real to millions of people today, as it has been in the past, in every country and culture of the world.

Religious experience is distinctive. It concerns an understanding of life based upon a fundamental belief that the world is more than a chance collection of molecules; that it is pervaded by, or given meaning by, a Reality or Power or Presence which is spiritual. Such conviction shows itself in behaviour and a way of life which for those who have such genuine conviction is primary. The social dimension of religion refers to the way in which other people, often whole cultures, attach themselves to such a way of life. Their involvement may however only be at a secondary level.

Although controversial, the claims made by those who have had what they call religious experience properly constitute an area of knowledge. If such claims are to be discarded it should be on the basis of real knowledge and not of misunderstanding or ignorance.

The study of religion is a fascinating pursuit, shot through with unusual and interesting information. It develops the skills of detection and interpretation in sorting out the various levels at which people may be said to be religious, and helps people to think clearly about controversial issues. It has been demonstrated over the past decade that religion can and does hold the attention of almost all children at whatever age, provided that, as with all other subjects, it is taught well. Dreariness and boredom in Religious Education has been due to deficiency in the teaching, not to what religion is about.

Religious Education can make a very positive contribution to world peace

The power of religion is frighteningly dynamic, and it has often been called the most dangerous force in the world. Some people who perceive its dangers have argued that therefore we should forget about it and try to steer people away from it. Yet this will not do. Time and time again religion has a way of coming back in new and insidious and more potentially damaging ways. The biologist, Sir Alister Hardy, used to say that the two most powerful drives in human beings are the sexual and the religious.[3] Just as it is foolish to deny the existence of the former, so it is foolish to pretend that the other is not there. Sexual appetite needs to be controlled and channelled for the mutual good of all societies and all individuals. The same is true of the religious urge. It must find a proper expression and contribute, like sex, to the immense benefit of humanity, not to its destruction. For if the dangers of religion are only too apparent, its creativity and impetus towards a qualitatively excellent approach to life are also well documented.

What is undoubtedly true is that the absence of understanding of religion can be very serious indeed. Situations which have developed in Northern Ireland, the Middle East and so forth readily spring to mind. Many people blame religious belief for such turmoil when in fact it results from lack of understanding or from insincerity. There are many counterfeit forms of religion. Prejudice and intolerance tend to go together and education *ought* to perform the humble but vital task of seeking to expose prejudice in favour of understanding. This will then allow students freedom to develop genuinely thought-out beliefs of their own. Ill-digested opinions and negative attitudes for or against religion need to be dispelled. It is not overstating the case to say that the peace of the world depends upon this.

Religious Education can help students in the search for their own convictions

Religious Education provides an excellent opportunity for learning to think clearly, especially about controversial issues and the development of convictions which can give purpose to life.

The value of such convictions has already been discussed in Chapters 4 and 5. Understanding of religion may offer people important criteria for guiding their judgment, and may provide an anchor in times of crisis and change, giving a sense of meaning and personal worth.

Even if a person does not find in religion a personal commitment – and it is *not* for Religious Education to tell children what to believe – the understanding of other people's commitment will be exceedingly valuable. In the shrinking world of the twenty-first century, with its multi-faith nature and increase in crisis-points, this understanding will be even more important.

If religion can provide motivation for living, then understanding of it should not be regarded as an option. Many parents, for example, are becoming increasingly worried about their children adopting strange cults and ways of life; yet often this reflects a deficiency in their education which has failed to help them develop powers of discernment in religion.

It is of vital importance that Religious Education should not be characterised by a dogmatic manner but should promote real thinking and disagreement, as well as possible agreement, by the student. Zealous religious believers have often failed to comply with the educational point made by Jeffreys: 'it is more important that our pupils should think for themselves than that they should think as we do'. It is all-important that Religious Education is taught in a way that promotes reflectiveness and does not make assumptions about the student's beliefs. It can then make a challenging and worthwhile contribution to the education of commitment.

Religious Education can protect students from being indoctrinated

Education takes place within a wider context than just that of the school or a particular lesson, and therefore the whole ethos of the society in which we live must be taken into account. It is here that the true indoctrination takes place, for children learn beliefs and values (such as those already discussed in Chapter 3) which are never questioned. Religious Education is an essential part of the syllabus, for to ignore it could result in indoctrination by the prevailing climate in which the child grows up, whether secular or religious. It may seem odd to take this stance, because so many people assume that Religious Education is indoctrination and that not to teach it is to avoid indoctrination. But I hold the opposite view. Do we really want children to be at the mercy of bits and pieces of information and opinions they pick up at home, on the television, among their friends . . ? For example, television, and the media generally, often present religious faith as a somewhat strange, even a somewhat fanatical, thing. This has on-going consequences.

Today in the West education takes place against a background of indoctrination into materialism. Solzhenitsyn, in a speech at Harvard in June 1978, commented that 'Spiritual life was destroyed in the East by the ruling party and in the West by commercial interest'. Like all generalisations one can immediately think of encouraging exceptions but the denunciation was sufficiently near the mark to prompt a defensive reply by the *New York Times*.[4] Few people would doubt that money and possessions and obtaining or enjoying a comfortable standard of living are predominating values today. Such materialistic conditioning is powerfully backed by positivistic reductionism, that is, an explanation of life which regards only scientific criteria as valid or valuable, everything else being a matter of mere opinion (see pp 23ff).

Symptomatic and illustrative of such ideological conditioning is the way in which Christopher Evans in his book *The Mighty Micro* dismisses religion. The book is about technology and there is no discussion of religion nor mention of his view as being controversial. His only comment on religion is where he predicts the rise of new religions to help make people feel safe in the new world of technology. He assumes that religion is a lie and that there is no God and no human soul; spiritual life is a mirage invented by man to make life more palatable. He ends Chapter 16 cynically with the comment:

> But there also remains the real chance that computers will be seen as deities, and if they evolve into Ultra-Intelligent Machines, there may even be an element of truth in the belief.[5]

The important point to be drawn from this is that such a dismissal comes close to atheistic indoctrination, for it is of the essence of indoctrination to prevent, whether intentionally or not, any understanding of, or reflection upon, certain issues. Much can be said about indoctrination, but I believe the point is often missed, as mentioned earlier on page 13, that by *omission* we most seriously inhibit the capacities of other people to understand. This effectively sends the mind to sleep on those matters to which attention is never directed, or which are skilfully avoided.

This results in a situation in which ignorance about religion is regarded as unimportant because 'no-one can know anyway'. People are generally aware of their lack of knowledge with regard to, say, quantum physics or the Roman Empire, but they imagine that they do understand all that matters about religion and therefore either accept it or reject it on a simplistic basis. I have met many children and adults whose thinking about religion is literally at infant level: for example, I recently heard a group of nine-year-olds talk with some sophistication about rockets and computers, yet they were quite content to draw crude pictures of God as an old man up in the skies. No wonder such absurd notions promote the belief that religion has been replaced by science. How can we expect children or adults to think straight about religion on the basis of such ignorance?

An important additional point can be made which relates to discussion of why a utilitarian approach is so pervasive. Material concerns exercise an inert form of conditioning by sheer distraction, quite apart from encouragement by commercial interests or possible anti-religious ideology. Day-to-day living, despite – or indeed increasingly because of – great technological advances is incredibly complex and time- and energy-consuming. Those on subsistence level are similarly preoccupied with the basic mechanics of being alive. All the great religions testify to the power of this distraction and the need to wage constant war against its temptations. This is why symbolism and the discipline of religious practices and ritual are so important in all the religions: they help to concentrate the attention on the spiritual dimension.

Religious Education has a powerful role in countering the conditioning, sometimes unconscious and sometimes deliberate, which afflicts our society and which is likely to do so even more in the technologically-dominated world of the future.

Religious Education also has a vital role in protecting children from any and all forms of religious propaganda, and from the narrowness and dogmatism of some of their home backgrounds. Many children, especially those from immigrant families, can feel a kind of isolationist schizophrenia when the values and beliefs they experience in their home environment are very different from those in the outside world. We are failing children if we do not encourage them to explore for themselves, in a thoughtful and sensitive way, the nature of religion, and if we do not help them to become aware of all forms of conditioning in the search for their own authentically-chosen commitments.

Our concern today for the rights of children, including especially the rights of children of diverse ethnic origins now resident in Western societies, makes this a particularly significant point which needs great emphasis. Education should be for *all*, not just for a privileged majority or minority, white or otherwise.

It will be noted that no mention has been made in this chapter of the legal requirement for Religious Education. This is because my concern is solely with the educational case for it. The law is a blunt tool with regard to promoting educational awareness. Neither the 1944 Education Act nor any subsequent revision or renewal of it will carry any weight as regards the educational importance of Religious Education. And only educational conviction can ensure that the subject has a proper place in schools and is taught well.

Nor has there been discussion of any special place for Religious Education in church schools, or of any arguments for the existence of schools organised by specifically religious bodies. This is because the chapter is concerned with the educational needs of young children and students, and these are the same, in principle, whether they are brought up in a religious or a secular milieu. Similarly, all schools, whether secular or religious, need a shared value-system which should form the basis for their educational activity; this should be increasingly open to children, as they grow older, to appreciate and scrutinise – with a view to their freely accepting or rejecting it, in part or in totality. This is not to say that the church school should not have its own special ethos; it both can and should, just as its secular counterpart can and should.[6]

An Aide-Memoire relating to commonly-heard comments

There isn't time for it

This rests on the assumption that religion is unimportant, but there are many reasons why this assumption needs to be challenged.

It's only of use to a few

Education is about opening up avenues for children to explore. Maybe only a few become, for example, musicians or scientists, but the rest have gained understanding about music or science if they have been well taught. Furthermore, religion is controversial and how can people reach a valid judgment about it unless they understand what it is?

It's a hang-over from the past – no longer relevant

If it is true it is supremely relevant, and in order to find out whether it is true or not a person should study it. It is always relevant also to seek to understand other people, including those for whom religion is real.

It's up to the churches, not the schools

This would leave probably 90 per cent of children out in the cold, including especially children who are deprived of any religious education in their home background. Nor is Religious Education just a matter of Christianity.

It's taught badly

No wonder, with the small amount of time and training given to it. More care and thought should be put into teaching it well. If mathematics or foreign languages, for example, are taught badly we do not argue for their removal but for improvement in teaching.

Most people don't want it

This is disputable, but in any case there is more to education than just supplying what the majority want.

Religion is false

This cannot be proved, nor can its opposite. People must choose for themselves but they need to do so on the basis of understanding, not of ignorance.

Religion is a matter of purely private concern

Not everyone agrees with this view, and the effects of religious belief affect other people and society at large.

It's a headache – you can tread on so many toes
Because Religious Education deals with controversial matters which can arouse passions and prejudices, it is the more important to help students to think straight and fairly about it.

If it hadn't been for the 1944 Education Act, RE would have gone already
Many would disagree with this and in any case it does not answer the question whether it is educationally desirable that Religious Education should go.

We live in a secular society
Religious Education is therefore all the more important because it can compensate for what so many children are likely to lack.

Teachers feel hypocritical doing it
Not if they are teaching understanding of religion and not trying to get converts to a particular viewpoint.

So many beliefs: where do you begin?
It requires care, skill and knowledge in the teacher and sufficient time to develop understanding, but the situation is basically no different from that in most subjects where there is so much to choose from, for example, history.

It's indoctrinatory
Not if it is religous *education* which seeks to teach understanding of religion and does not dictate beliefs. It is no more indoctrinatory, unless taught badly, than any subject can be if taught in the wrong way.

It's a dangerous subject
Surely, therefore, it is all the more vital that children have the chance to think clearly and fairly about it.

It shouldn't be a separate subject but be done across the curriculum
In a predominantly secular society Religious Education will tend not to happen in the teaching of other subjects, because of pressure of time, the need to cover a lot of material, and the fact that it may be seen as a distraction. Its distinctive concepts like 'God', 'Karma' and so forth need time when they can be properly developed.

It's too difficult
This view is debatable and even if true would be an argument for better and more careful teaching.

Notes and references

1 J S Mill *Nature, The Utility of Religion and Theism* (Longmans, Green, Reader and Dyer, 1874) p 69
2 See pp 160ff of Chapter 12 for information on such research
3 For example, Alister Hardy *The Divine Flame* Lecture VII (Collins, 1966), p 156ff
4 Quoted above (page 48)
5 Christopher Evans *The Mighty Micro* (Gollancz, 1979) p 221
6 How the ethos of the church school can or should be related to education is the subject of much discussion. See, for example *The Durham Report* on Religious Education (SPCK, 1970) p 205–271; *Signs and Homecomings* RC Bishops' Report (Geoffrey Chapman, 1983); H C F Beales 'The Struggle for the Schools' in *The English Catholics 1850–1950* (Burns Oates, 1950) p 399

9 What is Religious Education about?

The case for Religious Education given in Chapter 8 rests upon a particular view of how the subject should be understood. The rest of the book will consider this in some detail.

To begin with it is essential to be clear about what Religious Education is concerned with. There have been so many changes in the past decades, and such a lot of re-thinking, that what happens in schools today as Religious Education can be very varied indeed.

Here are four snapshots of Religious Education in practice. What impression would they give to a visitor new to the scene of what Religious Education is about? Is there a common denominator, and if so what is it?

A A class of school leavers

Teacher 'This week we shall continue the discussion about drugs. The video we saw about what drugs are and their effects gave us all a lot to think about, didn't it? One of the most frightening aspects of drugs is the way they seem harmless when you start off but can so quickly set up a habit. What do we call someone who just *has* to go on and on taking drugs, like Bob had to? . . . Yes, we say he's an addict. What happens if he tries to stop? . . . Yes he feels very ill and depressed – he gets what we call withdrawal symptoms.'

Gail 'But isn't the whole trouble that he can't stop? Bob only stopped because he had to – because he landed up in hospital following the crash.'

'Your're quite right, Gail. It's jolly difficult. I know because I once was on drugs myself and I can tell you I had a hell of a time getting off them.'

'How did you do it?' asked four or five voices at the same moment. A fascinating discussion followed in which the teacher shared with the group his own experience, and they talked about how people get hooked in the first place. Some of them confided how they'd tried some themselves. One boy stood against the feeling of the group as a whole in arguing that the risk was worth taking. 'It makes life worth living.'

'But at what cost?' said someone else.

B A class of 12–13-year-olds

Teacher 'Paul went on a second missionary journey. Do you remember where he went on his first one? . . . Yes . . . I hope you have all finished your maps. Now the second journey was so important because he was wanting to preach to the people in Macedonia. What was he wanting to preach? . . . Yes, about Jesus . . . '

Kevin 'Please Miss, how do we know all this happened? – it's a bit far-fetched.'

'Well, the Bible says so. Look we read about it in . . . '

'But the Bible's got lots of stupid stuff in it – like Adam and Eve and all that.'

'Kevin, that's nothing to do with Paul. Don't introduce red herrings.'

'Yes, but if you can't trust the Bible on one bit, why on another?'

'That doesn't follow, but we must get on with what we're doing. You've got to know Paul's missionary journeys for the end of term exams. We haven't time to go off the subject.'

'But why should we learn about Paul. It's boring, and he doesn't matter anyway.'

'Kevin, you will have a detention if you go on like this.'

Sullen silence resumed. Actually quite a number of children *were* interested in Paul's adventures even though they didn't know why they were studying him.

C A class of 10–11-year-olds

Teacher 'Today, children, we have a visitor. He is a member of the local Methodist church so some of you might know him or have seen him around. He's come just to talk to us a little about what he believes and why it means so much to him. Most of the time though will be free for you to ask him questions and discuss what he says.'

Turning to the visitor she said, 'Mr X ——— we're delighted to see you and thank you so much for coming. We've been doing quite a lot of work on Methodism – how it began with the work of John Wesley, how it's developed to the present day, and what seems to be special about the way Methodists see religion, compared with other Christians. In particular we've looked at some of the hymns of Charles Wesley which have been so important a feature of Methodism. We've sung one or two of these, thinking about their meaning, even though we're a mixed bunch of people as regards what we believe. I am in fact Jewish, some of the children in the class are Muslims and others come from Roman Catholic homes, but most don't know what they believe. One or two feel really sure there isn't anything in religion. But now we've got the chance of meeting a real live Methodist. Can you tell us something about what Methodism means to you?'

The children are very attentive as he's an interesting speaker who really talks to them as people. He tells them he became a Methodist because he found believing in Jesus Christ made absolute sense: 'It's the most important thing in my life' he said. He joined the Methodist church rather than other churches because 'I like the freer form of worship.' The children ask a lot of questions, many of them directly related to what he believes and why, and he is able to give direct answers as to what he thinks.

D A class of 6 – 7-year-olds

Teacher 'Now, children, you remember last week we talked about a special festival in honour of spring which Hindus enjoy? Can anyone remember what it's called? Yes James . . . Yes, Holi. Now this week there's another important festival, this time for Christians. What do we call next Sunday? . . . Yes, Easter Sunday. Does anyone know why Christians have this festival? . . . Yes, because they believe that Jesus rose from the dead and so they celebrate this. . . . So Easter is a very happy time for Christians. Often they send each other Easter cards. Have you seen some in the shops? . . . But what you *all* have seen I'm sure are Easter . . . ? Yes, eggs . . . Why do you think Christians give each other Easter eggs at Easter? . . . Well, what comes out of an egg? . . . Yes, young chickens or young birds, new life. So Easter is the festival of new life. So it fits in very well with the idea of Holi – winter is dead but spring has come.

Now let's look at the eggs which you've all brought along . . . '

There is much excitement in the class as these are proudly shown to the teacher. 'Oh, very nice, you've done extremely well. Did your mothers help you? . . . Now we're going to prepare a frieze as a background for our display of eggs. And we'll learn a song all about the coming of spring and what a happy time of year it is when the darkness of winter gives way to new life.'

The need for clarification

An enquirer may well be perplexed. If the four lessons purport equally to be Religious Education they seem to be operating on very different notions of what the religious element is.

There is indeed much confusion among teachers as to what Religious Education is about. Alongside more traditional ideas, some people talk as though it is really just about personal relationships and morality; others speak of it as basically a search for meaning in life; others refer constantly to the development of personal and social skills and awareness of community; still others see it as basically a contribution to an understanding of different cultures whose self-image is religious in that they adhere to special ritual, beliefs and forms of organisation.

Such confusion cannot be desirable. Is what constitutes religion simply the whim of individual teachers or the reflection of a prevailing trend? An 11-year-old I know was perplexed by the Religious Education lessons in his comprehensive school. He had no idea why he was learning about 'hands, last week, feet this week'. This kind of vagueness can bring any subject into disrepute.

Awareness of the difficulty of expressing in words what is fundamentally beyond words should not be an excuse for lack of clarity. Historians, for example, can argue intensively about what history is, but history can be characterised at an elementary level as a study of how human beings have lived in the past. This gives it a clearly distinct perspective for almost everyone. It is high time that Religious Education achieved such clarity about its basic subject-matter and intention.

What is religion?

Figure 15 gives a number of possible definitions. Is it possible to decide in favour of any of them? Here are some considerations:

1 The ideas given in the circle cannot serve as adequate description(s) because they are too vague. It is possible to substitute other words. Everyone may be said to have a way of life; what would make such a way of life religious? Are not all areas of the curriculum concerned with developing a sense of wonder? What is specifically religious about that?

2 The ideas in the square, however, though definite are too specific because they do not embrace all that religion commonly means. Not all religious people are involved, for example, in ritual in any organised way. The philospher, A N Whitehead, could argue that religion is what a person does with his solitude. Nor would all religious people say that they pray to God; many Buddhists, for example, would not. The required term must be broad enough as well as precise enough.

3 Wherever possible it is wise to use words in the way that they are commonly understood. Redefining words in a way different from common usage is hazardous. If I persist, for example, in calling a 'jug' what other people call a 'table', I cannot be surprised if communication presents a problem!

How, therefore, is 'religion' used in ordinary situations? Two remarks made

Figure 15 What is religion?

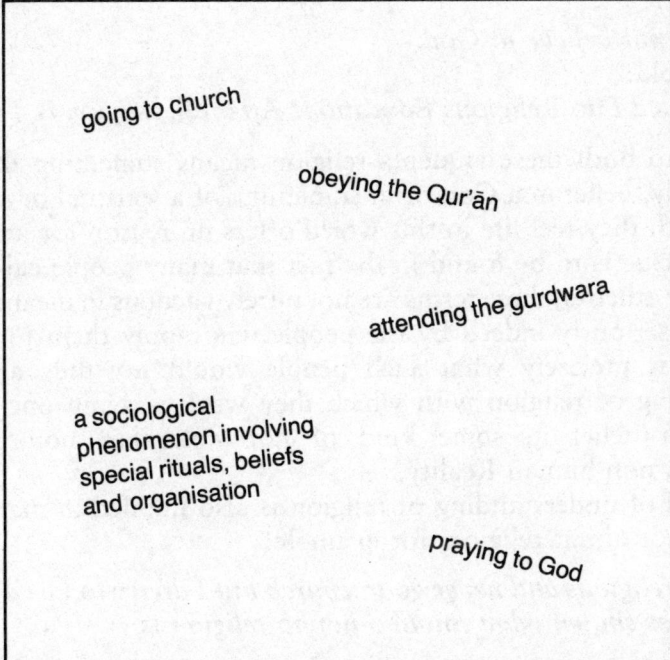

going to church

obeying the Qur'ān

attending the gurdwara

a sociological phenomenon involving special rituals, beliefs and organisation

praying to God

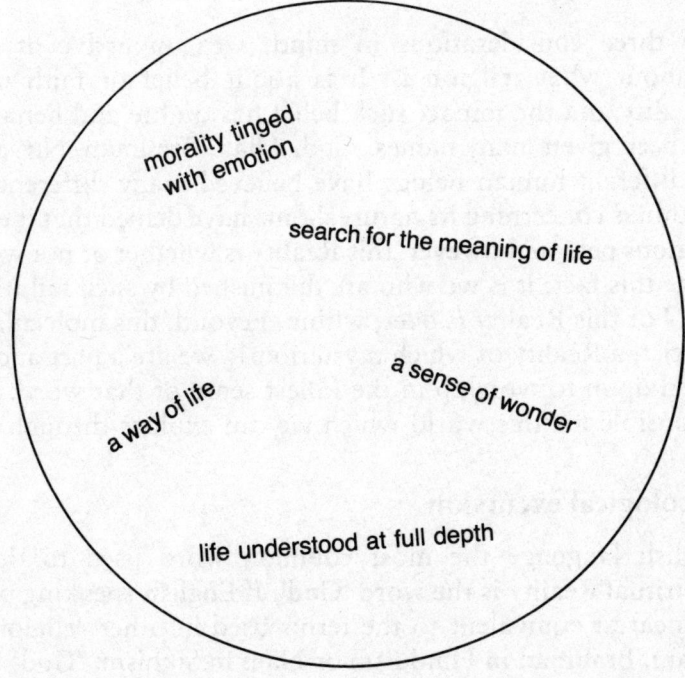

morality tinged with emotion

search for the meaning of life

a way of life

a sense of wonder

life understood at full depth

by students receiving Religious Education and recalled by teachers at a meeting I attended recently, indicate where we should look for a definition. An eight-year-old was reported as saying:

> *But I do not believe in God.*

A 14-year-old:

> *Why should I do Religious Education? After all, religion is a pack of lies.*

Clearly, to both these students religion means something they disagree with, namely, belief in a God or in something of a spiritual or supernatural nature which they feel life in this world offers no reason for accepting.

Another clue is to be found in the fact that many people call themselves agnostics or atheists; these terms are not purely vacuous in meaning, they are taken very seriously indeed by the people who apply them to themselves. 'Religious' is precisely what such people would *say* they are *not*. The understanding of religion with which they work is again one that sees it referring to belief in some kind of non-molecular, non-scientifically-explainable, non-human Reality.

This kind of understanding of religion is also implied in many everyday remarks made about religion, for example:

> *I am not religious and never go to church but I do try to live a decent life.*
> *Science has shown what mumbo-jumbo religion is.*

A minimal statement

With these three considerations in mind, we can arrive at a *minimal* statement about what religion is. It is about belief or faith in Ultimate Spiritual Reality and the impact such belief has on life and behaviour. This Reality has been given many names: God, Allah, Brahman, Nirvāna, and so forth, and different human beings have believed many different and often conflicting things concerning its nature. Some have denied that it exists at all. For the religious person, however, this Reality *is* whether or not we choose to acknowledge this fact; it is we who are diminished by such failure of vision, not Reality. For this Reality *is* over, within, beyond, this molecular world in which we exist, a Reality of which mysteriously we are a part and yet which we are called upon to worship in the fullest sense of that word. It contains and is responsible for this world which we can explore through Science.

A short theological excursion

In the English language the most common word used to denote such Ultimate Spiritual Reality is the word 'God'. If English-speaking people wish to find the nearest equivalent to the terms used in other religions, such as Allah in Islam, Brahman in Hinduism or Nām in Sikhism, 'God' is the most appropriate word. It will, therefore, be used in the rest of this book instead of more cumbersome and unusual phrases such as the ones already discussed, Ultimate Spiritual Reality. It must be understood, however, as embracing the focal-point of belief in all the world religions, not just in Judaism and Christianity.

The one religion which might seem not to fall within this understanding is Buddhism, which in its Theravādā form does not speak of Deity in any sense. Yet Buddhism is pervaded with a sense of the Divine. Buddhism arose within the context of Hinduism. The Buddha objected to the endless debates about what or who Brahman is. He believed these trivialised religion and were irrelevant to the pursuit of the right thinking and behaviour which would enable a person to attain Nirvāna. Nirvāna is a state of perpetual bliss and spiritual absorption in the Divine. It is not to be described because it so far transcends anything which finite human beings can begin to understand.

It is not therefore the case that Buddhism is atheistic in a Western sense of these words, denying the existence of God understood as Ultimate Spiritual Reality; nor is it agnostic, regarding such belief as debatable. Buddhism is impregnated with an awareness that the Divine exists. It simply believes that nothing which is not misleading can be said about it, and therefore that people's entire attention should be taken up with how they live their lives so that they may be in harmony with this Reality beyond description. (For further discussion see the Appendix to this section on page 127).

All the world religions demonstrate a similar reticence about speaking glibly of God, even though in some religions it may seem to the observer that this is not so. Yet the genuinely religious person who may seem to pronounce the word 'God' a great deal does this with devout humility and an awareness that God is infinitely greater than human understanding. Most religions, indeed, practise in some form or other what is known as the *via negativa* (the negative way) – that is, talking of God in terms of what God is not. Thus God is Indescribable, Infinite, Boundless, Unseen, Unknowable. Most religions however, except Theravādā Buddhism, do speak also of God according to the *via analogica* (the analogical way) that is, not talking of God as such and such, but saying that God is *like* something else. Thus God is Light, Power, Creator, Lord, King, Father, Shepherd, Judge, Saviour, Lover. Such terms are metaphors or analogies. Strictly they are not describing God but are pointers directing the attention of the believer towards God. (Figure 32 in Chapter 15 refers to the metaphorical use of prepositions to speak about 'God'.)

This apparent detour into theology is actually central to our purpose of discussing Religious Education. Theology, understood in its proper sense, is not a dry academic subject but a living and fascinating one. Theology, as the term implies, means 'God-talk' (*theos* – God, *logos* – word). This must feature as a key element in Religious Education. The kind of understanding about the *via negativa* and the *via analogica* which has just been discussed is a first essential in what it means to be religiously literate. It is as much part of

Religious Education as the concept of number is part of Mathematics. Children need to be helped to such understanding of 'God', just as they are helped to an understanding of 'number'.

Review of the four Religious Education lessons

If this element is omitted, Religious Education fails to be *Religious* Education. It may be history, sociology, cultural studies, art appreciation, personal and social education and so forth, but it is not helping people to appreciate what *religion* is. This is the element lacking in the lesson on drugs and the lesson on Easter customs. There was nothing in them which was designed significantly to help the students further forward in their awareness of what religion is. The personal, social and moral element in the lesson on drugs can be, although it need not be, related to religion. A religious person would certainly see its relationship, but a non-religious person would see no necessity whatever to bring religion into the discussion. The lesson on Easter customs may appear to the casual onlooker to have more to offer concerning religion, but in fact the mention of Jesus rising from the dead as being what Christians believe in was not related in any way to God but left as a purely miraculous statement concerning a human person. There was no discussion about this and no help given to encourage the children, whether they were from Christian, agnostic, Muslim or other homes, to think clearly about the content of this extraordinary Christian belief. The whole attention of the lesson was on the theme of new life for which the egg is a symbol. This was developing the children's aesthetic appreciation alongside the personal and social.

Is it possible to see the lesson on Paul's missionary journeys as Religious Education? Certainly the lesson fails as education. So many opportunities for developing understanding were missed. Yet even if it had been conducted by a teacher who was professionally sensitive and alert so that it was a 'good lesson' would it even so have been *Religious* Education in any significant way? Historical, geographical and sociological material may be as necessary for Religious Education as for, for example, English Literature or Art Appreciation. If, however, it is no more than this it cannot be judged in these three subject-areas as developing religious, literary or artistic awareness which was the purpose of introducing the material in the first place. In the lesson on Paul, his adventures were not related in any meaningful way to his overwhelming and life-transforming belief in God. The students were therefore not helped forward theologically at all. This is the classic, derisory image of what religion is about, and in fact the lesson was really reinforcing an archaic, imperialistic view of Christianity such as might readily prevent any understanding whatever of theology to emerge.

The only lesson which clearly focused upon what is central to religion was the one featuring the visitor from the Methodist church. This was clearly, for students as well as teacher, part of a learning experience in which fundamental beliefs of a specifically religious nature were being studied. The conversion experience of John Wesley, the hymns of Charles Wesley and the witness of a contemporary Methodist who is clear on the basically theological *raison d'être* for his religion, all point to education about what religion is.

The educational purpose of Religious Education

It should be noted that the lesson was exemplary in concerning the educational aspect of Religious Education as well as the religious. It was in no way assuming that students were religious believers, let alone Methodists. The atmosphere was a demonstration of openness, for many viewpoints were acknowledged to be represented in the classroom. What united them was a serious search for understanding about religion. This is the proper educational focus. It has nothing to do with evangelisation, propaganda or teaching for conversion. It promotes reflectiveness and knowledge.

At the same time the lesson did not assume that there are no answers, that commitment and convictions do not matter, that there is no evidence to be weighed or that the concern to try to find truth is irrelevant. Those in the class who came from, let us say, devout Muslim homes, or devout Roman Catholic homes, would not find their own religious outlooks questioned by the prevailing unacknowledged agenda of secular scepticism which features so prominently in Western societies today. Instead they would have the opportunity of extending their own experience to include that of other sincerely religious people, and in so doing would be likely to find their own faith deepened. There may indeed be a challenge, in that if their own faith is superficial and ill-understood, largely a matter of historical and cultural accident, then they would find themselves having to think more deeply about it. But this is the necessary risk which must be taken when education happens. People cannot remain at the level of infants in their outlooks and thinking if they are to be educated people, and if the faith cannot withstand the scrutiny of such enquiry in a sympathetic school setting it will be far more seriously at risk in the world outside, into which the student must emerge.

Problems of agreement about what constitutes religion

If a basic statement be accepted of religion as to do with a supposed Ultimate Spiritual Reality, or Presence, or God, and with the impact of faith in such on behaviour and way of life, it gives clarity and substance to the wholly educational purpose of Religious Education, namely, to help forward an understanding of religion. A guideline is established whereby Religious Education can make its unique contribution to the total curriculum.

Yet there has been considerable resistance to seeing religion in these terms. There has been a fear of accepting the fact that the very existence of such Spiritual Reality is doubted by large numbers of people, and that those who do believe, see this Reality in radically different ways which ought to be adjudicated between in the search for truth. The radically controversial nature of what is at the heart of religion is something from which people mostly run away. Emphasis on what is so controversial, furthermore, seems to open the floodgate to divisiveness. Peace and harmony are what every well-balanced human being longs for, and it seems to follow from this that occasions for dispute and disagreement in the classroom ought to be played down. Finally, teaching concerning beliefs is often suspected of being open to the charge of indoctrination, that is, of closing minds in acceptance of disputable views.

In response, however, one can argue that the radically controversial nature of religion should be openly acknowledged. Religion is controversial in a fundamental sense, for it may be that Spiritual Reality does not exist but is solely in the imagination of those who think it exists. But in order to decide, one must know what one is talking about, otherwise no proper judgement can be made.

Further, the controversial element can contribute very constructively towards the capacity to cope with the serious differences of belief which characterise the world. It is dangerous for individuals and for society not to be honest about disagreements, and to oblige people constantly to cover these up and pretend they do not exist. The hope of civilised society lies in creating a framework in which such differences may be accommodated and seen as part of the tapestry of life. Without discord there can be no harmony as we know it, but the discord must form part of the whole: it must find fulfilment, and in that ebb and flow music is born. Finally, indoctrination relates not to content but to manner of communication. (See pp 13f of Chapter 2 where this question is fully discussed.)

Two further reasons for not accepting that religion necessarily involves concern with a presumed Reality, or 'God', need closer attention because they promote an alternative view which takes the substance out of religion.

Is religion how people who call themselves religious behave and think?

Many people who say they are religious re-define what they mean by the term in order to retain continuity with their past, even though they have discarded the substance of religious faith. The sociological and cultural hold of religion on people is very tenacious, and rather than cut themselves off from the tradition they will re-define it.

In this way they come to terms with doubts about the truth of religion by saying that religion is a way of life, not in any sense something believed in.

Often this means taking religion out of it altogether. Many modern Jews, for example, say that Judaism is culture and does not involve any acknowledgement of the Divine at all. Yet they are happy for their customs to form the content of *religious* education. The same applies to many Christians who have serious doubts about the existence of God but who have re-defined their Christianity as a source of values for living and a raising of ultimate questions without any necessary relationship to God. 'God' has become for them another name for people's aspirations and ideals. It really does not matter whether God refers to anything objective or not.

In the light of this confusion from within the ranks of those who say they are 'religious' people, it is not surprising that the prevailing secular temper of our times should have seized on this as a neat way of avoiding the difficulties of teaching a controversial subject, especially because of the acrimony which has so often characterised those who make a stand on behalf of the truth of religion.

Yet any re-definition of words should itself be discussed as part of the Religious Education teaching. Dogmatism in re-definition is as inappropriate as dogmatism in traditional understanding. The issue must be opened up for students so that they can judge for themselves.

At this point, however, a relativist assumption is manifested in a reluctance to draw attention to the truth-claims on which religion is based. The assumption is that there is nothing knowable with regard to religion except the people who believe that there is something in it. Such relativism is pervasive in Western societies (as already discussed at length in Chapter 3). This is a major problem facing Religious Education today.

No-one disputes that there is a subjective element in religion, just as there is in subjects like history and science. But we do not limit history to the subjectivity of the historian or science to the subjectivity of the scientist. We say that history is about a real past and science about a real world of which we can acquire knowledge, however inadequate and limited that knowledge may be at present.

When such a definition is applied to religion it excludes from the start the possibility of there being an objective reality to its subject-matter beyond the simple fact of there being people who call themselves religious.

It is perfectly possible to disagree that there *is* such a Reality and to maintain that religious people are deluded, and that therefore religion must have deep psychological or sociological explanations. But no study of religion should *begin* with this assumption. That is hardly being open to the evidence. It is like a novice scientist saying that there cannot be any elementary particles, so that the only thing we can study is the behaviour and motivation of those scientists who say there are. The latter may be a consideration but it only becomes *the* major one if the scientist has already proved that elementary particles cannot exist. The almost exclusive concern in Religious Education with what religious *people* do or think reflects the same preconception – namely, that we cannot take seriously, or even entertain for a moment, the possibility that they may be right in what they say about Spiritual Reality. If we did, real discussion about the nature of that reality would form the centre of the attempt to understand religion.

Religion is focused on God (imagined or real, believable or not) not primarily on religious people

Genuinely religious people worship not themselves but God (see Figure 16). If we wish to understand what religion is about, we must concentrate on what religious people themselves see as at the heart of religion. To attend only to what *religious people* do and think is to attend to what is peripheral.

Truly religious people are usually conscious of their failure to express properly their faith in 'God' and are therefore aware that they are inadequate 'mirrors' of what religion is. An outsider is not going to get an adequate understanding of religion by looking at them, because their imperfection will stand in the way. Great effort is required of religious people if they are to live up to their faith. There is in most religions a consciousness of sin or failure to live as God wills people to live; in those where the concept of sin is not obviously present, there is nevertheless an awareness of the need for great moral and spiritual effort. This may take the form of renunciation of emotional involvement in the things of this world, its pleasure and pains and all its distractions.

Religious people do not normally say that religion is easy. It is something which has to be worked at. Religious people are like scientists, historians or writers in that they have to discipline themselves to learn and become more proficient. They are motivated by what they perceive as the objectivity of That to which they must relate.

Counterfeit forms of religion are many, for example, superstition, hypocrisy and formalism (see Figure 17). It is most important for the assessment of religion and development of convictions (whether for or against religion) that the difference between these counterfeits and genuine religion is appreciated.

Education which takes seriously assumptions and prejudice is vital when dealing with religion, for religion is the fertile soil for powerful and dangerous deception – both self-deception, and the conscious or unconscious manipulation of others. To fail to promote students' awareness of this is reprehensible.

If religion is conceived as being about people who happen to call themselves religious then this important dimension of Religious Education will be lacking. There will be no in-depth development of understanding concerning what is fundamental to religion, and therefore no criteria by which to evaluate what people say.

Figure 16 The focal point of religion

The heart of religion – the *content* of religious belief

The person who is 'outside' religion but who wants to understand it

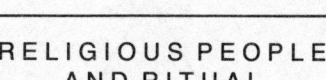

RELIGIOUS PEOPLE AND RITUAL

Getting to the heart of religion

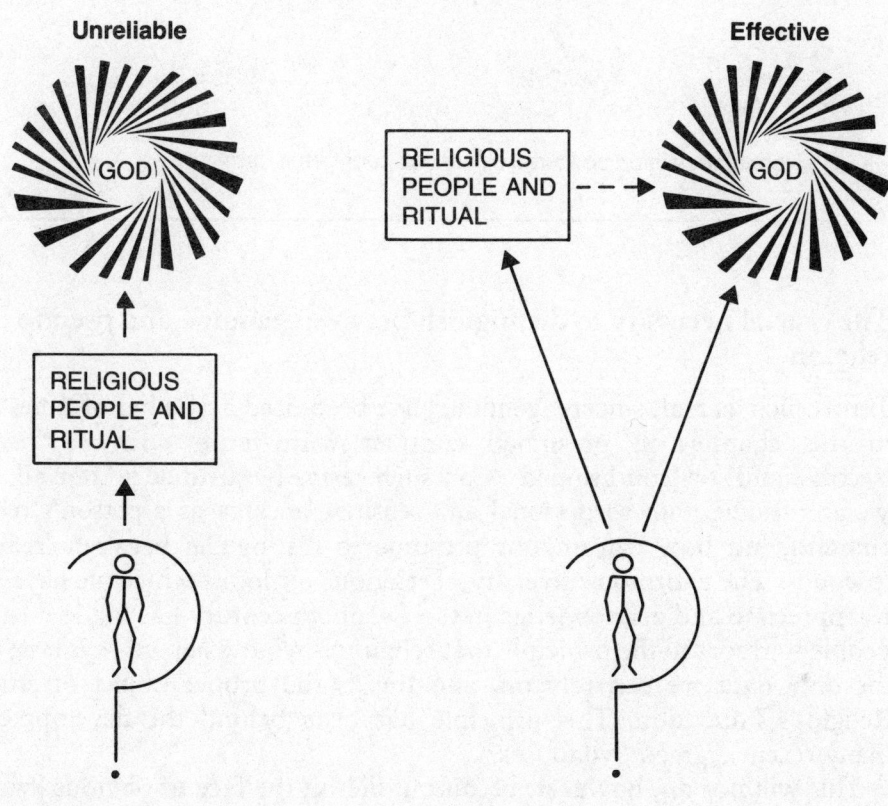

Figure 17   Counterfeits of Religion

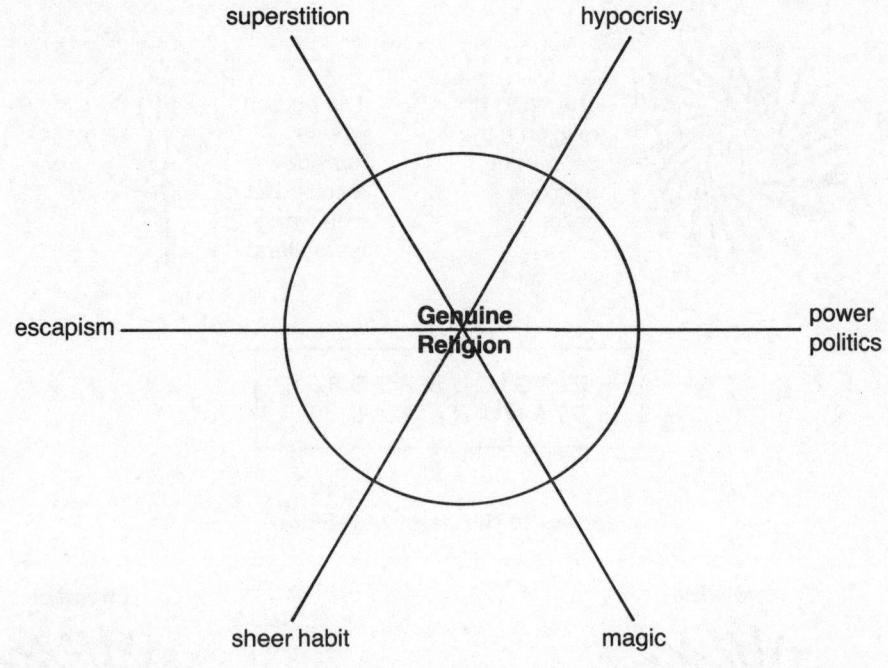

superstition   hypocrisy

escapism ——————— Genuine
Religion ——————— power
politics

sheer habit   magic

○ = genuine religion obscured by various counterfeit forms

The crucial necessity to distinguish between genuine and pseudo religion

Terms such as real, sincere, genuine have been used a number of times so far in this chapter, in presumed contrast with terms such as 'pseudo', 'secondhand' or 'conditioned'. Can such terms be justified? After all, when we are dealing with so personal and sensitive an area as a person's religious commitment, how can anyone presume to distinguish between 'real' and 'pseudo'? The enormous diversity of religious outlooks which we have learnt to appreciate and acknowledge in the twentieth century has made it easy for people to resort to the principle that religion is what a person *says* it is; this is the only data we can rely on, and this is the proper object of study in Religious Education. This principle has been behind the development of many recent Agreed Syllabuses.

This will not do, however, because it flies in the face of obvious evidence. We are familiar, in everyday life and in other areas of knowledge and experience, with the fact that some people are closer than others to the skills and understanding concerned with a particular area. For example, we speak of a good scientist, a good historian, a good writer, a good tennis-player, a good housewife, a good musician, and the school subjects associated with these areas of knowledge or skill are concerned with learning what makes them 'good'. To assume from the start that there are no criteria for such grading in religion as we automatically use in every other area would be indoctrinatory of this viewpoint. The possibility must be opened up. Anyone can set themselves up as an historian, or scientist, or writer, but not everyone is worth being considered as such. Education must be concerned with helping people to understand and handle the criteria by which judgment can be made. If the historian becomes a propagandist it is for the educated person to see through the propaganda and deny it the name of history. If the scientist does not bother to experiment, to study carefully the evidence and to consult with the scientific community as a whole, then however much he or she may claim to be a scientist we should not accord the status of scientific pronouncements to what he or she says. Similarly if a writer writes drivel without any sense of style, the same thing applies. This distinguishing is done on the basis of some idea of what the subjects ought to be; that is, on the basis of what science really is, what history really is, what literature really is. It may not be easy to put this into words, but a general concept of it is essential.

It is equally essential to distinguish between 'good' and 'bad' religious people. This distinguishing in religion is rendered peculiarly difficult but also peculiarly important, because of the many ways in which people can delude themselves and others with regard to high ideals and beliefs. Chapter 18 will discuss some of the criteria by which such genuineness can be discerned.

Conclusion

The discussion in this chapter has resulted in a view of how Religious Education should be conducted which can be summarised as follows.

1 It should be genuinely non-indoctrinatory both in intention and actuality, attending to understanding of religion and not to propaganda of any form. In particular this means presenting religious beliefs not in a way which assumes students' agreement or non-agreement, but in a way which stimulates people really to think about them for themselves.
2 What is presented in the classroom must be what is really distinctive and central to religion and this must relate to the *content* of belief. In this way it can help students towards genuine understanding and be free to be interesting, relevant and important.
3 It should help students towards making their own valid judgments for

or against religion by teaching criteria for discernment as to what real religion is.

4 It should help students work towards harmonious relationships between people, and to be able to distinguish between what is properly controversial and what is unnecessarily so owing to prejudice.

Finally, it is important to appreciate that if students conclude at the end of their Religious Education that there is no Ultimate Spiritual Reality, the Religious Education will not have been wasted if:

- it has helped to protect them from the effects of conditioning and any attempted indoctrination;
- it has given them some understanding of religion;
- it has shown up the complexity of issues and the problems of evidence;
- it has encouraged students to think about the commitments on which they wish to base their lives.

If properly taught, it will also have been an interesting and enjoyable subject of studies. If truth-claims are debated it is easy to make Religious Education live, and be an exciting and challenging subject.

Summary of argument of chapter 9

There is confusion about what the 'R' in Religious Education stands for. This is shown by extracts from four Religious Education lessons. A minimal definition is suggested as:

Belief in Ultimate Spiritual Reality (or 'God') and the impact of such belief on life and behaviour.

'God' is the most common word in the English language used to speak of Spiritual Reality and is the equivalent of words such as Allah in Islam, Brahman in Hinduism, Nām in Sikhism. Buddhism too assumes Spiritual Reality, although it does not talk about it.

'God' is indescribable (*via negativa*) but can in most religions be spoken of as 'like something else' (*via analogica*).

On the basis of this definition, a critique of the four lessons is possible.

A Drugs	R ✗	E ✓	
B Missionary journeys of Paul	R ✗	E ✗	
C Methodism	R ✓	E ✓	
D Easter	R ✗	E ✓	

Vagueness as to what religion is about

- can be due to fear of controversy, divisiveness, and indoctrination. Yet real harmony requires controversy to be openly acknowledged, and that people be helped to tackle these issues, and thus learn protection from indoctrination.

- can also be due to accepting, usually unconsciously, a definition of religion as in effect 'what people who call themselves religious say it is'. This puts the emphasis on so-called religious *people*, and is encouraged by re-definition of 'religion' by some 'religious' people themselves, and by the prevalence of a relativist assumption. Yet re-definition and relativism should themselves be discussed – not assumed and therefore indoctrinated. Understanding of religion, which is the proper educational aim of Religious Education, is not possible except on the basis of taking seriously the concept of 'God' (real or imaginary) and not just studying 'religious' people.

a) This is what is important to genuinely religious people

b) Religious people are generally aware of how inadequately they point to God

c) There are many counterfeit forms of religion which need to be distinguished

Implications for Religious Education

1 It should be non-indoctrinatory in intention and manner.
2 It should focus on what is central to religion.
3 It should teach criteria for discernment, for students to make their own valid judgements themselves.
4 It should help students to cope with controversy creatively.

Appendix: Note on Buddhism and the understanding of religion as centred on 'God'

The objection may be raised that in the text (p 117) I am misinterpreting the nature of Buddhism. I would reply that to the extent that Buddhists wish their way of life to be considered a religion they do subscribe to the view that there is more to reality than what the atheist or the agnostic would concede. This 'more to it' is the demarcation line between what religious and non-religious people believe in.

I would reiterate that although the word 'God' may be interpreted by some people in crude anthropomorphic terms, this is

a a travesty of theism as it manifests itself in the lives of holy people and scholars within theistic religions, and therefore;
b not properly what the word denotes.

St Anselm, for example, both saint and scholar, developed his ontological argument for the existence of God on the understanding of 'God' as 'that than which a greater cannot be conceived'. Easy definitions of 'God' reveal rather the distance between believers' understanding and the reality they claim to believe in.

I write this after a very helpful discussion with a Buddhist whose 'atheism' a theist could also affirm, because by 'God' he meant some finite being, describable and domesticated. The theist may easily agree that such does not exist, for it is very far removed from how St Anselm used the word 'God'. I therefore maintain that the term 'God' is appropriate as the nearest English equivalent to the real centre of all religions, whether so-called theistic or non-theistic.

The distinction between theism and non-theism remains important. It refers to whether or not a religious person's understanding of the reality signified by the term 'God' includes, or does not include, a personal connotation. A theist may say that it is not misleading to speak of God in personal terms even though God is infinitely greater than what we mean by personal. A non-theist, on the other hand, would be likely to say that such language is totally misleading, because 'God' is not 'personal' in any form whatever.

Peggy Morgan, in a recent article on 'The place of Buddhism in the religious education curriculum'[1] notes that Buddhists cannot agree to 'belief in a personal God'. She then raises the counter-question as to what is meant by 'God' and suggests a link with *Advaita Vedanta* Hinduism without developing the argument further. This suggestion in fact supports my line of reasoning because in discussion with Professor Mahadevan of Madras University, himself a practising advaitin, he both accepted the understanding of 'God' I have outlined above and believed that this was a way of bringing many different religious traditions into a meaningful relationship.[2]

Notes and References

1 *BJRE* Vol 9, No 1, Autumn 1986, p 18
2 Private conversation with Professor T M P Mahadevan at his house in Madras, January 1979

10 A Threefold Approach to Religious Education: Experience, Imagination, Thinking

The previous two chapters have drawn attention to the proper aim of Religious Education, namely, to help students understand the nature of religion, not to make students religious. This leaves all the question-marks in place beside even the most fundamental problem: whether there is anything in religion at all.

In order to achieve this aim in Religious Education, a threefold approach is helpful. Religious Education needs to promote:

a experience;
b imagination;
c the capacity to think.

Experience

Sine experientia nihil sufficenter scire potest (without experience, nothing can be known sufficiently). So runs an inscription outside the University Botanic Gardens in Oxford. The importance of relating education to student experience has long been appreciated; structuring experience as a basis on which to build understanding and competence in skills is familiar in all subject areas taught. With regard to Religious Education, however, two problems present themselves. First, there is often confusion as to what constitutes experience which can be properly termed religious. Second, most teachers are inhibited from relating Religious Education to experiential work by the fear of indoctrination.

What is religious experience?

Religion is concerned with a distinctive type of experience, which is not infrequently confused with other forms of experience. Figure 18 distinguishes five kinds. Most experience has more than one component, and may include all five. It might indeed be said that a distinguishing feature of religious experience is that it includes all the others, at least implicitly.

Figure 18 Five kinds of experience

Personal

about myself, my
feelings, my reactions,
what happens to me

Aesthetic

about the beauty of the
world and the wonder it
arouses. This is basically
a way of looking at the
world which is so powerful
that people may say that
they are grasped by it

Social

about myself as a member
of a group, what I share
with others, or receive
alongside them

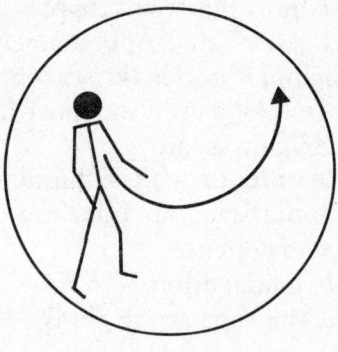

Religious

about a Presence or a Power
with which I interact in some way

Moral

about the obligation of myself
to others, and of them to me
and to each other: the awareness
of 'ought'

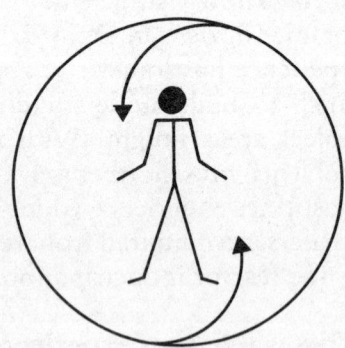

What makes an experience distinctly religious? Not just that it is meaningful to me, nor just that I share it with others, not just moral consciousness, nor just a sense of wonder, but at the very least an awareness of 'some Power beyond themselves' as Sir Alister Hardy expressed it when inviting people to contribute to the initial research of his Religious Experience Research Unit.[1] The accounts sent in show that people clearly understood this 'power' not to be that of society, or of other scientifically or humanly explainable phenomena, but to have other elements:

- giving a sense of oneness; this power is seen as that which gives meaning and significance to *life as a whole*.
- giving a sense of extraordinary certainty; the experience is so direct and immediate that it is impossible to doubt it – it is *self-authenticating*.
- giving a sense of belonging, of relationship to this power. While there is a feeling of being passive, there is also a feeling that an active response of some kind is required – that there is *interaction*.

The following account describes an experience which someone had at the age of 5.

When I was about five I had the experience on which, in a sense, my life has been based. It has always remained real and true for me. Sitting in the garden one day I suddenly became conscious of a colony of ants in the grass, running rapidly and purposefully about their business. Pausing to watch them I studied the form of their activity, wondering how much of their own pattern they were able to see for themselves. All at once I knew that I was so large that, to them, I was invisible – except, perhaps, as a shadow over their lives. I was gigantic, huge – able at one glance to comprehend, at least to some extent, the work of the whole colony. I had the power to destroy or scatter it, and I was completely outside the sphere of their knowledge and understanding. They were part of the body of the earth. But they knew nothing of the earth except the tiny part of it which was their home. Turning away from them to my surroundings, I saw there was a tree not far away, and the sun was shining. There were clouds, and blue sky that went on for ever and ever. And suddenly I was tiny – so little and weak and insignificant that it didn't really matter at all whether I existed or not. And yet, insignificant as I was, my mind was capable of understanding that the limitless world I could see was beyond my comprehension. I could know myself to be a minute part of it all. I could understand my lack of understanding.

A watcher would have to be incredibly big to see me and the world around me as I could see the ants and their world, I thought. Would he think me to be as unaware of his existence as I knew the ants were of mine? He would have to be vaster than the world and space, and beyond understanding, and yet I could be aware of him – I was aware of him, in spite of my limitations. At the same time he was, and he was not, beyond my understanding.

Although my flash of comprehension was thrilling and transforming, I knew even then that in reality it was no more than a tiny glimmer. And yet, because there was this glimmer of understanding, the door of eternity was already open.

Every single person was a part of a Body, the purpose of which was as much beyond my comprehension now as I was beyond the comprehension of the ants. I was enchanted. Running indoors, delighted with my discovery, I announced happily, 'We're like ants, running about on a giant's tummy!' No one understood, but that was unimportant. I knew what I knew.

This inner knowledge was exciting and absorbingly interesting, but it remained unsaid because, even if I could have expressed it no one would have understood. Once, when I tried, I was told I was morbid.[2]

This account from Edward Robinson's book *The Original Vision* may help to clarify the distinction between different sorts of experience, as it in fact demonstrates all five. It was *personal* in that the little girl was on her own in the garden when she felt a great sense of peace and elation come upon her. The *social* dimension was present in that she was aware of herself as one of a huge number of other human beings as she contemplated the sheer multiplicity of the ants. The *moral* element was not so much to the fore but was implied in that just as ants work together and cooperate, so should human beings. It was an *aesthetic* experience in that she was appreciating the beauty of the world, its order and its mystery. But it was also *religious* because she thought in terms of a giant responsible for the world in relation to whom we are like ants; the three elements outlined above of a sense of oneness, certainty, and belonging, were part of the experience.

Can Religious Education relate to experience?

An immediate problem, however, is that to assume religious experience on the part of students, or to teach in order to arouse such experience, would be indoctrination, not education. Many people appear to have no religious experience to draw on, and to try to induce it in those who must compulsorily attend school is to be guilty of foisting on to students something which it is possible to regard as illusory and untrue.

It is clear that we should not assume that people have such experience. Nor should we assume that they do not, or that they are incapable of it. This would be to fly in the face of much evidence. Many children, especially among immigrant families, come from homes where explicitly religious experience is not entirely excluded, and some from homes where it is the focal point of life. Furthermore, children's capacity to understand bears a direct relationship to their exposure to the use of explicitly religious language and concepts. It will not do to assume they lack the capacity to understand even if given some help. (See Chapter 12 for a detailed discussion of this.)

The fear of indoctrination can be overcome provided that the teacher is aware, and constantly helps students to be aware, of the two levels of student-experience possible. One is at the level of actual religious experience and the other that of empathetic trying-to-find out. The distinction between these two levels is further developed in Chapter 13 on Worship in School, for assemblies giving opportunity for such explicitly religious experience can be an important partner to classroom Religious Education.

Religious Education neither should nor can work towards students having religious experience, but it should relate to such experience in two ways. First, it should give opportunities for students, as David Hay notes, to 'open their personal awareness to those aspects of their experience which are recognised by religious people as the root of religion'.[3] This is not indoctrinatory because it is not assuming that students will achieve such awareness, or that if they do they will interpret it in religious terms. Such an aim, however, does seek to sensitise them to what religion is about and thus to contribute powerfully to their understanding of religion and their ability to evaluate its truth or falsity for themselves.

Second, Religious Education needs to perform the humble but crucial task of giving students a vocabulary which they can, if it seems proper to them, relate to their own experience. On the basis of their understanding of this vocabulary they can then make judgments with regard to the experience of others. It is important to note the often-forgotten truism that we are all inter-dependent and cannot get very far entirely on our own. This is obvious in the case of technology. How many of us would have discovered how to make fire, clothes, the wheel, the micro, entirely on our own? So it is in religion. A person needs to be able to relate his or her own private experience to that of others, otherwise that person is imprisoned within limited horizons.

Bridge-building of this kind, however, requires expression. Words are by far the most complex, sophisticated, adaptable and potentially precise of such tools. This necessarily involves introducing students to theological language.

It is a marked feature of British society today to keep experiences like that of the five-year old recorded above completely private. A cultural taboo is at work which also affects a person's inner life, in that, lacking any kind of linguistic or symbolic vocabulary, the insight arising out of experience is, as it were, still-born. Edward Robinson notes how one man, recalling an experience he had had more than 50 years before, 'actually thanks us for having brought him to reflect on this long-buried experience, and so having enabled it to germinate'.

This person had written:

The remarkable thing, as I now see, about such seeds, stored as bare memories of experiences which in the past have fallen on unreceptive ground, is their capacity to remain dormant for long periods, perhaps waiting inertly for an auspicious change in the soil which contains them.[4]

Imagination

Religious Education should help people to make sense of their own experience in the light of other people's and to find a measure of communicable expression.

Imagination is needed in order to be aware of the experience of others and open to the possibility of making such experience one's own. Imagination has tended to be undervalued in schools for a very long time. It is seen as a pleasant extra – perhaps something good to say about a student in an arts subject – but not as an essential ingredient for understanding. This may be because of its association with fantasy, with make-believe. There is a kind of use of imagination which is just escapism and which encourages an air of unreality – if, for example, I go round imagining that I am Cleopatra! But imagination can be directed towards understanding, towards knowledge, towards reality, as when, for example, I imagine what it is like to be living now in the slums of Calcutta, in a room with other families, with no electricity and only one water tap for about a hundred people.

Yet even this clearly desirable use of imagination does not receive conspicuous encouragement in our educational system, in part because of its absence of academic rigour and its non-examinable nature. Glancing through back numbers of the journal *The Twentieth Century* I came across an article in an issue dated May 1901 with the interesting title *The Blunder of Modern Education*. It made almost humorous reading because of the ardent way in which the writer warmed to his subject. He lamented the mental dullness produced by too much reading, too much stress on pumping out the same factual information, too much uniformity engendered by class-teaching, syllabuses and examinations. Near the end he remarks:

> The imagination is killed in early childhood; ideas are allowed no room to expand; the mind is forced to remain within rigid limits, like a fowl's beak bent to a chalk line.

This unusual simile is in many respects as relevant in 1987 as in 1901, despite the much greater emphasis on creativity in education. The stifling effects of the pre-arranged syllabus, the examination ritual, the importance of testing, of comparison of the individual with a norm, still operate and take their toll.

Einstein wrote in his treatise *On Science*: 'Imagination is more important than knowledge.' That one of the greatest scientists of all time should have made such a comment is in itself impressive. In what ways may it be considered meaningful, especially within the context of Religious Education? I suggest three ways.

1 *Imagination educates the emotions*: it enables individuals to leave the

confines of their own exceedingly limited experience and enter into that of others. It can give rise to empathy and to putting oneself in the place of another; realising that here there is another living centre of reality of the same value as oneself.

In Religious Education imagination allows students to enter into the experience of religious people. For the dilemma is this: only if a person is 'inside' a situation can it be understood. Thus it is frequently noted by Muslims, for example, that only a Muslim can understand Islam. But most people are 'outside' Islam, and if they were to become Muslims the problem would not be solved because they would then be 'outside' so much else. No-one can be a Muslim, Hindu, Humanist and Christian all from the inside. The necessity to specialise, and the inevitably limited nature of any one individual's experience, means that understanding has mostly to be achieved from outside, however unsatisfactory this may be. The bridge can only be crossed by imagination. The strangeness and subtlety and complexity of religious experience calls for a conspicuous exercise of this faculty.

2 *Imagination can extend the frontiers of knowledge*: it is needed to provide the starting-points for reason and the hypotheses for experiment. Vision is a prerequisite for knowledge: the greatest scientists have the creativity of artists. Imagination sees a range of possibilities to be explored.

All this applies with especial force to religion, which deals with that which lies beyond ordinary sense-experience and categories of thought. The ability to perceive what religion is about, quite apart from the ability to affirm it – that is, to be religious – requires a generous use of imagination. This is not to assume that religion is make-believe. Such a view may itself reveal a lack of imaginative capacity, for whether religion is make-believe or not is a judgment which should be made only on the basis of understanding what it is, and for that imagination is necessary. If Spiritual Reality exists, it cannot be directly perceived, touched and handled but rather intuited. For example, the question about the origin of the cosmos as a whole is utterly meaningless to many people because they cannot conceive even the possibility of a non-empirical mode of being.

Imagination is needed not only as a starting point for thought and for questioning, but throughout the process of reasoning and experimenting. Imagination sees the implications of arguments, the dangers lurking in half-truths and over-simplifications, the possibility of hidden factors and so forth. Imagination refines awareness, and helps to overcome the dull, pedestrian way of thinking which boxes everything in unrelated compartments and sets up many false 'either/ors'.

The either/or mentality is particularly unfortunate with regard to the attempt to understand religion, for religion is full of seeming contradictions, difficulties and controversial statements. The complexity of issues must be brought out in Religious Education with all age groups including the youngest. So often people seem to think that religion is straightforward; they may warm to it, ignore it or oppose it, but their choice is based on serious misunderstanding.

In Religious Education, therefore, imagination is needed to develop vision and awareness of possibilities so that the truth of religious claims can be thought about authentically.

3 *Imagination can activate will-power.* Napoleon, for example, understood this well enough when he remarked 'Humankind is wooed by the imagination.' We are all so limited by our own horizons, our feelings, our moods, our interests, our innate laziness, that we need stimulus to progress, to move, to change. Imagination helps to awaken our sleeping will-power – that faculty which so signally distinguishes a person from a thing, from a bundle of molecular reflexes. It does so by projecting possibilities and keeping fresh in the attention what is past while giving confidence to move into the future.

The exercise of imagination is important with regard to an understanding of religion. Without it, most people have little motive to take religion seriously; they are subject to the pressure of a predominantly secular society and can easily be distracted from religion, which makes no direct appeal to the senses. Some kind of jolt or effort is required even to start out to be religiously educated.

At a deeper level, Religious Education should enable people to realise the importance of commitment, and should give training in decision-making. The actual content of Religious Studies includes impressive examples of the use of imagination both in the power engendered by commitment, and in the endeavour to live up to the very high standards taught by all the great religions.

Religious Education ought properly to raise the question of what makes people tick, what gives them purpose, and what *ought* to do so: that is, what corresponds to reality. It is not the place of Religious Education to direct the will; any such attempt would justifiably raise the charge of indoctrination. Its role is, however, to raise the issues, to familiarise people with questions of evidence and so forth, and to encourage real thoughtfulness as to the choices of faith which, if not made consciously, will happen unconsciously. Imagination is needed in order to appreciate in others and consider for oneself questions of motivation, purpose, commitment.

Thinking

Experience and imagination both stimulate and call for reflectiveness. A creative circle needs to be formed in which the passive element of experience, allied with the motivational power of imagination to see possibilities, is corrected or reinforced by intellectual reasoning.

The traditional picture of schooling has placed such stress on the intellectual that there is a tendency today to go to the other extreme from the fear of imposing on a largely unacademic majority what is suitable only for the academic few. This false polarisation between life and academic matters, however, is a misunderstanding of what the intellectal side of understanding is about.

Thinking is what everyone does well or badly, profoundly or superficially, every time they say anything to themselves or to others, and every time they make connections between things or ideas or images in the mind. In practical terms, it is not possible to be human without thinking. The aspect of Religious Education concerned with thinking is therefore simply seeking to develop this essential aspect of all learning. It has relevance for all students, whatever their age or intellectual ability.

Any explicit development of theological thinking in primary children has, however, been dismissed by many Religious Education experts. Consequently, unlike, for example, in mathematics, hardly any attention has been given to building up educationally acceptable concepts. This has resulted in teenagers being expected to make judgments regarding religion when they are operating with concepts appropriate perhaps at infant level but seriously inadequate for adolescents. Until primary Religious Education takes theological thinking seriously the situation cannot be expected to improve dramatically. The limitations imposed on secondary school timetables, the greater problem of motivation and the undoubted fact that failure to develop understanding in childhood can seriously inhibit the capacity ever to understand at all, means that the secondary school ought to be able to build on solid foundations and not have to try, belatedly, to do all the construction-work itself, in unfavourable circumstances. (Chapter 11 discusses this in more detail.)

The thinking of Religious Education, as in all other areas of the curriculum, should build on the experiencing side and the imagining side. A careful programme which builds on the inter-relatedness of these three aspects can enable students to gain insight into the nature of religion, and this is the proper end of Religious Education. The question of commitment can then safely be left in the hands of the individual who has such insight, and the Religious Education will be clearly seen as non-indoctrinatory – either for or against religion.

The importance of thinking can be expressed even more strongly. In all spheres of life it is thinking which protects students from being indoctrinated by the content of experience and imagination. Experience is passive – the individual has no control over it. Imagination also, by its very nature, is uncontrollable. Reason applies controls and enables a person to make sense of and evaluate, and to say Yes or No to what experience and imagination throw up. Teachers who fail to equip students with the ability to think clearly about the experiential and imaginative capacities which they promote *are* indoctrinating, whether they intend to do so or not. The emotions involved are extremeley powerful, and great care is needed in awakening them.

It is particularly serious, therefore, that Religious Education – which raises such dangerous emotions – should have a reputation for being intellectually weak. Often Religious Education is thought of as a soft option where opinions can be expressed without evidence, and regurgitation of a few obvious 'facts' is all that is required of a cognitive nature.

It is possible to identify six fundamental questions concerning religion. Religious Education should constantly raise such questions and give help to students in learning to think about them; if any of these is missing the development of understanding about religion is inhibited. None of these questions admits of an easy or straightforward answer and the teacher should draw attention to this. But just because proof, understood in a scientific sense, is not possible, this does not mean that 'anything goes'; that people can hold whatever opinion they like with educational validity. The need for clarity of thought, honest argument, fair assessment of evidence and so forth is just as necessary in understanding religion as in understanding science or history. The six central questions are as follows:

1 What does religious language mean?
Just as in mathematics the concept of 'number' is taught, so there are certain central and distinctive concepts of religion such as 'God', 'soul', 'prayer' and 'salvation'. These need to be the subject of continual teaching, both with regard to meaning and to how they can be expressed. (For some discussion of how these can be introduced with younger children see Chapters 12 and 15.)

2 How do actions and visual symbols express religious belief?
The way in which religious belief transcends straightforward logical talking should be brought out under question 1 and developed with regard to non-verbal forms of expression. Exciting work can be done with students at all stages in this area, but care must be taken that it does not stop at the level at which it may be considered in some other subject, for example, sociology, history, or art. The proper content of religious understanding is an appreciation of what the symbolism is pointing towards.

3 What is religion?
This is fundamental, otherwise neither teacher nor taught knows what the subject is about. But it is, like the other questions, one which needs constant discussion. No rule-of-thumb answer can be given and the deeper one looks into this question the more involved and challenging it becomes. Something of the excitement of this search can be conveyed in the classroom. The basic understanding of religion argued for in Chapter 9 is a starting point only.

4 Is this person or action genuinely religious?

This is vitally necessary as a preamble to questions 5 and 6. Religion is so often simply dismissed as irrelevant, mistaken, or indeed dangerous, because no help is given to people on how to discriminate between the genuine and the sham. To fail to recognise the abuse of something makes it impossible to properly weigh up its use; to discard or accept religious belief on grounds of the failure of others to be truly religious or live up to these beliefs is ludicrous. Chapter 18 discusses this in some detail with regard to secondary school work.

5 Are religious beliefs true?

This is a question which must be studied because there can be no understanding of religion without the realisation that religious believers are convinced of the truth and absolute significance of religion. The most direct and simple way to appreciate this is to take beliefs seriously enough to debate their truth. Furthermore, it is fascinating to students of all ages, for they do ask deep and fundamental questions about the nature of reality. Much can be done even with young children (see Chapter 15 pp 211ff especially).

Figure 19   A Threefold Approach

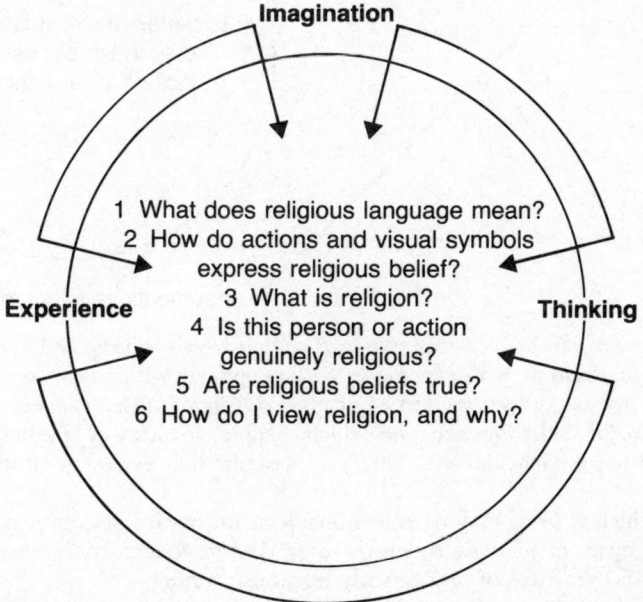

Experience should be understood through imagination and thinking.
Imagination should be stimulated by thinking and experience.
Thinking should be informed by experience and imagination.

Figure 20 Religious Education and Experience

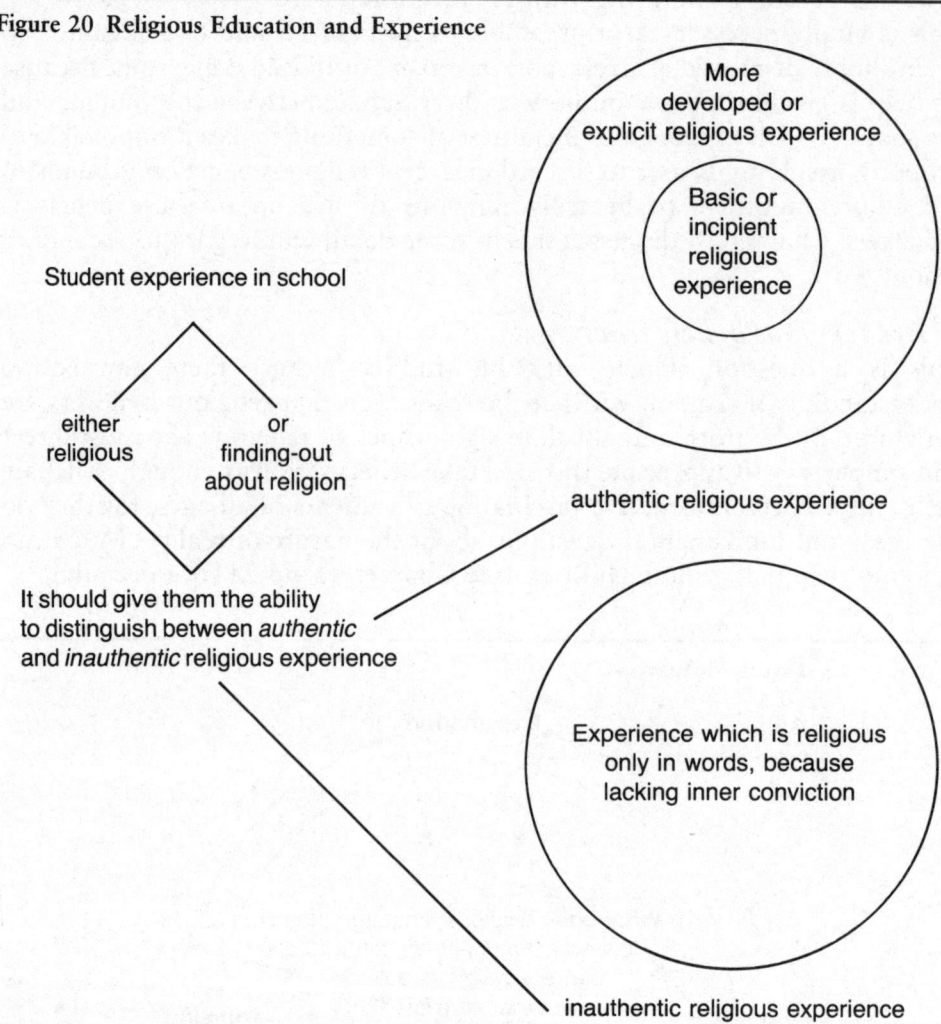

Religious experience can be seen fom two angles, that which is basic and that which is more developed. The first is to do with experience welling up from within a person's life, with what is personal and private and yet seen to be of universal significance. The second is to do with explicit worship or enlightenment in which people consciously participate in shared experience, and use a particular vocabulary to describe that experience and invoke further experience.

Experience which is *basic* may be called incipient, in that it does not usually get very far unless nurtured or given encouragement by some kind of attachment, however loose, to the thought-forms and practices of an explicitly religious tradition.

Experience which is *more developed* unites individuals to the experience of others, and gives them the wherewithal to act upon the experience and develop from it.

Experience which is described in religious terms but which is not part of a person's inner life is not religious at all. This can be explained in terms of psychological needs, of social conditioning, of moral motivation or of aesthetic awareness. The religious language or ritual is used simply as a vehicle for something which can be described in these other terms. The 'religious' description is superficial and basically redundant.

It cannot be too strongly emphasised that the purpose of raising the truth-issues and sharing with students questions of evidence is not to gain their adherence to this or that viewpoint, but to open up the issues so that they can make up their own minds on the basis of some knowledge rather than on ignorance. This leads to the next question.

6 How do I view religion, and why?

Discussion of Question 5 tends to be sterile unless both teacher and students are genuinely engaged with the themes in such a way that they are *really* thinking and relating the discussion to their own experience, convictions and insights. Failure to do this is largely responsible for the rift between academic study and real life already referred to. One way of expressing the purpose of education as a whole is to describe it as the process of unveiling preconceptions and examining them in the light of reason, with the intention of gaining wisdom, as discussed in Chapter 3. With regard to religion this is paramount because emotions and conditioning can so easily carry all before them, whether for or against religion.

Figure 19 gives a summary of the chapter and Figure 20 an additional note on Experience.

Notes and references

1 The research of the Religious Experience Research Unit is described in Alister Hardy *The Spiritual Nature of Man* (Clarendon Press, 1979).
2 Edward Robinson *The Original Vision* (RERU Manchester College, Oxford, 1977) p 12f.
3 David Hay 'Suspicion of the Spiritual: Teaching Religion in a World of Secular Experience' *British Journal of Religious Education* Summer 1985, p 142.
4 Edward Robinson *op cit* p 145.

11 On Content

Chapter 8 has looked at the *raison d'être* of Religious Education, Chapter 9 at what religion is and Chapter 10 at the purpose of Religious Education. It is time to consider by what subject-matter this aim should be achieved in the classroom.

Emphasis on skills

It is first important, however, to examine how content is related to skills. A skills-based approach to Religious Education is sound, liberating and exciting. Three main arguments can be put forward in favour of this:

1 The task of trying to communicate the mountainous volume of content which an understanding of religion requires was always a hopeless one, even in the days when Religious Education centred on Bible teaching. If any group of people are asked to write down what they consider essential or desirable as Religious Education content, there is usually disagreement. By concentrating on skills the teacher is released from a heavy burden.

2 Religion deals with dynamic, controversial and potentially explosive material. A content-based approach to it, therefore, calls for extreme care in selection and simplification, together with very wide knowledge and great powers of discernment. Otherwise, the teacher may be guilty of misrepresentation and prejudice. To promote in pupils the skills with which they can discover and evaluate for themselves, however, renders this dilemma much less acute. The teacher must still be aware of how teaching may be over-burdened by his or her own viewpoint, but attention to skills acts as a safeguard.

3 Skills concentrate on what the pupil is *doing*, and this encourages a real engagement with the subject-matter. The 'detective' approach applied to the teaching of the Bible, for example, is extremely fruitful: pupils can become involved and excited as they pursue clues and learn to weigh up evidence. Presentation is no longer teacher-dominated, and pupils' motivation is stimulated by their pursuing problems and goals themselves.

Distinctive skills necessary for understanding religion

Many of the skills needed in Religious Education are of a general nature but they are applied to religion in asking and following up the six fundamental questions just outlined in Chapter 10. These questions may be summed up in three groups of two: the first relating to the outward phenomena of religion in words, visual symbols and ritual, the second to discernment as to what is genuinely religious and the third to matters of evidence and judgment. There is a natural progression through these questions but they are also part of a spiral, all being related to each other.

The ability to handle such questions requires skills of discernment:

- the recognition and use of specifically religious terms;
- appreciation of the way religious ideas are frequently expressed through symbolism;
- awareness of the difference between religious and secular experience;
- the ability to discriminate between religion and its counterfeits such as superstition, hypocrisy and formalism;
- the evaluation of the kind of evidence upon which religious beliefs rest;
- the ability to relate to what is being studied and especially to one's own experience.

Applied to a common theme used in Religious Education today at all levels, that of Festivals, this would mean asking:

- What do the religious words used in the Festival mean to believers?
- What beliefs in fact lie behind the practices associated with the Festival?
- What would make taking part in a Festival a religious experience?
- How could an outsider tell whether a person taking part in a Festival does so from genuine devotion or from superstition?
- Are there good grounds for the beliefs expressed in the Festival?
- Why would I, if opportunity presented itself, take part or not take part in such a Festival?

The importance of content

Emphasis on skills does not mean that content is irrelevant or unimportant. There can be no education in skills without content. But the principle of selection is different. Instead of suffering from the nightmare of trying to be comprehensive and convey all that students need to know, the teacher is now free to develop just a few themes which are particularly appropriate, related to the students' own expressed interests or the teacher's own enthusiasm and expertise. This can promote work in depth, instead of the superficial canter through an amazing amount of material which has so often characterised unsatisfactory Religious Education. Great care is needed to ensure that the few topics which are chosen for this detailed work in developing skills really are important and central to an understanding of religion.

The content discussed and studied in Religious Education, therefore, both matters and does not matter at the same time. It matters in that the content should not focus on what is peripheral and secondary. It does not matter in that there is such a vast amount of suitable and adequate content from which to choose.

In the teaching of history it is better to study a little well, provided it is done within the context of an awareness of breadth, than to try to cover a lot of material and do it badly. The same is true in literature; to read one book properly will engender more understanding than skipping through dozens of books and not allowing any of them to make any impact on the reader, or permitting the reader to have, as it were, any conversation with them. It is the same in Religious Education.

The importance of a World Religions dimension

A few years ago it may have been necessary to argue forcibly for the inclusion of world religions in Religious Education. Now, however, such an approach is taken for granted in many areas of Britain and those where it is not are widely regarded as out of step with contemporary developments.

The case for the teaching of world religions rests on four main considerations. The first is that in many schools in Britain today there are children whose home backgrounds reflect a multi-faith presence in our society. It is axiomatic of good teaching to relate to that which is important and familiar to those one is teaching. If therefore there are, for example, Muslims or Sikhs or Hindus in the class it is a lack of courtesy as well as educationally undesirable not to relate to those faiths in Religious Education and help all students forward in their thinking about them. Even if, however, no other world faith is represented in a classroom, it is important that students are aware of such faiths, and not completely ignorant of them, because they are likely to need to relate to them in other, future contexts. The diversity of world faiths is clearly represented in British society today.

Second, Religious Education has a most important role to play in promoting an international and world-wide consciousness. Our world is becoming a global village, and people must be helped to a positive and creative appreciation of otherness and differences and of ways in which these can be contained without arousing fear and enmity. Religion features as a central, and potentially very dangerous, factor in many of the tensions of the modern world; straight thinking concerning religion is not optional.

Third, if taught well the study of world religions can be fascinating, challenging, demanding and illuminating. Just as travel can enhance people's understanding and feed the imagination, helping them to see in a different light what is familar to them, so can the study of world religions.

Fourth, the teaching of world religions can help to prevent any feeling of attempted indoctrination in Religious Education. Because a number of views are presented, the impression that there is only one is guarded against. Few children, parents or fellow members of staff would suspect the Religious Education teacher of trying to make converts in the classroom on behalf of two distinctive religions. This is not to say that the inclusion of world religions cannot be in its own way indoctrinatory. It can in two respects: with regard to biased comments and selection of material and with regard to the attitude to religion upon which that selection of material is based. But if the teacher is educationally committed and alert (as in the profile given in Chapter 6) the world religions perspective does help to open up Religious Education and promote students' genuine thinking.

Problems in teaching world religions

The case for teaching about world religions is impressive. Unfortunately, however, the problems of doing it have not been adequately weighed up. There has been a precipitous rush to re-model syllabuses and examination work within the wider mould without appreciating sufficiently the dangers. These include the superficiality of what has been lampooned with some accuracy as a 'Cook's tour' of religions, due to lack of understanding by teachers, the minute amount of time available for dealing with very complex and difficult themes, and the difficulties which students experience in relating in any helpful educational way to what may and often does appear as strange and unintelligible. Moreover, as already mentioned, the question of bias and indoctrination can still enter in.

Members of the different faiths, fairness to whom is often cited as a major reason for including world religions, have also been highly critical of the way in which these faiths have often been introduced in the classroom.

First, serious misunderstandings as well as sheer errors have often been conveyed. In a recent article, Rabbi Douglas Charing drew attention to a number of pitfalls in the teaching of Judaism. He argued that 'it would be better to *unlearn* if the right approach is to be achieved.'[1] The dangers of generalisations, of stereotyping people, and of indulging in giving fascinating but irrelevant details which are then remembered while what is important is forgotten – all these are common to the teaching of any religion, and they need to be guarded against. It is exceedingly difficult to be accurate, fair and balanced.

Second, so much of the teaching of world religions has contributed little to *Religious* Education; rather, it has amounted to lessons in history, geography, sociology or anthropology, and what is distinctive of religion *per se* has been ignored or glossed over in favour of peripheral matters and absorbing external practices. To teach that Muslims pray five times a day, or that Orthodox Jews wear prayer-shawls with tassels when praying, is describing an aspect of human behaviour. Such information only becomes *Religious* Education when the reasons for this behaviour are explored at length and a real attempt at understanding the underlying motivation is wrestled with.

This inevitably takes teacher and taught into the realm of beliefs, as does indeed frequently happen in the classroom. But to understand religious beliefs requires far more than 'factual' information of the kind 'Muslims believe there is one God, Allah, and Muhammad is his prophet'. Yet for all the reasons given in Chapter 3 such discussion of truth-claims tends to be avoided.

Third, and not unrelated to the difficulties already referred to, is the use or misuse of the teacher's own religious or ideological commitment. Many teachers find this a source of perplexity if not of embarrassment. Enough has been said in Chapter 4 on this issue and the suggestions given in Figure 11 (page 65) for the teacher in the classroom are particularly useful with regard to teaching world religions. Yet many teachers do not feel secure enough in their own commitment or in their knowledge of other religions to put themselves in such a vulnerable position in the classroom.

Fourth, world relgions have often been presented in a relativist, secular garb which has rendered such teaching suspect by members of other religions. Many Hindu and Muslim parents, for example, prefer to send their children to a church school which is explicitly Christian-based, rather than have their children taught a humanistic version of religion which they see as erosive of faith in an insidious way. Much of the discussion on the adequacy of critical openness, for example, has arisen from protests from immigrant parents (see pages 41 and 177).

Fifth, while the difficulties of teaching the concepts associated with Christianity have long been appreciated, it is often forgotten how much more difficult it is to come to terms with those of a religion arising out of a different culture other than that which surrounds one. In some ways, this applies with as much force to immigrants, especially in the second and third generations, as it does to those for whom the culture is indigenous. The ethos of their new environment can quite quickly make them feel distanced from their original culture.

In the light of these considerations, how should the teacher approach the teaching of world religions? I would suggest the following strategy as an aid towards avoiding the dangers outlined above – of mis-representation, trivialisation and indoctrination.

1 Limit the field of study to work in no more than *two* religions, or in *one* topic relating to a number of religions. Superficiality is the enemy

of learning. To try to cover too much ground increases the dangers of unwarranted generalisations. Work in depth is what counts.

2 Share with students the difficulties of the task. Involve them in the process of education by directing their attention to it, to what is happening to them, and to how we as teachers treat them and treat the subject.

3 Try to appreciate the religion in question at its very best and its highest level. Find out what it means to the truly devout, indeed saintly, believer. This involves concentrating on the 'luminous centre' of the religion, on why it has been able over the centuries, and still is able, to sustain such saintly and good people, and on what underlies their belief.

4 Limit the attention given to external details of behaviour and ritual by always discussing as fully as possible their meaning and value or validity. Basic factual information is readily available in textbooks, library books and audio-visual form, and much of it can be discovered by students for themselves. The teacher should devote most attention to the question of *why* this or that is done.

5 Acknowledge that there is much in the religion which appears to be contradictory, ignoble, corrupt or evil. Wrestle with the relationship between these manifestations and the luminous centre which sustains the saintly believer. If there is discontinuity, then the negative elements must be discarded as inauthentic expressions of the religion. If, for example, the central teachings of a religion are to love God and one's fellow human-beings, but some practitioners pursue persecution and violence, the latter is a distortion, a cancerous development which must be acknowledged as such.

6 Analyse what means you adopted in order to begin to appreciate something of the luminous centre of the religion, and then share this methodology with students. By what criteria does one distinguish between the good and the bad, the saintly and the impostor?

7 Relate your own commitment to that of the other religion. The beliefs at the heart of that religion are deemed to be true by the believer. In wrestling, therefore, with the question of truth one can come much closer to appreciating what being a believer means. This wrestling also makes the study of the other religion a meaningful and challenging experience in itself – which is precisely what Religious Education ought to be for the students. One can then raise these questions in the classroom and continue the thinking-out process, ready to receive fresh insights from the discussion.

8 Cultivate an attitude of critical affirmation towards views and beliefs other than one's own. This means *wanting* to make their insights part of one's own experience, *wanting* to appreciate their truth, believing that what has meant and does mean so much to other human beings of

integrity and moral worth cannot be wholly illusory. Such an affirming attitude, however, must also take seriously the discrepancies, contradictions and inadequacies which any study of people's views and beliefs reveals. It is worth asking the question, and constantly encouraging students to ask the question, as to whether these negative elements are not all due to misunderstanding and a negative attitude towards the beliefs of other people.

9 Be prepared to be vulnerable in the classroom, by sharing one's deepest convictions in a spirit of allowing them to be criticised and challenged. This will demonstrate for students how *valid* beliefs come to be held: that is, by allowing such beliefs to be scrutinised and argued against and for. This kind of teaching not only makes Religious Education fascinating for students but also teaches them to think for themselves.

10 Take seriously what the students and/or their parents believe, and have it as one's aim in teaching to lead students on in their own authentic thinking and awareness. Help them to articulate for themselves what makes them tick by helping them to appreciate what is so meaningful to people of other religions. In this way students' own personal experiences and insights can become linked to the great traditions which are the birthright of every human being and which schools should try to make real for them.

I hope I have been able to offer a positive approach to the teaching of world religions which at the same time really considers the problems involved. Such an approach fully acknowledges the need for openness, tolerance and acceptance of other people as people; however it also seeks to take seriously the truth-claims of the different religions as seriously as do the believers themselves within the various traditions; furthermore, it recognises the need for confrontation where contradictions, hypocrisy and negativity are involved. Even young children are capable of appreciating something of this positive and yet critical approach if it is constantly demonstrated by the teacher.

The necessity for teaching concerning Christianity

While a world religions dimension is important, the case for teaching Christianity does not just rest (in Britain) on its being one of the major religions.

First, Western civilisation has been deeply and lastingly influenced by Christianity. There is therefore a cultural obligation to help the young understand Christian belief and practice to the extent that they are then able to make sense of the civilisation of which they are a part, or to which they have come. It is impossible to understand either western literature or western history without this basis. Fifteen years ago an atheist lecturer in English bemoaned to me the fact that the widespread lack of adequate Religious Education was resulting in such ignorance that the great classics of English literature were becoming almost impossible to discuss, even the simplest bibical allusion, she said, was missed by students. In the intervening years the situation has deteriorated considerably. In a century of incredible change and insecurity, it is even more important that people can tune in to great literature, music and art, so much of which has been impregnated by Christian idealism. No society should allow its cultural heritage to be dissipated by default; the older generation owes it to the young to provide them with sufficient knowledge to be able to come to terms in their own way with the tradition.

Second, helping students to an understanding of religion involves their appreciating its challenging nature. In this task, Christianity has a special role to play. For the reason just discussed it is still largely true that the religion which children in Western societies are most likely to come up against, and either espouse or reject, is Christianity. By and large, when people make judgments in Britain about religion, these are usually based on an understanding or misunderstanding of Christianity.

It is difficult to establish accurately the percentage in Britain of those practising religions other than Christianity.[2] In addition to a long-established and strong Jewish presence, the number of representatives of other world faiths has greatly increased in recent decades. The numbers, however, should not be exaggerated. A generous estimate of recently settled ethnic minorities would not number them at more than five per cent of the total population, and that includes a significant proportion of Caribbean immigrants who are Christian. Furthermore, this percentage is highly concentrated in certain areas which clearly call for separate consideration. Apart from those areas, Christianity still remains the most live religious option for most people in Britain. The numbers of Westerners who seriously weigh up the possibility of becoming Jews, Muslims or Hindus, for example, is very small and is usually associated with conversion after prolonged contact with the corresponding culture. For most people in Britain the real challenge of religion is likely to be felt only with regard to Christianity. Ignorance, prejudice and half-digested bits of information regarding Christianity can cause people to switch off religion *per se*.

Third, the chances of such ignorance today are high, because of the increasing secularisation of our society. Children develop certain opinions about the religious language and practices which they come across in a haphazard fashion, and these opinions are often very inadequate, simply because of their lack of experience. It is easy for young children, for example, to acquire the idea that the Christian 'God' is a sentimental Santa Claus figure, or that he is just a God of 'All things bright and beautiful' who has nothing to say about the nastier aspects of life. At a more sophisticated level it is easy for people to acquire the idea that 'God' is simply the reflection of the highest qualities and ideals, or that 'he' is wish-fulfilment, and so forth. The teacher has a very clear-cut and important role to play in leading students on in their thinking, in helping to correct misunderstandings and to build up more adequate concepts.

Fourth, the positive side of an environment which has some connection with Christianity ought also to be appreciated. It is a fundamental educational maxim to proceed from the known to the unknown, and the search for relevance means that it is desirable to find starting-points in students' experience. Christianity presents many such. Even young children get glimpses of Christianity all round them – they see churches, Salvation Army bands etc; they celebrate Christmas; some go to Sunday school or know children who go; they see programmes referring to Christianity on television and pick up odd remarks in conversation.

Fifth, The acquistion of skills of discernment with regard to what is genuinely religious is a major requirement in Religious Education. It is particularly important that this be practised with regard to what is closest to the home tradition, because of all the emotional overtones (favourable or unfavourable) which this aquires. Western civilisation has been largely formed by those who claimed allegiance to Christianity. I phrase it in this way because the distinction between an outward allegiance and the actual practice of its inner meaning has unfortunately always to be borne in mind. As Chesteron commented when someone blamed Christianity for all the ills of modern society 'The Christian ideal has not been tried and found wanting; it has been found difficult and left untried.'[3] Nevertheless, certain principles and attitudes have given rise to a distinctive kind of outlook, however distorted or neglected its Christian heritage may be. The very concept now subscribed to in Britain of the ideal of a pluralist, multi-cultural society bears silent witness to the impregnation of Christian ideals within the culture. The notion of the equality of all people everywhere, regardless of colour, sex, race or creed; and the concept of the responsibility of a host culture to foster the means by which immigrant cultures can be maintained in their own cultures both owe a great deal to Christianity, and its insistence on the ideal of *agape* or 'love of neighbour', which prevents exclusivism.

As the world becomes a smaller place, ideas mingle and sharp distinctions tend to disappear. To try to claim that Christianity has a monopoly on such an attitude of love would be grossly unjust. The more what is genuine within other religions, for example, is appreciated the more such idealism surfaces. But what can and should be claimed is that many of the features in Britain today which are most concerned with promoting real respect for all people are in direct line with Christian teaching, and historically have arisen within its setting.

A particularly interesting example of this Christian influence relates to the dialogue between world religions. The Christian initiative here has been most marked. The desire for relationship, for understanding, for affirmation of the other, for genuine repentance at former injustice or unkindness, and for forgiveness of injuries received and hurt sustained, has been largely pioneered by Christians.[4]

Sixth, this last point leads to another important consideration. Christianity should be taught because its historical manifestation has spanned all cultures and it has demonstrated the possibility of powers of reconciliation. The retort that Christianity has been responsible for great hatred, persecutions, inquisitions and wars does not remove the validity of its basically universal and evil-transforming potential. The failure of Christians to be Christian has indeed been very serious indeed, and the note of imperialism in the missionary enterprise has caused great distress, yet fundamentally this has been non-Christian. Those Christians, for example, who have been involved in anti-Semitism have been failing as Christians. They stand condemned by their own teaching. Authentic Christianity, however, opens up the way of forgiveness and repentance, and the possibility of a fresh start. Freed from imperialist associations, many Christians are already pointing to a new order of relationship between those of different faiths and ideologies, one not of conversion from, but of acceptance and deepening of, the respective commitments, within a sense of real community and learning from each other.[5]

Finally, it is important for immigrants as well as natives to gain understanding of Christianity because this will help them to feel more at home in their new environment. Unless they are going to remain in isolated ghettoes in a strange country, this is vital. Many in fact, *do* want to learn more. They are both interested and also aware of how important it is. It is not helpful for such children to be kept in ignorance about much of their host's culture, just as it is not helpful for them to lack the ability to speak English. The adjustments which they need to make are in any case taxing. We often seriously underestimate the strain on, for example, Sikh children growing up in this country. Understanding can ease the situation.

I wish to argue therefore for a 'both/and' approach to content: both a world religions dimension and the teaching of Christianity. The latter should be taught with the same degree of care for accuracy and depth of study as is called for with regard to other religions. It is not an easy option. The influence of the secularisation of society means that there is a widespread, basic and alarming ignorance of what Christianity is about.

The place of the Bible

Forty years ago, it would have been taken for granted that the Bible should occupy a central place in Religious Education. Now, however, it is frequently bypassed altogether. One reason for this has been the major influence of

Goldman's research in the early 1960s, in which he effectively drew attention to the difficulties of teaching the Bible to children. The validity of his research can be questioned (see Chapter 12). But there is no doubt that the misleading and deficient Bible-teaching which he so castigated was widespread, and still does happen in some areas. The explosion of interest in so many other directions, including world religions and themes of relevance to modern living, has resulted in further demotion in the place of the Bible.

Recently there has indeed been an awareness by many Religious Education teachers that the Bible deserves more consideration, but it is not always easy for them to see how this can be done without resorting to what may be termed old-fashioned and discredited Bible-teaching.

For the understanding of Judaism as well as of Christianity, students need to be introduced both to the Bible's content and to problems of its interpretation. Figure 21 lists the main arguments against teaching the Bible and possible responses to them. I believe that there are more than adequate replies to all these objections. I would insist, however, that it all depends on the quality of teaching, which must not be simplistic, but rather focus on helping students to relate authentically to what is of central importance. For Christianity, the person of Jesus is crucial. Even a minimal understanding of authentic Christian experience is impossible without knowing about the life and teaching of Jesus, the events surrounding his death and the reasons why Christians believe in his resurrection and unique divinity. Even if the starting-point in the classroom is contemporary Christian practice, it still remains essential for students to discover more about this person whom Christians claim to follow and worship. Of necessity this involves biblical work, because the New Testament provides the source material *par excellence*.

Coming to terms with this material is by no means easy, and even young children should be helped to be aware that different interpretations are possible. Gaining skills of biblical criticism is not a luxury reserved for an academic sixth-form but a basic requirement for all students, and considerable work can and should be done on this in the primary school. Such skills involve an appreciation of the different ways in which language can be used; the ability to appreciate the nature of historical evidence; and the development of a 'detective' approach in trying to find out how trustworthy the sources are.

The historical dimension is especially important in Christianity, not only for discovering about Jesus as a historical person, but also for understanding the development of the Church. Study of churches today will be little more than a sociological survey unless there is appreciation of the theological and historical reasons why they exist and function as they do. Questions which need to be raised with students include:

- Are the churches being true to the mainstream Christian tradition?

Figure 21 The Bible in the classroom

WHY NOT?

Factors which might inhibit the teacher from embarking on any serious Biblical work in the classroom:

a The Bible has been associated with an 'old-fashioned' pre-Goldman approach to religious education.

b It has often been regarded as boring by children.

c It is remote and irrelevant to children unless they have a highly developed sense of history.

d The concepts necessary in order to understand it are beyond the capacities of most children.

e The complexities and contradictions of Biblical criticism make the teacher's task impossible.

f The Bible raises the 'confessional'/'objective' dilemma: a detached, historical approach is dificult, often dull, and not true to the material, while an enthusiastic, committed approach runs the danger of attempted indoctrination.

g The Bible is relatively unimportant, because discussions of the truth-claims of Judaism and Christianity, which would require appeal to its evidence, should not receive particular attention in the classroom; religious education is concerned with what people believe, not with the possible validity or otherwise of their beliefs.

h Any stress on the Bible is symptomatic of a parochial approach to Religious Education in today's pluralist society.

AND WHY?

a Goldman's research showed up an educationally poor way of teaching the Bible. A different approach is needed and is possible.

b The Bible is not boring, but the way it has been presented has often been boring.

c Study of the Bible is valuable in helping to develop a sense of history and in discovering whether it has insights both psychological and spiritual which hold good for every age.

d This can be disputed (see pp 160ff) As in all other subjects, time is needed to develop concepts adequately.

e The teacher needs to share the problems and skills of biblical interpretation with the children, so that it becomes exciting detective work.

f This is a false either/or. There is no such thing as a detached, historical, approach. The only safeguard against indoctrination lies in arousing peoples' interest, often by expressing views strongly, and encouraging them to think for themselves and probably disagree.

g Truth-claims are central to religion, and understanding is therefore inhibited without dealing with them.

h Only if it is assumed that little time should be devoted to the study of Judaism or Christianity, and the reasons for such an assumption are weak (see pp 148ff).

- Has that tradition in itself become corrupt?
- Would Jesus be likely to feel at home among such Christians today? and so forth.

The study of Christianity can take on depth if students are encouraged to wrestle with such questions and to relate them to their own ideas and experiences, whether these are Christian, within the orbit of another religion, agnostic or atheist. Work on the understanding of God as Father, can, for example, be both fascinating and illuminating for people whether or not they choose to accept this understanding as true. One of the greatest Hindu saints of this century, Gandhi, acknowledged Jesus as 'the greatest source of spiritual strength that man has ever known.'[6] The teaching of Jesus has ingredients of directness, controversy, humour and simplicity which can make the encounter both stimulating and challenging.

Religion and general issues

Teaching either world religions or Christianity will not get very far unless Religious Education first attends to a different area of content altogether, namely, that of life in general: the interpretation of life in scientific terms, and the reasons why people decide for or against religion. Neither Islam nor Christianity, for example, have much chance of being understood without this element. Furthermore many of the problems of tackling religions as such, including Christianity, can be bypassed by looking at what religion is in itself, quite apart from any official organisation of it.

It is most important that religion is not presented simply in its institutionalised form. Serious doubts indeed can be raised by people who are compartmentalised into Hindus, Christians and so forth as to the validity of this understanding of religion. Religious experience in all forms, particularly mystical experience, transcends all the artificial boundaries which human culture and accidents of birth have thrown up. Furthermore there has always been a tension within great religions as to whether such compartments are really important at all for the religious person. Karl Barth, for example, an outstanding and deeply committed Christian theologian who was one of the first to oppose the rise of Nazism, saw religion, including Christianity, as 'the drunken blurring of the distance between God and man.'[7]

If we add to these considerations the importance of making education relevant to the situation in which students find themselves, we must clearly pay considerable attention to what does preoccupy them today, and work to see what theology has to say about that. Thus moral issues, experiences of all kinds, other areas of knowledge, philosophical questions of how we know anything, all need to find a place in Religious Education.

This is not an unwarranted extension of content, nor is it promoting a stance of vagueness, provided that the basically theological nature of the enquiry is constantly to the fore. Chapter 18, for example, discusses how the lesson on drugs first considered on page 111 could be rendered Religious Education. There needs to be explicit opening up of the question of how religion and attitudes to life and moral issues in general are connected.

The relationship between moral issues and religious insight is a complex one, and this fact itself needs to be brought to students' attention, even at a very early age. Religion relates to morality at the level of reasons for morality, and of motivation actually to be moral. However religion should never be *equated* with morality, for people can be moral without being religious, and religious without being moral. Very much to the fore should be the possible distinction which must always be borne in mind between what people say and what they do; and the value of ideals which are not lived up to needs to be thoroughly discussed.

One of the most important themes which deserves a wide coverage in Religious Education is that of the supposed conflict between Science and Religion. This is important because it relates to the pervasive -isms which affect the way almost everyone tends to think about religion today (see Chapter 3). Serious study of the relationship between Science and Religion can be very fruitful in guarding against prevailing forces of indoctrination, and in promoting clear thinking. Such work as well as being stimulating and interesting, can demonstrate that integration of the curriculum which educationalists are increasingly acknowledging as desirable.[8]

The science and religion issue relates closely to what needs today to form a major part of any Religious Education work, namely, discussion about the question of knowledge, and about the grounds for believing or not believing in God. Religious Education will rarely appear relevant, meaningful and alive for students unless it challenges them to think in an open way about the evidence on these matters. For truth is always relevant if it concerns ultimate questions. The anxious search to find material which will interest students can be bypassed if teachers listen to the questions actually being asked, or the unexamined grounds upon which religion is dismissed or accepted.

What is needed is not simply vague discussion of opinions, but real help in helping students learn to think theologically, so that their judgments concerning religion can be based on knowledge.

Cults and the occult

There is much debate on how far cults, especially those concerned with spiritualism, should form part of the content of Religious Education. It may seem helpful, and perhaps necessary, to deal with these areas when thinking about what constitutes false or pseudo religion. There are, however, three basic problems which need careful consideration if more than a reference to cults is made.

First, unless a great deal of time is available, study of cults, the occult or other such developments will be at the expense of what is properly central to an understanding of religion.

Second, the absence of knowledge concerning main traditions, and views which have been tested and found acceptable by those traditions, will cause a vacuum with regard to the essential ability to evaluate the validity of developments in or departures from those traditions. If one's purpose is to study oak-trees, a study of mistletoe is only marginally helpful.

Third, the lack of criteria for discernment concerning the truth and validity of cults and the occult can have serious repercussions for students, which is why many responsible teachers and parents are wary of their being studied. A little learning is certainly a dangerous thing. Emotionalism and psychological immaturity can trap some young people with regard to these matters. In particular, the occult is extremely dangerous. If there is truth in it, it relates to a dark power which people should not be encouraged to meddle with. If it is harmless then it is also unimportant, and so attention should not be given to it when there is so little opportunity to study properly what *is* important.

My response therefore to questions of whether such-and-such a cult should be included in Religious Education is: how far is it going to help students forward in understanding and appreciating the main issues concerning religion and its most distinctive and central manifestations? If it is eccentric, bizarre, peripheral or potentially damaging, the fact that students are interested in it is not sufficient educational reason for its inclusion. Education is not about entertainment, even though the good educationalist knows how to present material in an interesting way. If the teacher is extremely competent, knowledgeable and sensitive, even topics such as witchcraft can yield insights into what is important in religions, but the proviso is a very important one.

Postscript on anti-racism

Sometimes the teaching of world religions is promoted on the grounds that this is anti-racist, and areas where such teaching is not very conspicuous are referred to scathingly as the White Highlands. Similar connotations of racism are sometimes attached to those who argue that the greatest amount of time allotted to Religious Education in schools should be concerned with Christianity. To argue that this is being racist is, however, a serious *non-sequitur*. Clear thinking is called for, especially because the anti-racist issue can arouse strong emotions.

There are at least two reasons why it is inappropriate to argue for world religions on these grounds. First, the inclusion of world religions handled in a certain way may serve to reinforce racism, while a properly educational and sound study of Christianity alone may help to render the possibility of racism remote when students do meet with those of other faiths.

Racism properly means the holding of an attitude of superiority, dislike or hostility towards someone on the sole grounds of his or her being of another race. It does not refer to absence of attention being paid to the traditions of other races. It is true that the latter *may* sometimes spring from an attitude of racism and that ignorance concerning other races *may* contribute to racism. But racism can also occur when much is known about other races, and when what is known is disliked or feared. It is probably true that knowing about such matters as dress and eating-habits can counteract instinctive feelings of anxiety over what may appear strange, but greater knowledge about certain matters, for example, attitudes to women, or particular religious practices, may increase the possibility of there being points of conflict.

Second, the obstinate predicament in which all human beings find themselves is that of limitation. If I attend to one thing I cannot be attending to something else at exactly the same time. I cannot listen properly to a Beethoven symphony and a Yiddish folk-song at the same time. Choice is inevitable. The implications of this very obvious fact are often not sufficiently appreciated. I take for granted the desirability of breadth of knowledge, of knowing everything that is to be known, and of being an expert in every field of human endeavour and achievement and of being steeped in the culture of every race which has ever inhabited the earth. Equally however, I acknowledge that this is unattainable. It takes years to understand deeply the music of Beethoven, and to begin to appreciate Hinduism would necessitate years of study. Priorities have to be made. It is therefore not being racist but sensible and realistic to limit horizons.

What is vitally important, however, is to teach the limited area within a perspective of awareness that the broader exists, and that it is fundamentally time, energy and capacity which prevent one from studying it, not lack of interest or of a sense of its importance. Concentration on just one area can lead unintenionally to the viewpoint that what I know and understand is superior to what other people know and understand. Because of the danger of such an illogical but easily formed attitude emerging I would argue strongly for the inclusion of a world religions dimension in Religious Education. It is important that children grow up with an awareness that there are other religions, and that they should be prepared to be fair and positive towards them. But given the limited time normally allocated to Religious Education, care must be taken that this is not to the detriment of other important areas of Religious Education.

Notes and references

1 Douglas Charing 'Teaching about Judaism' in *TES* 13 December, 1985.
2 Ethnic minorities in Britain. In July 1986 the following is up-to-date information:
  People of Indian origin – 673 700
  Caribbean – 545 700
  Pakistan – 295 400
  Asians from East Africa – 181 300
  Mediterranean – 170 000
  Southeast Asia – 120 100
  Bangladesh – 64 500
  Others – 156 000
  TOTAL: 2.2m (of whom 40 per cent were born in UK) – around 4 per cent of the population.
  Some of the religions represented include Judaism, Islam, Hinduism, Sikhism and Buddhism.
3 G K Chesteron: *What's Wrong with the World* part 1, ch 5, (1910).
4 With regard, for example, to Hinduism, there have been many Christians engaged in non-proselytizing dialogue. For example, E Stanley Jones *The Christ of the Indian Road* (Hodder and Stoughton 1925); A G Hogg *Karma and Redemption* (1909); K Klostermaier *Hindu and Christian in Vrindaban* (SCM, 1969); R Panikkar *The Unknown Christ of Hinduism* (DLT, 1981); Abhishiktananda *Guru and Disciple* (SPCK, 1974); S J Samartha *The Hindu Response to the Unbound Christ* (Bangalore, 1974).
5 In India, for example, the Christa Prema Seva Ashram, Pune, and the Kurisumala Ashram founded by Father Bede-Griffiths and Father Francis Mahieu.
6 Gandhi 'What Jesus Means to Me' *The Modern Review* October 1941.
7 Karl Barth *Epistle to the Romans*: October 1941, Romans 1 23f.
8 The four-year project on Science and Religion to be completed in 1988 will produce a textbook for secondary schools *At Home on Planet Earth*, videos and background material for teachers.

12 Conceptual Development and Religious Education

It has become almost axiomatic among teachers concerned with Religious Education for younger children, that the development of any kind of theological understanding as such is impossible, because children lack the necessary cognitive capacity. Particular attention therefore has been drawn to two kinds of Religious Education: implicit Religious Education, designed to encourage pre-religious experience; and explicit teaching about religious customs or what religious people do, without any serious attempt to consider what they believe and why. Almost all the Agreed Syllabuses reflect this two-fold approach. Usually indeed the stress is on the first.

This exclusion of any concern about helping children learn to use theological language correctly is extremely serious because it actually makes it impossible to help children begin to understand religion. For such understanding there is no avoiding the importance of religious concepts, whatever religion is being studied. Even in a religion like Buddhism where such concepts are transcended, they have to be understood before being left behind: to use a favourite Buddhist analogy the raft is needed to enable people to embark on the quest across the sea of knowledge (see pp 104ff, 116ff, 124–6, 136ff for further discussion of the importance of the thinking element in Religious Education).

One reason for the flight from theology has been over reaction against the typically catechetical approach which used to prevail in so many schools, and which does still in some. The catechetical approach was – and is – damaging on two scores: first, to treat a captive audience of young children in such a way is to indoctrinate them, or to try to indoctrinate them. Second, it involved using words which made no personal sense to the vast majority of the children (exceptions only prove the rule) and which therefore tended to lead to merely surface knowledge, often with some very serious misunder-standings. The catechetical method historically arose within communities of faith, where what was taught in this way was related to the experience of faith and worship all around the catechumens. This is an altogether different situation from that obtaining in our primary schools. It is right and proper that the method should be eschewed in them.

This does not mean, however, that theology should go, only that it should be presented in a way which children *can* make sense of, and in which they are encouraged to think about it for themselves as they grow older. The style of teaching must not be dogmatic, in the sense of 'This is what you must believe', but clarifying: 'This is what Christians believe, or Muslims believe'.

A futher reason however for the abandonment of theology in the primary classroom has been the influence of Piaget. The impressive research of the Swiss psychologist early in this century resulted in his identifying a series of stages in cognitive development. In some very influential work in the early 1960s Ronald Goldman[1] applied a Piagetian-style analysis to Religious Education. His findings have been almost universally understood as predicating that children are incapable of theological thinking until they reach the stage of 'formal operations' at around the age of puberty.

Children's thinking capacities

There has been considerable debate concerning the validity of Goldman's research. But this has largely remained at an academic level and has not reached the majority of practising teachers. As one example, Ken Howkin's critique, published in 1966, which pointed out many of the limitations and misleading effects of Goldman's research, received very little publicity.[2]

In a brief but potentially important paper, addressed primarily to teachers, Dora Ainsworth calls for a re-thinking of the significance of Goldman's research. It may be, she says, that his findings 'demonstrate not the level of children's capacity to understand but the inadequacy of their language and/or experience and imply their lack of adequate religious education.' argues that 'just as children need to learn the language of mathematics, they need to learn the language of religion' and that we cannot assume that children do not have relevant experience. She considers that deferment in helping children to learn to use religious language 'may be detrimental to their growth of understanding'.[3]

Her thinking is in line with recent work in child psychology by Margaret Donaldson, Gill Barrett and others. Margaret Donaldson, a professor at Edinburgh University, devised a series of experiments involving simple variations of some tests used by Piaget. The research showed that children's performance improved significantly if the content of the task made sense to them and interested them.[4]

I am reminded of my father's teaching experience in Newcastle in the late 1920s. One eight-year-old, the son of a baker, seemed incapable of doing mental arithmetic until my father translated the sums into buns and loaves of bread, whereupon the child could do them easily.

Gill Barrett has done experimental work using groups of children at the ages of 5, 7, 9, 11, 13 and 15. She found that the five-year-olds were able to use higher level concepts or abstractions about the things they knew well. She concludes 'Higher level thinking, whether it was conceptual or functional, seemed more related to language and thinking *experience*, that is, exposure to them, and opportunity and confidence to practise them, than to age or 'intelligence' *per se.*'

She went on to identify six cognitive learning skills, and notes:

> I see all these skills as relevant and usable at all ages but I recognise that differences may lie in the degree to which they are 'usable' at any point in the individual's learning process, both because of lack of experience or opportunity to use any one skill and/or because of personal style in relating to the world.[5]

It is significant that one of the factors she mentions as inhibiting children's cognitive skills is lack of opportunity to use them. The distinguished educationalist Jerome Bruner noted that 'the growth of mind is always growth assisted from the outside' and 'The intellectual nurturing that makes it possible eventually to use language as a tool of thought requires long years and complex training.'[6]

The concept of number, for example, is developed through innumerable instances, as is the concept of chronology in history. The same is likely to be true in religion. Children will never learn how to use theological language correctly, as they learn to use mathematical or historical language, if they are not introduced to it.

There is indeed a further problem with regard to religious language. Children are frequently introduced to it in a highly misleading manner. They may, for example, hear words like 'God' used as expletives, or in fun, or by people whose own understanding of such language is naive and undeveloped. John Hull, in a recent editorial, commented:

> It is from de-theologised adults that young children pick-up such clichés (these are little more than verbalisms). God is male, is old, looks after us, makes flowers grow, and that we go to be with Jesus when we die, etc. What we find in this repertoire of child-like religiosity is very little intrinsic to childhood but a great deal which indicates the puerilization of adult religious life.

He makes a plea for introducing young children to religious vocabulary conversationally. This, he maintains, will 'widen the repertoire of the children. Experience suggests that far from confusing children, this approach encourages delight, play and curiosity.'[7]

Major inadequacies of Goldman's research

The inhibitions imposed by uncritical acceptance of Goldman's work may be further removed by summarising the major inadequacies of his research.

First, as already noted, the Piagetian theory of biologically conditioned stages of cognitive development has been seriously challenged, together with the philosophy of which it was a part.[8] Yet Goldman made this the basis of his research into *thinking*. Second, Goldman did not make clear how or why the Piagetian theory should apply to *religious* thinking. Should not research about religion have terms of reference which also take account of what is distinctive and unique to religion?

Third, Goldman's understanding of religion has been criticised as biased towards a particular brand of Protestantism with an undue stress on interpretation of the Bible in a rationalist manner. Obvious bias of this nature should be removed from research if it is to be valid.

Fourth, Goldman actually works with two quite different definitions of religion which he nowhere explicitly relates. Nicola Slee has pointed this out in an important article following her research on children's religious thinking.[9] She notes that for accumulating data Goldman saw religion as 'characterised by formal adherence to traditional patterns of religious belief and practice,' while his wider argument about religious development and how this applies to Religious Education is based on an implicit concept of religion. Here, she notes:

> religion is continuous with 'ordinary' life, but provides a frame of reference or perspective through which ordinary life is turned into something else . . .

> . . . this extraordinary dualism within Goldman's model of religion receives no explanation and obscures the relationship which obtains between Goldman's research claims and his educational arguments.

These arguments, developed in Goldman's more popular book *Readiness for Religion*,[10] require

> empirical verification of quite another kind than that which Goldman gives in his analysis of children's understanding of Bible stories and religious practice. Such verification would need to establish the child's ability to generalise from 'ordinary experience' to a religious 'frame of reference' rather than the child's ability to interpret explicitly religious material. Goldman has not provided such evidence.

Fifth, the method Goldman used to accumulate his data has been challenged. He interviewed children on their understanding of three biblical narratives, which were told to the children without a context and in a modified version. These were: Moses and the burning bush, the crossing of the Red Sea and Jesus' temptations. The criticism has been three-fold: that the choice of narratives was an unhappy one and not representative, that modifications distorted the original and being presented out of context made it extremely difficult for children to understand, and that the questions asked actually encouraged the kind of naive literalism which the children apparently showed. F H Hilliard expressed this as early as 1965 in an article in *Learning for Living* when he commented on the question:

> 'Supposing Moses had got over his fear and looked at God, what do you think he would have seen?'

... It would need an exceptional theological maturity in a child or adolescent to point out to the questioner that he could not really give any answer to this kind of question in the terms in which it is asked and with all the assumptions it seems to make.[11]

The conclusion of Nicola Slee's article is that Goldman's importance rests not on his research or suggestions for Religious Education but on his highlighting major issues for future research.

For the teacher, the value of Goldman's work is perhaps rather different. It has alerted people to the need for care in the way in which children are introduced to religious language. Limited experience and limited vocabulary can easily lead children to form wrong impressions, not because they are illogical but very often precisely because they are devastatingly logical, as the following conversation shows. It took place between a six-year-old and his mother on the way back from school one day:

David	'Is God a Jew?'
Mother	'Why do you ask that?'
David	'Well, Jesus was a Jew, wasn't he?'
Mother	'Yes.'
David	'And Jesus was God's Son, wasn't he?'
Mother	'Yes.'
David	'So that means God must be a Jew too.'

The conversation just recorded in fact relates to the Christian doctrine of the Trinity. Most readers may be inclined to respond immediately that this is too difficult for so young a child. Yet Jerome Bruner could say

any subject can be taught effectively in some intellectually honest form to any child at any stage of development ... No evidence exists to contradict this hypothesis. Considerable evidence is being amassed that supports it.[12]

If something is really understood it can be communicated in its essential simplicity, without distortion, to even very young children. A major problem in helping young children to think clearly about religious beliefs is that many adults themselves cannot make sense of them. If they talk about them at all, therefore, they will tend to use technical language which they do not themselves really understand. This points to the need for far more adult education and in-service training.

An argument often put forward against *any* serious work on religious concepts is that religious beliefs are 'beyond adults' understanding, let-alone children's'. This expresses something extremely important which should be communicated to children, namely that the mysterious transcendence which religious believers see as at the heart of religion *is* something infinitely beyond anyone's human capacity to understand. Children can often appreciate this much more easily than adults, who may be conditioned into thinking they ought in principle to be able to understand everything. This fact of ultimate incomprehensibility however does *not* mean that nothing can be said or known. There is as great a difference, for example, between the way a trained theologian and a beginner discuss the concept of the Trinity, as between the way in which a trained physicist and a beginner discuss electrons.

Helping young children towards some understanding of the Christian concept of God

It may be helpful to take an example of the kind of theological teaching possible. Crucial to any understanding of Christianity is some awareness of how Christians understand God.

It is also important that children are taught that this is something which they must think about for themselves as they grow older. It should be explained that while Christians believe that it is true, other people do not or do not feel very sure about it. The simple point can be made that we cannot know for ourselves whether it is true or not unless we first understand what it is about, otherwise our opinions about it are likely to be foolish.

It would, however, be indoctrination by omission for teachers to withhold teaching children understanding of something on the grounds that they do not think it is true, when there are a great many people who do think it is true.

A special use of language

It would be helpful to begin by noting with children that when Christians speak of God as 'Our Father' or use the term in the different sense of referring to Jesus as God's Son, they do not mean that God is a parent in the way that human fathers and mothers are. Christians are using words in a special way to point to something which they feel certain is true but which cannot be described, only pointed towards. They are saying that God is *like* something else.

Simple examples can be discussed: 'The cushion is green as an emerald' or 'the lion is king of the jungle' or 'the man is an ass'. In each case we do not mean that the cushion *is* an emerald, the lion *is* a king or the man *is* literally an ass; we mean that they have something in common: greenness, power and stupidity (however unfair the latter is to asses!).

Once the children have grasped this, one can go on to discuss with them how easy it is to 'stretch' the analogy, that is, to make it mean more than it should. To offer the man oats because he has been described as an ass is a humorous case in point. This may seem frivolous, but the very same mistake can easily be made without realising it when this use of language (that is, analogy) occurs in religion. Analogy has to be interpreted within the whole context which gives it meaning. Common human experience and use of language help people to understand correctly 'the man is an ass'; this is also, or should be, the case in religion.

If there are Muslims in the class, examples could be given from the Qur'ān. Allah is spoken of in analogies such as, *Al-Malik*, Lord or King, and *Al-Hakam*, Judge. Muslims believe that Allah is beyond any adequate description by human beings: He surpasses in an infinite way all that we have experienced. When a word like 'king' is used to describe Allah, therefore, it does not mean that Allah is in all respects like earthly kings, but that He is supremely what is central to the word 'king', namely, that He has authority and power; it does not mean that Allah has a literal throne to sit on and holds in His hands a literal sceptre! Furthermore, it is necessary to understand the idea of authority and power at its very highest: any hint of selfish aggression or tyranny must be subtracted from it before we can properly use 'king' as a Name for Allah.

Christians speak of God as Father in two senses of the word. Firstly, they pray to Him in the Lord's Prayer as 'Our Father who art in Heaven'. They do not mean that God is literally our father in the manner of a human being begetting children, but that He is *like* a good father, that is, that we have all been created by Him, that He loves us and that He guides us as a good human father cares for his children. Just as children can have relationships with their fathers and mothers as persons, so we can with God.

The term 'mother' may be more appropriate for many children who come from homes where they cannot develop a positive concept of 'father'. A problem may indeed present itself in that so many children lack a stable home background; for some, neither 'mother' nor 'father' may have any overtones helpful for their understanding the Christian idea of God. The teacher can use such awareness to help children appreciate the *analogical* nature of language here. It is the idea which matters, the idea of love and consideration and ability to look after those who are dependent on others for support. It may be a relative, a friend, or a teacher who can supply what the concepts 'father' or 'mother' lack for that child.

It is important to remember, too, that older children can begin to develop a more general understanding of words like 'father'. Even if they have not experienced what it is like to have a 'good' father, they can and do become aware of what other children have experienced and what they have not.

Objections that Christians are being sexist in speaking about God as Father rest on a failure to appreciate the analogical nature of the language. The fourteenth century Christian anchoress Julian of Norwich,[13] for example, found no difficulty in speaking of God as Mother. She took for granted the generic use of such words. It remains true, however, that Christian theology, like Jewish and Muslim theology, arose in a male-dominated society where it was more appropriate *for them* to speak of God as Father. In our society a wider terminology is probably important, but this can be evolved only on the basis of understanding the earlier language. Such questions can be discussed effectively with older children. Problems can themselves become stepping-stones to understanding, provided the problems are shared with the children.

The second way in which Christians speak of God as Father is in an altogether different sense. God is described as 'the Father of our Lord Jesus Christ' and Jesus is spoken of as God's Son. In this sense Jesus is different from all other human beings, so Christians believe. This again is an analogy. It does not mean that God is literally a parent. Christians do not believe that God has a physical body and therefore can have children.

With young children there is often confusion between God and Jesus. To help them to see that language is being used in a special way can help to prevent muddled thinking. When Christians speak of Jesus as God's Son they mean that they believe Jesus was in a special way close to God.

It cannot be too often stated that the teacher must be sensitive to the ability, experience and interest of the children, so that opportunities for introducing them to religious vocabulary and concepts are not lost. Small group and individual work is a very effective approach, especially as it can take account of the very great differences in background and capacity to understand which children exhibit. Some six-year-olds are capable of understanding work usually thought suitable for 11-year-olds, just as some 11-year-olds need simple vocabulary and a method of teaching more appropriate for infant children.

Introducing the doctrine of the Trinity

With children of junior school age it is possible to begin to develop some understanding of the doctrine of the Trinity. This may sound outlandish to many adults! The following lengthy extract suggests one possible way of dealing with the subject, and also expresses some difficult points in an exceptionally clear way.

Teachers will doubtless be able to think of many variations to develop the story-line and make it more relevant to the children they teach. If it would be more helpful, Johnny could become, for example, an eight-year-old.

The thing on Johnny's plate and the way Christians talk about God
Extracts from an article by W H Vanstone,[14]

> Once upon a time there was a small boy who was so neglected by his parents that he was taken into care in a children's home. His birth certificate showed that his fifth birthday was coming soon and Matron promised that, when he came to breakfast on his birthday, there would be a present on his plate. But it seems that, never having had a present before, he did not know what a present was. So when his birthday arrived and he saw a large red ball on his plate, he said with some amusement, 'That's not a present: I know what that is – it's a ball.'

He had supposed, it seems, that a present is one thing and a ball is another – just as a bat is one thing and a ball is another. He had to learn that one and the same thing can be both a present and a ball – and, indeed, more besides. For it happened that what was on his plate was not only a present and a ball but also, since it had been made in Hong Kong, an import. So that morning there was a present on his plate; there was a ball on his plate; there was an import on his plate. But there were not three things on his plate – only one thing. When at school he heard God referred to as 'Father', 'Son' and 'Spirit', the lesson he had learned on his fifth birthday saved him from the error of supposing that there are three Gods. He realised that it was possible that the words 'Father', 'Son' and 'Spirit', all referred to one and the same God.

But Johnny had a further lesson to learn on his birthday. Having learned that the words 'present', 'ball' and 'import' all referred to the same thing, he first of all thanked Matron politely for the nice import; then, having taken it to school, he got up a football match and was heard calling urgently to a team-mate, 'Give the present to Tom; he's not marked!': and later, in a geography lesson, when he was asked what is the opposite of an export, he said 'a ball.' The Headteacher had to be brought in to straighten things out. 'Yes,' he said, 'these words "present", "ball" and "import" do all refer to the same thing – the thing which was on your plate this morning; but you can't pick and choose any one you like to use about it. For they refer to it in different ways. If your're talking about it as something the kind lady gave to you, you must call it a present; if you're playing with it on the school field, you must call it a ball; and if you're talking about where it came from, you must call it an import.'

This second lesson which Johnny learned on his birthday also proved helpful in Religious Education lessons. He realised that, although the words 'Father', 'Son' and 'Spirit' all refer to God, you can't pick and choose whichever word you like. Each word refers to God in a different way, and you must use the word that is appropriate to how you're thinking about God and what you want to say about Him.

Later, he produced a better analogy because one which was more closely related to God as personal:

'I've been using,' he said, 'the model I learned on my birthday. Since then I've found another that actually works better – and this one is personal. It's Mr Smith: as you know he's Tom Smith's father and also his Headteacher and also his Scout Leader. There's only one Mr Smith, of course; but Tom has different words – Dad, Sir, Skipper – which he uses to and about him at different times. Tom gets into trouble if he says "Dad" in class or "sir" at home; it must be difficult for him. It must have been very difficult for him last week when they were both in that play and Tom had to call him something else again – "Caesar": but of course Mr Smith wasn't really Caesar – they were only acting. But Mr Smith isn't acting as Tom's father or Headteacher or Scout Leader: he really is all three. And he never stops being all three. One day Tom called him "Skipper" at home, and Mr Smith said, "I'm not your Scout Leader now". Tom was surprised and said, "Aren't you? Who has taken your place?" but Mr Smith said, "You've got me wrong, I'm still really your Scout Leader but you mustn't call me 'Skipper' at home". So Mr Smith really is all three all the time.

Once when he'd been cheering up a lad who was very upset he said, half to himself, "The father often has to come to the aid of the Headteacher": and when I thanked him for the smashing games he arranged at Tom's birthday party he said, "Ah, that was because the Scout Leader was helping out the father".

So you could say that, while Mr Smith is not three different people, he is three persons: and perhaps this point in the model helps us to understand the 'special and peculiar' way in which 'person' is used when Christians say that there are Three Persons in One God.

Sometimes you're not quite certain in what way you want to refer to something, or it doesn't seem to matter very much in what way you refer to it. After a football match I sometimes think "I mustn't forget to take my present home" and sometimes "I mustn't forget to take my ball home": and it doesn't seem to matter which I think. And when Tom is walking home from school with Mr Smith I don't suppose that there's an exact point when he must stop calling him 'Sir' and start to call him 'Dad'. Surely too, when we are talking about God there must be some occasions when we can't be sure whether we should say 'Father', 'Son' or 'Spirit; and when it doesn't matter very much which we say. For surely it would be very odd if we could discover or invent rules for speaking about God which were more precise and detailed and comprehensive than are the rules for speaking about things like balls and birthday presents, fathers and Headteachers – about which we speak so much more often and with which our language is so much more at home.'

Such analogies may help children to think straight about the doctrine of the Trinity. This of course is *not* the same as believing it. That can only come as a later question, and only after much exploration can firm convictions for or against such beliefs be reached.

Notes and references

1 Ronald Goldman *Religious Thinking from Childhood to Adolescence* (Routledge and Kegan Paul, 1964)
2 Kenneth Howkins *Religious Thinking and Religious Education, a critique of the research and conclusions of Goldman* (Tyndale Press, 1966)
3 Farmington Institute Discussion Paper No 1 on 'Religion and the Intellectual Capacities of Young Children' by Dora Ainsworth. Her research on the teaching of parables to young children was quoted by Goldman
4 Margaret Donaldson *Children's Minds* (Fontana, 1978) gives details of her experiments and conclusions
5 Gill Barrett 'Structure of knowledge and the learner' *CJE*, Lent 1986, p 73f
6 Jerome Bruner *The Relevance of Education* (Allen and Unwin, 1972) pp 52, 50

7 John Hull, editorial in *BJRE*, Spring 1986, p 60f

8 The philosphy known as Structuralism. An article by David Heywood in *BJRE*, Spring 1986 on 'Piaget and Faith Development: A True Marriage of Minds?' discusses this and provides a useful bibliography

9 Nicola Slee, for a PhD at Cambridge University. Her article 'Goldman Yet Again: An Overview and Critique of his contribution to Research' *BJRE*, Spring 1986, p 87f) is an excellent summary

10 Ronald Goldman *Readiness for Religion* (Routledge and Kegan Paul, 1965)

11 F H Hilliard 'Children's religious thinking: the need for more research' *Learning for Living*, 1965, p 15

12 Jerome Bruner *Beyond the Information Given* (Allen and Unwin, 1976) p 413

13 There has been a great revival of interest in this Christian mystic. Her *Revelations of Divine Love* (available in a shortened version as *A Showing of God's Love* edited by Anna Maria Reynolds, published by Sheed and Ward, 1958) has a depth and originality which makes it especially relevant today. See also *Julian: Woman of our Day* edited by Robert Llewelyn (DLT 1985), and *Julian of Norwich* by Brenda Watson, a wallet of materials (booklet, notes and cassette) for use in schools, available from Norwich Cathedral Bookshop (1981)

14 W H Vanstone 'The Present, the Ball and the Import' in *Quarterly Review of the Community of the Resurrection* No 332, Lady Day 1986, pp 10–14

13 Syllabus: Agreed or Otherwise

'Nothing is more hopeless than a scheme of merriment' once exclaimed Dr Johnson. Happiness is something over which people have no direct control: it comes or it does not. Can one perhaps parody this as 'Nothing is more hopeless than a syllabus for education, especially Religious Education'?

Nevertheless, it is equally true that while happiness cannot be guaranteed by planning, its occurrence is encouraged by the presence of sufficient structure. Aimlessness is not in fact fertile soil for happiness. In education, syllabus seeks to provide that sense of purpose and order which can best facilitate understanding. Often, however, syllabuses do not do that; instead they restrict and inhibit.

It is the purpose of this chapter to discuss what a syllabus needs to be like in order to help forward Religious Education. This will involve: looking at the present situation and how it has developed; noting what topics need further development in syllabuses; and summarising useful principles for evaluating or drawing up syllabuses.

An agreed syllabus

The present situation and its background

The concept of an Agreed Syllabus is a peculiarity of Religious Education. Each local education authority has for use in its schools a Syllabus which meets with the approval of four groups of people: representatives of the Church of England, of other religious denominations, of the Local Education Authority and of teachers (1944 Education Act Section 29). The Act laid down that the Agreed Syllabus for county schools 'shall not include any catechism or formulary which is distinctive of any particular religious denomination' (Section 26). In voluntary-controlled schools such an Agreed Syllabus may be augmented 'in accordance with the trust deed relating to the school' (Section 27) and in voluntary-aided schools replaced by such instruction approved by managers or governors (Section 28).

Why an Agreed Syllabus?

The concept of an 'Agreed' syllabus is mute testimony to the unfortunate legacy of bitterness and contention bequeathed to present-day Religious Education by the controversies of the nineteenth and early twentieth centuries. One or two extracts from pamphlets published in the early years of Queen Victoria's reign will illustrate the long history of the problem.[1]

The relationship between education and religion was being hotly debated at that time in the light of possible legislation aimed at extending education to children of the working classes. The Rector of Liverpool, Rev Augustus Campbell, hoping 'to abate the enthusiasm of those amiable visionaries who seem to think that mere education is a cure for every material ill'[2] argues that religious instruction based on the authority of the clergy of the Church of England is the only safeguard against the dangers inherent in education. But a dissenting minister of Winchester, Rev W Thorn, inveighed against the teaching of the Anglican catechism to children as constituting 'defective and pernicious instruction . . . fearfully adapted to lead their minds into the ways of error, iniquity and everlasting destruction'.[3] A Mr Wyse however, offered a relativist-sounding solution:

> As much food for your own taste as you like, but no forcing it upon others. Remember the fable of the fox and the crane; they both gave good dinners but not for mixed company. You have no right to set your polemical springs guns and soul traps on the manor of another.[4]

Irritation over intransigent attitudes regarding Religious Education prompted Lord Brougham to appeal for a spirit of tolerance:

> Or shall it be said that between the claims of contending factions in Church or in State, the Legislature stands paralysed lest offence be given to some of the knots of theologians who bewilder its ears with their noise, as they have bewildered their own brains with their controversies.[5]

To overcome the dilemma posed by such contradictory views of what Religious Education is and how it should be conducted the concept of an Agreed Syllabus was eventually to gain ground. It was pioneered in 1923 in the West Riding of Yorkshire and in 1924 in Cambridgeshire, and these and other syllabuses became widely used throughout England. The 1944 Education Act prompted much activity in revision of syllabuses and the drawing up of new ones. They were seen as the means by which religious instruction could take its place fairly in the school curriculum.

How effective were these earlier and post-1944 Agreed Syllabuses in improving Religious Education?

One clear benefit was the reduction of sectarian squabbling. A wide-ranging survey undertaken by the Institute of Christian Education and published in 1954 saw little evidence of any doctrinal or denominational controversy.[6] It welcomed the democratic and decentralised procedure for drawing up Agreed Syllabuses. This procedure yielded another benefit in that the necessary involvement of a large number of people created wider interest in Religious Education and stimulated much discussion about its nature.

Many of the syllabuses were a source of inspiration to teachers and a mine of information and suggestions. Current educational thinking found its way into them and helped to ensure educationally desirable aims and objectives with regard to Religious Education.

However, there has always been considerable criticism of particular syllabuses. The ICE Report of 1954, mentioned above noted, among other points, neglect of attention to the needs of less able pupils and of sixth formers, as well as the inclusion of too much detail for easy assimilation by the teacher.

A later Report emerging from meetings of lecturers and teachers at the University of Sheffield Institute of Education between 1956 and 1960 considered that the standard of Religious Instruction was 'clearly very poor' and that most Agreed Syllabuses must take some share of the blame for this situation. For these syllabuses, if taught adequately, 'would demand not only the services of an accomplished theologian but also six or more teaching periods a week.'[7] Many schools, it noted, seemed to ignore the advice given in most syllabuses to be selective.

An Agreed Syllabus renaissance

The quarter of a century since then has seen great changes in educational thinking, in society, and in understanding of religion. It is not surprising therefore that the need for a quite fresh approach involving the compilation of new Syllabuses has been increasingly acknowledged. Mostly the concept of an Agreed Syllabus as desirable, important and necessary has not been challenged, despite the great irritation felt by many at what has sometimes been seen as an embarrassing historical anomaly.[8] The last decade has seen a renaissance of interest in bringing Agreed Syllabuses up to date and making new ones.

The legislation of 1944 has proved capable of immense extension. The requirements of the Act related to the teaching of religion, not specifically of Christianity, and the mechanism for drawing up the syllabus included a committee of religious denominations which can, and does where appropriate, include other religious traditions. The compilation of the Birmingham syllabus in 1975 demonstrated this. The Agreed Syllabus became the instrument for bringing in a multi-faith approach. Other syllabuses since have made this a major feature, such as those of Bradford (1983) and ILEA (1984), but all the new syllabuses include other religions whilst still retaining a special place for Christianity. The inclusion of secular lifestyles has proved more controversial, but the awareness that religion must be related to life as a whole and not stand out as some erratic boulder has found its way into all the syllabuses.

The new-style syllabus has thus emerged as a potent instrument for curriculum innovation. Once again the West Riding of Yorkshire was in the forefront of syllabus planning when it perceived the role of the syllabus to be supportive rather than directive. The title of the new syllabus brought out in 1966, *Suggestions for Religious Education*, initiated freedom and encouragement to schools to discuss their own programmes of work. Another particularly influential syllabus was brought out in Hampshire in 1978. This has been adopted in as many as fifteen other LEAs. Examples of more recent syllabuses are those of Durham (1981), Humberside (1981), Berkshire (1982), Bedford (1985) and Sheffield (1986), the latter based on the Durham syllabus. In addition, many authorities are issuing support materials for their own or their adopted Syllabus. This may take the form of a Handbook of practical material relating to the syllabus with examples of actual classroom work, or of regular mailings to schools of supplements as in, for example, Avon.

The purpose of the new-style Agreed Syllabus

The new syllabuses set out to be 'enabling' documents. That of Durham County may be taken as an example. Its Preface expresses clearly a radical shift in intention: the new syllabus

> is different from its predecessors in many ways, but particularly in that it does not seek to impose one prescriptive scheme of work on all schools. Instead, it is expected that schools will shape their own schemes of work.

The means by which it has been able to do this while still exercising its function of providing structure is by abandoning preoccupation with content in favour of concepts, skills and attitudes which can be developed through a variety of subject-matter.

> The former Durham County Agreed Syllabus (1946) was conceived in terms of content, of factual subject matter to be imparted to children. Within that context teachers were allowed a limited freedom of choice but essentially they were expected to teach the facts of biblical knowledge and of the history of Christianity. The present Syllabus moves away from the idea of a content-based Syllabus to one which is directed towards the development of the concepts involved in understanding religions.[9]

By 'concept' it means a fundamental idea. The result is a short document unlike most of the unwieldly older syllabuses. Practical classroom suggestions are reserved for a handbook described as *Aids to Religion* which is to accompany the syllabus; it discusses in some detail the nature of these concepts.

Other syllabuses have made the same point by concentrating on aims and objectives. The Hamphsire Syllabus, for example, is almost entirely taken up with these.

Some syllabuses have expanded this approach to offer teachers a mini-guide to recent developments in Religious Education thinking. The Humberside Agreed Syllabus of 1981, for example, includes sound summaries on 'Commitment and Indoctrination' and 'The Relationship between Religious Education and Moral Education', as well as providing a very clear statement of the intention of Religious Education. This it summarises in visual form.

Humberside Agreed Syllabus (1981) p 9

THE INTENTION OF RELIGIOUS EDUCATION

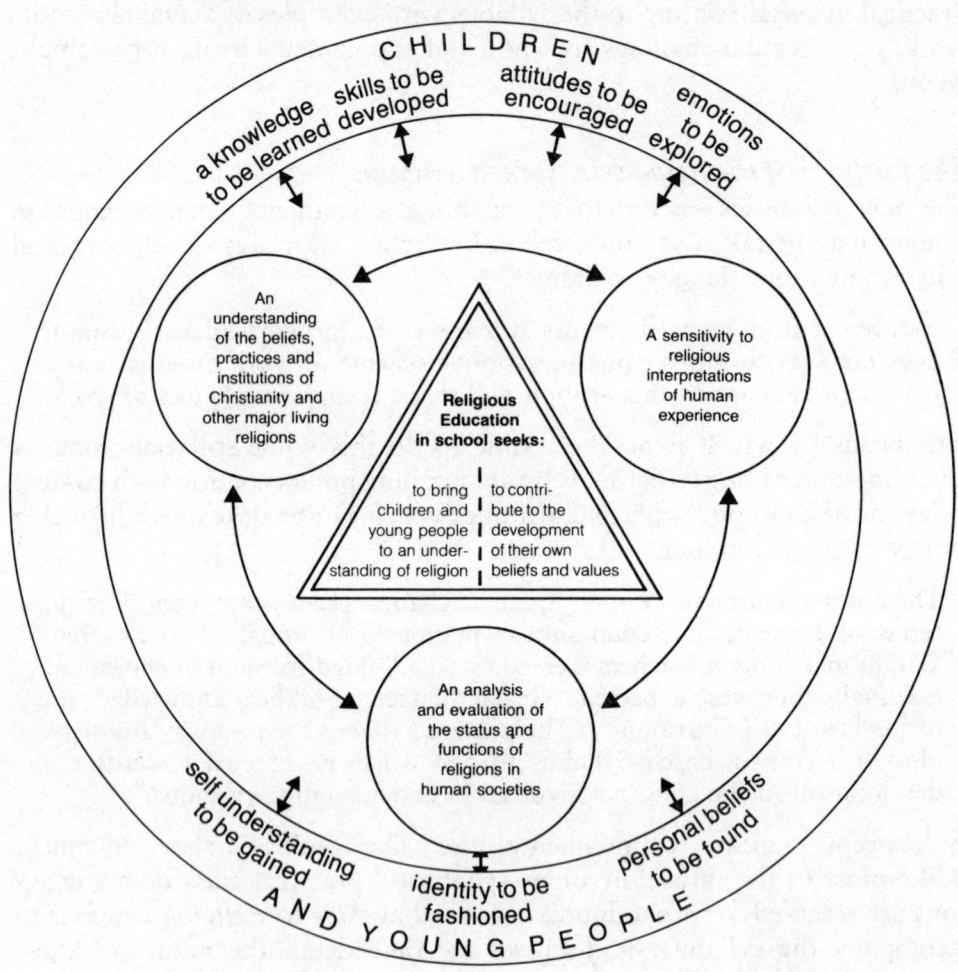

The Berkshire Syllabus of 1982 seeks to do the same kind of thing. It too has a helpful section on Openness and Commitment. Its most distinguishing feature, however, is the emphasis it places upon the idea of 'personal quest', relating this to 'religious heritage'. It wants teachers to develop in students the ability to respond to what it sees as the seven dimensions of religion through developing eight appropriate attitudes and six necessary skills.

Berkshire Agreed Syllabus (1982) Page 32

A VISUAL SUMMARY

In the centre of the diagram there is reference to the religious heritage which pupils are to see and experience, and to which they are to make a personal response . . .

In the circle round the edges of the diagram there are the three separate aspects of personal quest – feeling, knowing, doing, the development of attitudes, of knowledge, of skills. The two-way arrows in this circle emphasise that these three kinds of objective are of equal importance, and that each affects, and is affected by, each of the others.

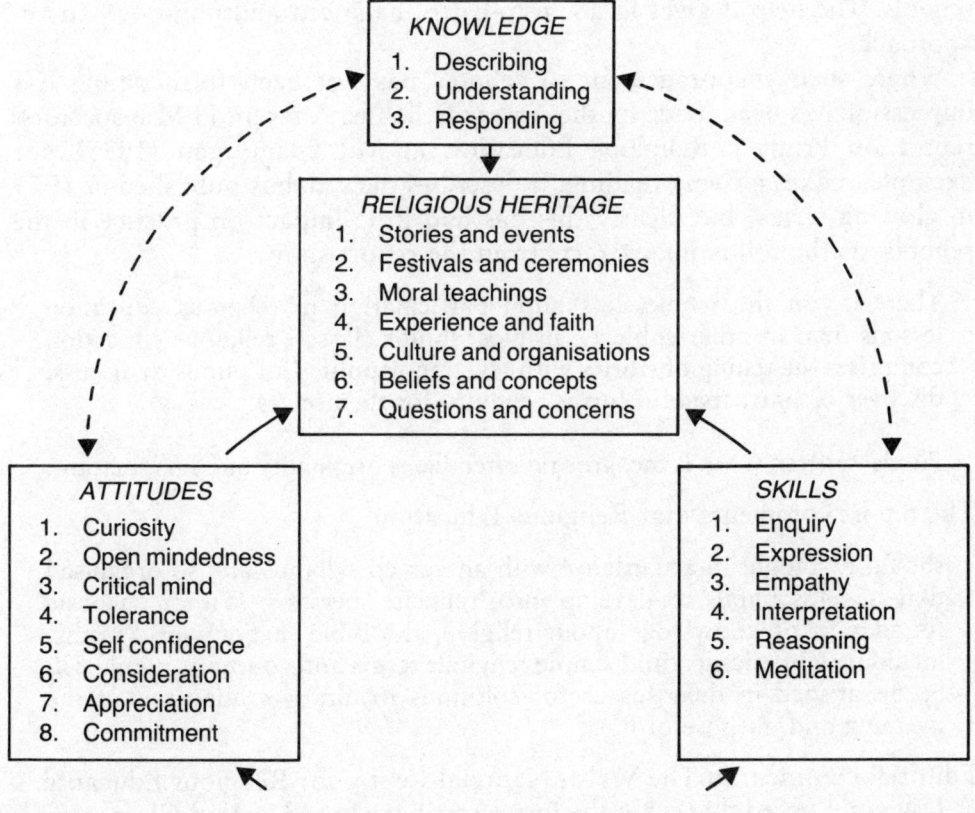

This emphasis on quest takes up one of the pointers in the Birmingham and Hampshire syllabuses. Students should be helped to a really meaningful Religious Education by its being related to their own personal search, arousing appreciation and eventually the capacity to make a full critique of the meanings and values enshrined in religion.

The implementation of an Agreed Syllabus

One of the great strengths of the influential Birmingham and Hampshire syllabuses was the manner of their launching. They were prepared for by energetic and dedicated advisers and teachers who developed in-service work and teacher-involvement.

A less well-known but equally striking example of the kind of effective on-going activity possible in enthusing teachers to adopt a creative approach to the Agreed Syllabus, developing their own schemes of work, is to be found in the publication in Newcastle of *A Modular Approach to Religious Education* edited by the Adviser, Gerald Miller.[10] This was the result of teachers' own thinking together. It is realistic, taking account, for example, of the gross lack of time afforded to the subject, and it takes seriously the problem which hardpressed Religious Education staff face in secondary schools. The help it gives is down-to-earth, balanced and non-dogmatic in approach.

Where such encouragement to schools has not been forthcoming less impression has been made by the Agreed Syllabus. A recent H M Inspectors' report on Primary Religious Education in Mid-Glamorgan (1985), for example, makes gloomy reading. It describes the syllabus published in 1979 in glowing terms, but clearly this has had little impact on practice in the schools, as the following extracts from the report show

> There is, on the whole, less pupil participation in religious education lessons than in other subjects. In most junior classes, religious education comprises the telling of stories with few opportunities for pupils to discuss, discover or participate in further enquiry for themselves.

> Pupils' written work is meagre and often lacks originality and imagination.

The report comments that Religious Education

> should be taught in accordance with an agreed syllabus and so organised that it helps pupils to develop into 'religiate' persons. Without a basic foundation of knowledge about religion, the Bible, major world faiths, including Christianity, and simple religious terms and concepts, pupils will be dissatisfied in their search for solutions to ultimate questions of the meaning and purpose of life.

Editorial comment in The Welsh National Centre for Religious Education's *R E News*[11] noted that what the Inspectors have found in Mid-Glamorgan is a nationwide problem. It concludes by noting that syllabuses and guidelines must be far more explanatory in communicating with teachers and that such documents need supporting by courses, advisory work, new textbooks and audio-visual materials.

Some failings in recent Syllabuses

The task facing compilers of Agreed Syllabuses is an unenviable one, for the syllabus must be like an umbrella under which every variety of religious and non-religious stance represented substantially in an area can find its place. Because religion is so controversial a matter, about which people can feel very strongly indeed, this exercise can generate great tension. This in turn creates a real dilemma: in the interests of peace and of arriving at some kind of agreement shall a lowest common denominator approach be adopted? Or shall the document give a clear lead, which will be unacceptable to many? If the first solution is adopted, the danger is that the element of inspiration will be jettisoned and the result will be a rather anaemic, superficial treatment. If the second approach is favoured and also if the four committees drawing up the syllabus really represent the shades of opinion among their constituents, it is likely that the term Agreed is not appropriate.

The ILEA syllabus of 1984 reflects such tension clearly. This is one of the reasons why it has been much criticised. In a heroic effort to be fair to all, a hornet's nest of other problems has been uncovered.

A multi-faith approach which erodes faith
The whole purpose of the ILEA syllabus is 'promoting understanding and harmony between different religions'. Yet many immigrants of other religions have protested against what they see as an erosion of their faith. They see the new-style Religious Education as destructive. Most Muslims, for example, are offended to see the Prophet Muhammad relegated to a list of Key Figures in what is itself one of seven suggested topics in one-third of the syllabus.[12] Many Christians feel similarly about what they see as 'selling out' on Christianity.

It is interesting to reflect that although the Humberside Syllabus is meagre in what it says about the inclusion of world religions, the general tone is far more evocative of what religion is really about. It would be likely, therefore, with some emendation, to meet the approval of most devout worshippers within other faiths (excluding extremists) far more readily than the ILEA syllabus, even though the latter sets out to do this. Not only is it sounder in its understanding of religion, but it seeks to communicate in a clear way what Religious Education is trying to achieve. The problem of communication with parents unfamiliar with British notions of education is crucial.

Emphasis on legal requirements
The ILEA Syllabus has not helped itself by its general tone, which is somewhat legalistic. To begin a Preface with the words 'Religious Education

is in the curriculum by law. The Agreed Syllabus is the method by which that law is implemented' is not likely to endear itself to readers. Nor is it helpful in promoting a truly educational approach to Religious Education. Further, although responsibility is laid on each school to devise its own scheme of work, the insistence that this 'should be made available to the governors of the school and will need to be kept under review', though legally correct, reinforces the non-educational tone. A three-page Appendix on the legal background in a slim document which allots only five and a third pages to the Secondary Stage of education and six to the Primary, further underlines the same view.

Unrealistic extension of subject matter

There are other weaknesses in the ILEA Syllabus. There is a dogmatic requirement to include in the Secondary Scheme of work 'an ethical non-theistic tradition such as Humanism' (page 16). A similar requirement in the Birmingham Syllabus came under heavy fire and had to be withdrawn on the grounds of unwarrantable extension of content. Nor is it clear how stating what religion is *not*, can help forward the educational aim of Religious Education – namely, understanding religion (see Chapter 9 for further discussion of this).

Furthermore the extension of content with regard to world religions, which is required, is unrealistic:

> Each scheme of work should include these living faiths: Buddhism, Christianity, Hinduism, Islam, Judaism, Sikhism. They should be dealt with as rich and diverse world religions.[13]

This sounds commendable until it is remembered what a small amount of time, resources and expertise is available for teaching Religious Education. The 1944 Education Act laid down a 'statutory minimum' of 35 minutes a week but as Richard Acland commented in 1963

> The statutory minimum is a formal insult, how can any assistant teacher be expected to convey the impression that religion really matters, when the headteacher has proclaimed on his timetable that it matters half as much as physics, one third as much as PE, one quarter as much as geography and one fifth as much as maths?[14]

The position in most schools has altered little since then. The ILEA injunction is therefore a recipe for disaster or non-implementation. It clearly fails to take seriously the academic rigour with which Religious Education ought to be concerned, whatever the age or ability of the students being taught.

Lack of intellectual rigour

The Durham Syllabus promises to focus a proper amount of attention on the intellectual side of the subject. It analyses the concepts involved in understanding religion in two lists: A and B; A relates to common human experience such as *Awe and wonder*, and *Self* while B is theological and includes concepts such as *Deity, Worship and Ritual*. Yet it fails to show how these are related, that is, how the general experiences feed into an understanding of religion, and how the theological tradition illuminates the common human situation.

In the accompanying handbook *Aids*, a clear example of this breakdown between the concepts is given on page 83.

Stage 3 of *A Possible Outline Scheme of Work for Third Years on Self* reads:

My spiritual capabilities and needs.
a) I have no need for God – atheist
b) I will only believe if I have proof – the agnostic
c) I have a need for God – believer
d) The effect of belief on Individuals and Society[15]

The first three sentences are misleading generalisations. With regard to c), if the first of the A concepts (awe and wonder) had been related meaningfully to B concepts such as worship, faith and prayer, a far more careful analysis of why people are religious would have ensued. Some people may indeed embrace religion in order to satisfy some personality need, but at the heart of genuine religious experience lies awareness of the transcendence of God. The syllabus does not alert its users to the difficulties and complexities of any talk about religion.

The Berkshire Syllabus may be taken as another example. It helpfully distinguishes between different aspects of Knowledge: Describing, Understanding and Responding. There is, however, no mention of the crucial skills of interpretation of evidence. The effect is not to take religion seriously in its claim to truth but to represent it only as something about which it is good to have an opinion.

The same weaknesses appear in the Hampshire Syllabus. Indeed there is much family likeness in all recent Syllabuses owing to common influences such as the Schools Council reports and material with its strengths and weaknesses.[16]

Missing from the Hampshire Syllabus is any reference at all to questions of evidence. Students' own judgment-making is encouraged without a proper wrestling with the problems involved. The assumption is that straightforward factual description of religion is possible and that that is sufficient for informed judgment.

Vagueness as to what religion is

The Berkshire Syllabus is in many ways imaginative and thoughtful and attractive in tone. A major criticism however is that it fails to make clear what is distinctively religious. It contains copious photographs of a variety of human activities – for example playing a recorder and dressing up for a special occasion – which create an immediate impression that Religious Education is really general education.

Similar vagueness as to the relationship between explicit and implicit Religious Education is one of the weaknesses of the Hampshire Syllabus which have emerged in a research project by Alan Brine, published by the Schools Council.[17]

Brine did case-studies of 13 schools, examining how helpful the new Agreed Syllabus had been in improving Religious Education for 8–12-year-olds. He was able to report many positive findings, but concluded that a number of schools revealed key areas of continuing uncertainty which had not been resolved.

This question of what is meant by religion is the first he notes. Lack of clarity on this matter is in fact common to most syllabuses.

Other weaknesses

Brine goes on to note that more help is needed regarding:

- the approach to Christianity to take account of the unique reaction most pupils have to their own tradition
- the rationale for the inclusion of material on non-Christian traditions and the implications for classroom teaching and resourcing. This is particularly important in schools with no children from minority ethnic/religious background.
- the concept of 'skills' in RE

The first of these weaknesses relates to a major presupposition of the syllabus: the distinction between Religious Education as 'exploring religion' and as 'Christian nurture'. Brine writes that an 'over-precise' distinction here will not

help in developing an approach to RE which recognises the validity of the pupils' existing framework of religious ideas and experiences . . . It is arguable whether the Hampshire Agreed Syllabus has helped to clarify this difficulty.[18]

This comes close to the criticism concerning erosion of faith which is made by many faith-communities (see page 146 above). (All the criticisms related in the last few pages are discussed elsewhere at some length.[19])

An Ideal Syllabus

Discussion of the failings of syllabuses perhaps puts a question mark beside their usefulness at all. It is to be hoped that in practice teachers use discretion and initiative.

This draws attention to the crucial role of the teacher in education. It is more and more appreciated that the value of any syllabus in the end depends upon the quality of the person using it. A syllabus cannot guarantee excellence or even competence; its role can only be supportive. Is a syllabus of any kind indeed the best way of supporting the teacher? May it have a detrimental effect? The concept of having a syllabus, whether Agreed or not, has hardly ever been seriously challenged, but perhaps it should be. In the light of criticisms of the concept it may be possible to guard against the inadequacies of a syllabus.

The case for and against syllabus

a A syllabus can give a sense of purpose and progress, and build up confidence that something positive is being done.

b A syllabus can co-ordinate work between different teachers and classes, and perhaps between different schools.

c A syllabus can guard against an over-idiosyncratic approach by ensuring a minimum of balanced content.

d A syllabus can provide some guidelines as to skills, attitudes and content and where appropriate information can be found.

e A syllabus can give encouragement to curriculum innovation.

Other considerations, however, ought to be weighed.

a A syllabus is bound to be selective, and yet by being written down can give the impression of being authoritatively balanced and comprehensive.

b A syllabus inevitably reflects an overall viewpoint whether of a specifically religious or non-religious commitment, and this may cause it to be rejected by some teachers.

c A syllabus can encourage a secondhand approach to the subject; teachers who lack confidence and/or motivation may simply comply with it in a perfunctory manner, distancing themselves from any meaningful engagement with the subject.

d A syllabus is pre-arranged and may be aesthetically and educationally very pleasing to the compilers but in fact irrelevant to the intended recipients; the heart of communication lies not in what is offered but in what is received.

e A syllabus may inhibit that flexibility and fluidity which is extremely important in teaching, for each person taught, and each class, is unique; the immense problem of inspiring motivation to learn means that the teacher must be very responsive to the particular atmosphere, interests and needs of each class; over-adherence to a syllabus can damage this sensitivity.

Principles to bear in mind when evaluating or drawing up a syllabus

None of these considerations demolishes the case for syllabus. Aimless meandering, following individual whims without regard to what anyone else is doing, is hardly educational. Teachers do need support and suggestions, especially in a subject like Religious Education where so many non-specialist staff are involved.

The considerations referred to amount to abuse of the syllabus either by the compilers or by those using it. Are there, therefore, guarantees against such abuse which can be built into the syllabus or which teachers can bear in mind when either evaluating or adapting one? I suggest the following considerations:

1 Non-dogmatic tone and style
The syllabus should be the servant not the master, suggesting guidelines without being dogmatic. It should actively encourage those using it to alter and adapt it freely. The dangers of misuse should be articulated throughout, and therefore to some extent guarded against, and teachers should be encouraged really to engage with the ideas and the materials given in the syllabus and indeed to criticise its proposals. The syllabus should seek to open up issues, not foreclose them, so that no teacher who is concerned about real education is alienated from it.

2 Acknowledgement of limitation and complexity
The syllabus should draw attention to its own inadequacies and invite criticism, but in a positive way, noting the complexity of issues and the problems of selection. It needs to get across, if possible, the exceedingly important point that the more one knows the more one knows what one does not know. This is not an admission of defeat, but rather of the only success which counts; the ability to acknowledge one's limitations, difficulties and failures in the light of one's real insights. If the syllabus incorporates this element it will help to give confidence to many teachers who lack it because they feel inadequate.

3 Individual/group-tailored content
The syllabus should cater for *all* abilities and therefore allow for individual and group work and non-uniformity of content in a class. The syllabus should give help on organisation of classes so that different topics can be pursued according to varying levels of perceptiveness, interest and need.

4 Encouraging depth of study
The syllabus should promote depth of study, suggesting ways in which the ramifications of a topic can be explored and appreciated. The thought should

always be uppermost that it is quality not quantity which matters: not how much is covered but how well it is done.

5 *Three-fold approach*

The syllabus should draw attention to the three interlocking approaches of experience, imagination and thinking. Often the effect of syllabus has been to ignore experience, stifle imagination and pedestrianise thinking. The balance needs to be redressed; the syllabus should be inspirational.

6 *An educational framework within which controversy can surface*

The syllabus should exemplify a well-understood and openly acknowledged rationale for Religious Education such as that outlined in Chapters 8 and 9. Within such a consensus the controversial nature of the subject can and should be brought out. Without a definite boundary, the artist is inhibited; similarly without an overall agreed strategy, individual freedom cannot flourish.

7 *Giving confidence to the teacher to educate through structured situations*

The syllabus should give help to the teacher in responding to the spontaneous questions which good teaching raises. The syllabus should be flexible enough to allow time for unstructured conversation and discussion, and it should give sufficient background for teachers to be able to use fully the opportunities which such chance occasions present. (For an example of the kind of thing needed see the analysis of some classroom conversations in Chapter 15 on pp 214ff).

8 *Working towards self-education of pupils*

The syllabus should seek to render itself redundant by working towards the self-education of students. This involves seeking to develop appropriate attitudes and skills, and promoting powers of imagination which can enable the individual to relate creatively to his or her own experience and that of other people.

9 *Focusing attention on what is fundamental*

The syllabus should alert teachers to those fundamental issues concerning religion which crop up over and over again, whatever the topic or starting-point. Understanding is gained through constantly coming back to the same points and seeing them in a new light. The syllabus should make clear that this is not repetitious presentation of content, and that different content can and should be used to discuss these fundamental issues.

Figure 22 The Agreed Syllabus?

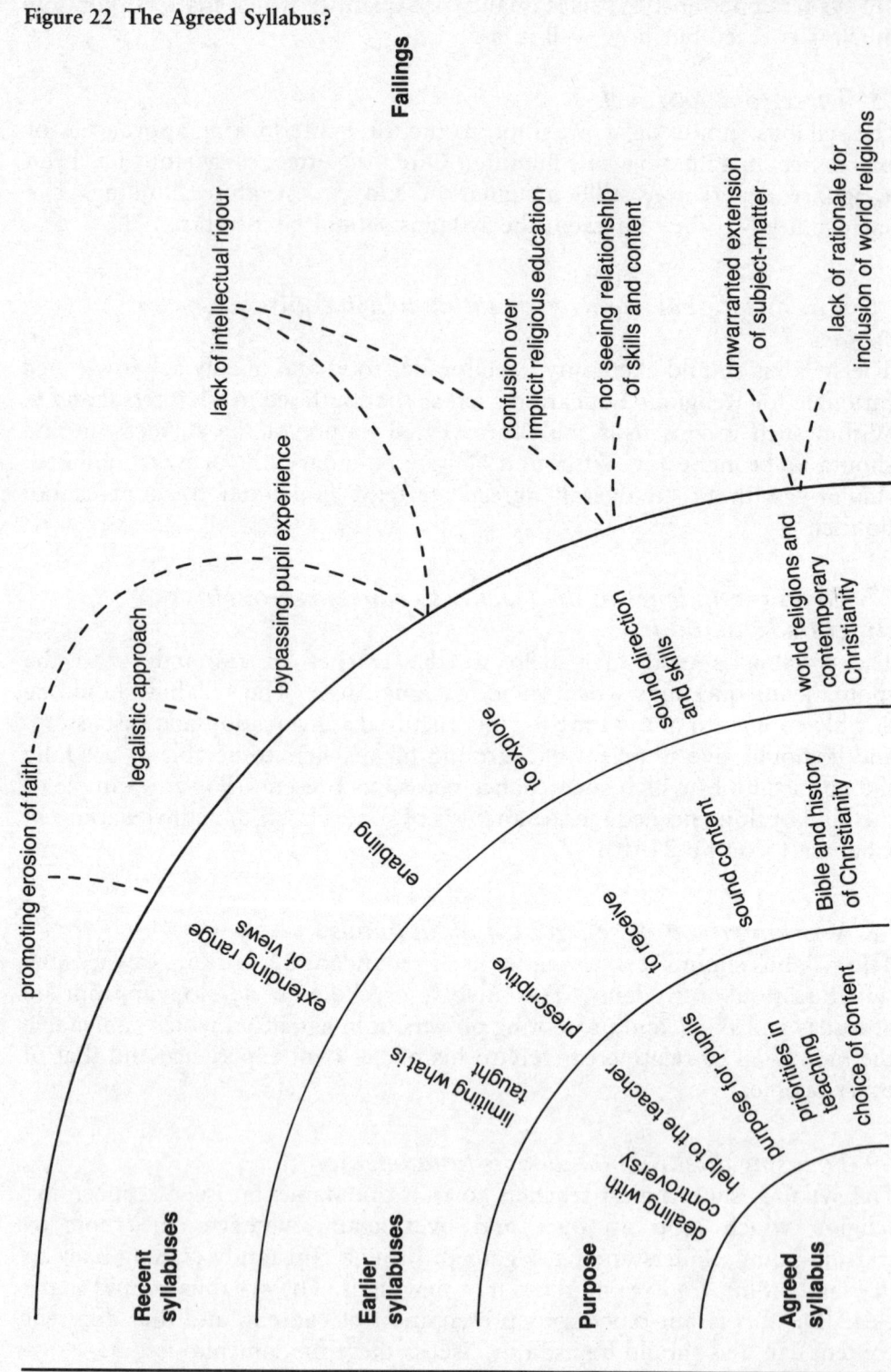

10 *Developing an understanding of principles for selection*
The syllabus should draw attention to what is of central importance for understanding religion. Without attempting to specify precisely what should be covered, the syllabus should ensure that the overall impression conveyed by the teacher's choice of material is not one of superficiality and of peripheral themes and information. It is not a question of banning, for example, work on the Moonies or on some obscure religious festival, but of seeing that the central issues of religion are raised by concentrating most time and thought on content which draws attention to them.

Figure 23 The Ideal Syllabus

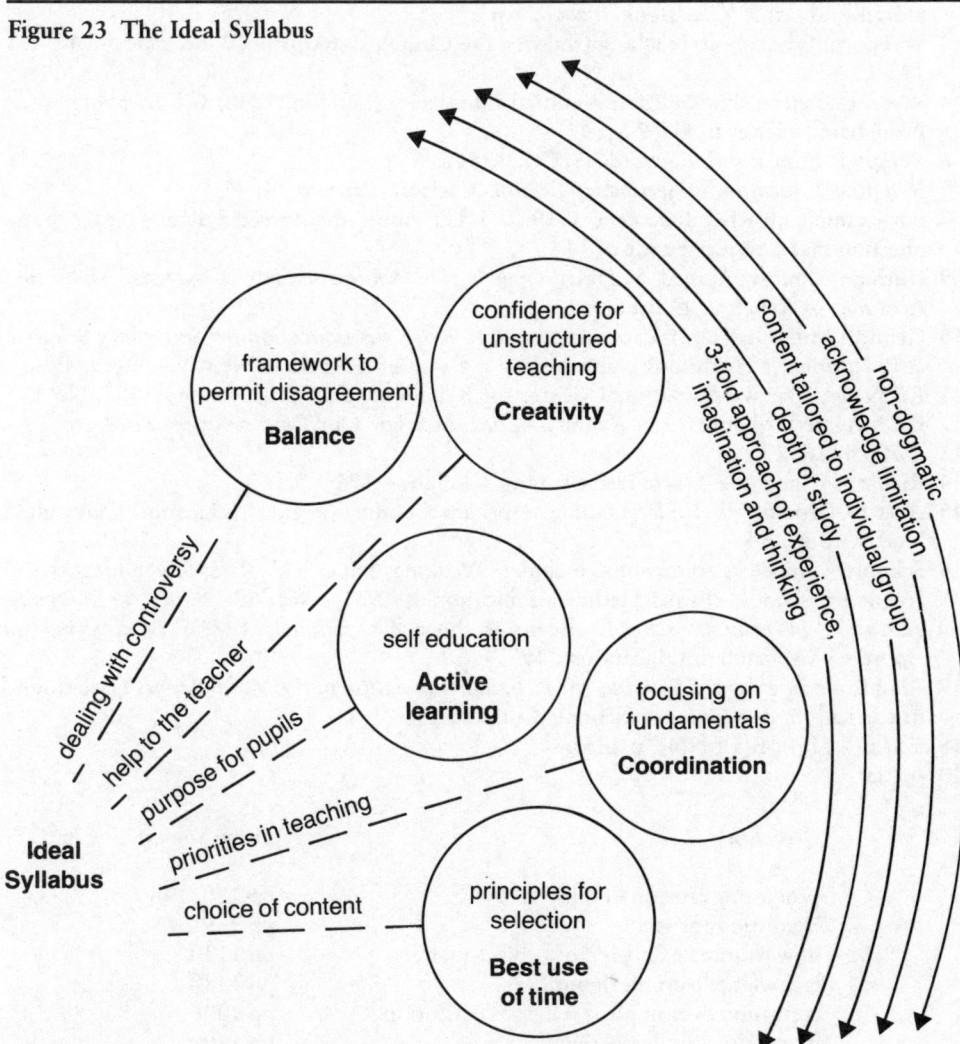

Relating the ideal syllabus to the purpose of the Agreed Syllabus

If applied to syllabus-making these ten principles would help to ensure that the failings, already outlined, in some Agreed Syllabuses are overcome. (Figures 22 and 23 offer a resumé of the chapter.)

Notes and references

1 The extracts which follow are from Gladstone's collection of tracts on Education, from St Deiniol's Library, Hawarden
2 Augustus Campbell 'A speech on the subject of National Education delivered at a public meeting in Liverpool, 3rd April 1839 with an Appendix as to the influence of education on morals and crime' *Gladstone Tracts* 25 p 35
3 W Thorn: 'The Sin of Teaching Children the Church Catechism' (Winchester, 1840) *GT 121*
4 Wyse, quoted in 'Principles of National Education' (London, 1840) *GT* 25 p 41
5 Brougham: a letter in *GT* 24 p 47
6 *Religious Education in Schools* (SPCK, 1954)
7 *Religious Education in Secondary Schools* (Nelson, 1961) p 44, 47
8 For example an REC document of 1975 'What Future the Agreed Syllabus Now?' put a question mark beside the idea
9 Durham County Agreed Syllabus *Growing in Understanding: Concepts, Skills and Attitudes in Religious Education* 6
10 Gerald J Miller (ed) *A Modular Approach to Religious Education for Secondary Schools: A Practitioner's Handbook* published by a group of teachers in Newcastle-upon-Tyne
11 *RE News,* The Welsh National Centre for Religious Education, Autumn 1985, No 13
12 ILEA Agreed Syllabus 1984 *Religious Education For Our Children*, pp 12–14
13 *ibid* p 4, 16, 17
14 Richard Acland *We Teach Them Wrong* (Gollancz, 1963) 35
15 *Aids to Growing in Understanding* (Durham County Religious Education Curriculum Study Group) p 83
16 Schools Council publications include: Working Paper 36 *Religious education in secondary schools* (Evans/Methuen Educational, 1971); Working Paper 44 *Religious education in primary schools* (Evans/Methuen Educational, 1972); *Discovering an Approach* (Macmillan Educational, 1977)
17 Alan Brine *The Agreed Syllabus for Religious Education in the Middle Years* Case studies in curriculum development (Schools Council, 1984)
18 *ibid* B(4), I(3), B(5), H(4), p 135f
19 p 128f

Criticism	*discussion on*
promoting erosion of faith	pp 25ff, 146
legalistic approach	pp 96f, 107
unwarranted extension of subject-matter	pp 113ff
lack of intellectual rigour	pp 137ff
confusion over implicit religious education	pp 100f
by-passing pupil experience	pp 129ff
lack of rationale for inclusion of world religions	pp 145ff
not seeing relationship of skills and content	pp 142ff

14 Assembly and Worship in School

One of the most direct ways of pursuing Religious Education is through assemblies. This was doubtless the intention behind the 1944 Education Act, Section 25 of which states:

> The school day in every county school . . . shall begin with collective worship on the part of all pupils in attendance at the school.

Much has changed, however, since 1944. Not only has Britain become a more secular society and more self-consciously pluralist, but there has been far greater refinement in our understanding of what education is. It is not surprising therefore that many, indeed perhaps most, schools feel uneasy about the whole question of school worship. Not only is it very difficult to do properly, even where attempted, but it is widely seen as an anomaly, indeed as an intrusion, in the school curriculum – usually on the grounds that it is hypocritical, non-educational and indoctrinatory.

An increasing number of schools ignore the question altogether by seeing assemblies as a time to bring the school or a number of classes together for administrative purposes and to foster an *ésprit de corps*. These assemblies lack any specifically religious element. Such infringement of the 1944 Education Act can, if questioned, be argued for on the grounds that the provision is now unworkable.

I do not however think that we can let the matter rest here. The wholly educational case for school worship has hardly been given a hearing. In order to appreciate what this is, it is helpful first to look at the objections raised against the possibility of bringing anything genuinely religious into assemblies.

Three objections

1 The first objection is that compulsory worship compromises the integrity of most, if not of all, participants in today's maintained schools. An article in the *Sunday Times* in January 1984 was humorously headed: 'About turn, all you Christian soldiers'. It reported the decision by Manchester Education Authority to call for a ban on the singing of hymns like *Onward Christian Soldiers* in school. It quoted from the Manchester Religious education

guidelines:

> Attempts to force children to pray and sing hymns of praise to a God in whom they do not believe can easily become an act of hypocrisy.

Radical agnosticism more closely describes the prevailing climate of opinion today than religious faith. The presence of increasing numbers of people of other cultures in cities like Manchester does not remove the charge of hypocrisy, for children from such homes would not be able to participate with integrity in Christian-based worship.

2 A second argument is that compulsory school worship compromises the openness with which education is concerned. Worship, by its very nature, embodies a commitment to a particular view of reality. This is acknowledged by people as diverse in their approach to religion as Evelyn Underhill in her classic book on *Worship,* and the members of the British Humanist Association. The BHA's booklet entitled *Objective, Fair, and Balanced,* expresses it like this:

> Worship presupposes an object of worship; and the detailed practices involved in worship presuppose various truths about the nature and activities of this object of worship[1]

Evelyn Underhill began her book:

> Worship in all its grades and kinds, is the response of the creature to the Eternal . . .
> it is always a subject-object relationship . . .
> an acknowledgement of Transcendence . . .
> Worship, then, at every level, always means God[2]

Education, on the other hand, is felt to be based on notions of exploration and the use of critical acumen; thus it cannot assume religious faith as a starting-point. As one Religious Education teacher put it to me recently: 'My approach in religious education is open, in assembly it is closed – the two are irreconcilable.'

In *School Worship: An Obituary* John Hull expressed the tension in this way:

> Worship is committed to its content and is passionate and adoring while education is detached from its content and is enquiring and reflective.[3]

Worship indeed, if well conducted, can make a powerful emotional appeal very different from the more rational approach proper to the classroom study of religion.

3 A third objection is that compulsory attendance at an assembly for worship constitutes and unwarranted infringement of a student's freedom: however well-intentioned, it is an attempt at indoctrination, at exerting undue and educationally-damaging pressure upon the captive audience.

Nearly twenty years ago Loukes, in *New Ground in Christian Education* recorded this conversation between a schoolgirl and her headmistress:

Girl 'You have no right to make us pray'
Head 'But I don't; nobody can *make* you pray.'
Girl 'But you try to; you say 'Let us pray'.[4]

The girl clearly experienced worship assemblies as claustrophobic – a time when she felt 'got at'.

A letter from an 'Anxious parent', published in the *Times Educational Supplement* (14 June 1985) expressed the view very forcibly:

At my five-year-old daughter's maintained primary school, they hold daily assemblies in which it is assumed, without argument, that God exists and that He is benevolent (my daughter sings 'I'm very glad of God. His love takes care of me'). The children are also told, as matters of fact, that Christ was born of a virgin, that he walked on water, that he came alive again after being killed and other things which only a tiny minority of fanatics believe to be true.

These assemblies take place every day. Can you advise me what to do about this indoctrination . . . ?

Inappropriate responses to these objections

a Re-defining worship as 'celebration of value'

Etymologically this is possible. *The Shorter English Dictionary* testifies to the following usage in 1610: 'Respect or honour shown to a person or thing'; The word is derived from the Old English *weorpscipe*, (*weorp* 'worth' or 'value', *scipe* 'ship'). Thus, in worship something of value is being acknowledged in an appropriate manner, or celebrated or given honour. These can be general values or matters of common concern which have nothing to do with religion.

This is not, however, how the religious believer views 'worship', nor what agnostics or atheists would choose to say they engage in. Such a redefinition is therefore misleading and can become almost empty of any content as one Headteacher showed in a letter to *The Times* (7 June, 1984).

'Collective worship' connotes a wide range of activities: listening quietly to a reading or a piece of music, saying 'Amen' at the end of a prayer, applauding a school football result or simply being together in visible community.

This simply will not do, as another Headmaster pointed out on 13 June.

b Making worship assemblies voluntary

This seems an obvious solution, because it is the element of compulsion which is responsible for their offensiveness to the educationalist. It is not, however, as simple as it seems. Such a view assumes that there is no *educational* case for worship assemblies, that it does not matter whether children are introduced to the possibility of worship or not. If they happen to have parents who are religiously-committed or if they chance to be interested themselves, opportunity for worship is provided. But what about the uncommitteed, those who see no point in religion and the (probably) vast majority who never really think about religion one way or the other – those who come from homes where religion is never mentioned, or if it is, with a sneer, and those who do not know what they think? Meetings for worship which are voluntary in effect deprive most children of opportunity to get on the wavelength of worship. The social pressures on children, fear of being thought to belong to a 'God-squad', plus the delights of the playground and other activities or even getting homework done, operate very effectively against such choice being real choice.

It is also important that the opportunities for worship be seen as an integral part of the total curriculum, and not relegated in the eyes of students to the status of an optional extra. Were mathematics, English, history, PE etc, *all* made voluntary, of course Religious Education and attendance at assemblies for worship could be voluntary, but we are a long way from such a concept of education in the running of our schools.

All children have a right of access to worship in schools, or, to put it the other way round, children are seriously deprived in their education if they are not given regular opportunities for worship. Schools should be places which extend invitations to discover something of the wonder and richness of life. They exist to open up avenues for people and this should include religion. No-one is obliged to go down any of those avenues, and no-one should try to *make* anyone explore them. But the school is not doing its job unless it opens them up for people to see.

Looking again at the objections

Objection 2, which contrasts worship and education, is not valid because it sets up a false either-or on the question of openness. Complete openness is not possible in education for all the reasons discussed in Chapters 3 and 4 (see especially pp. 40ff). Understanding, which is the object of education, requires imagination and experience as well as critical faculties (see Chapter 9). Similarly, worship, if truly worship and not hypocrisy or any of the other counterfeits possible, encourages not a closed but an open mind, receptive to fresh insights (see Figure 17 on page 124, Figure 25 on page 197).

That school worship can be 'open' education is perhaps demonstrated in a remark from an aetheist teenager whom I used to teach. Several years later I met up with her again and reminiscing about school she said that what she had missed most was the assemblies with the hymns and Bible readings and prayers: 'Even though I didn't believe them then and don't now they gave me something challenging and inspiring to think about.' What better educational reason could you find for opportunities for worship in school?

Objections 1 and 3 are, however, valid if they are a true picture of what assemblies giving opportunity for worship necessarily have to be. Hypocrisy must be discouraged, and attempts to force children to praise a God in whom they do not believe are wrong, both from the point of view of education and of worship. Indoctrination is a very real and serious danger and the traditional assembly *has* been guilty of it, even though mostly unintentionally. The conversation which Loukes recalls above sums this up very neatly.

It should be noted, however, with regard to the first objection that it is equally wrong to assume that all or even most students lack any religious faith, and it is important that faith where it occurs be integrated within the experience of the students concerned (see Chapter 10). One of the unsatisfactory aspects of much modern Religious Education has been the failure to take seriously this possible element of religious faith in students (see pp. 177, 180 of Chapter 13).

Furthermore there is no need for the opportunities for worship to be provided only within a Christian framework. The 1944 Education Act has shown itself capable of expansion to include all religions (see Chapter 13 p. 172).

With regard to the third objection 'Anxious Parent' unwittingly displays how easily indoctrination happens. 'Anxious Parent' appears not to be concerned with opening up the issue for the child of whether or not any religious beliefs are true. 'Anxious Parent' is assuming they are not, is wishing to pass on this assumption to the child, and is angered by the school's operating on a different assumption. Both school and Anxious Parent are at fault in not sharing with the child the controversial nature of beliefs, whether religious or non-religious. Children should not be told as a matter of fact that God exists and so forth, but neither should they be kept in ignorance about so potentially important an area of knowledge. Ignorance is a poor basis for the informed evaluation for which education should prepare the child.

Educational assemblies which are religious in content

I wish to argue that it is possible to hold assemblies which positively encourage integrity and freedom of thought and are in no way indoctrinatory. Such assemblies are capable of commanding the respect of all students and teachers whatever their religious or non-religious persuasions. Their purpose is wholly educational; they aim

- to help people to understand something of the nature of religion; they can be an integral part of Religious Education; • in order to do this, to try to create a time and place where students (and teachers) are free to reflect and be quiet without any assumptions being made about them.

Taking seriously the nature of religion and how understanding about it may be reached

In order to understand about religion it is essential to try to understand what is its nerve-centre – worship. As Ninian Smart wrote

> . . to gain an inkling of the nature of the concept of God it is surely requisite to look to the worshipping activities that surround, so to speak, belief in the divine.[5]

Without some sensitivity to the experience of worship it is easy to think of God as an abstract idea, without any sense of the absolute commitment of the religious believer in the presence of what he or she believes is Reality – typically the pose of worship or meditation. Somehow a way must be found to help children to appreciate this; otherwise they have not begun to understand what religion is.

The path to understanding has to be governed by the nature of what is to be understood. A poem cannot be appreciated in the manner of a military campaign, skills like swimming have to be practised really to be understood – and so forth. Real understanding involves personal participation in some sense. Thus I think the Durham Report quite correct in saying that

> While the analogies are not wholly exact, religious education without worship is like geography without field studies, the learning of a language without trips abroad, science without its experiments, the theory of music without singing or playing an instrument, literature without reading books.[6]

The problem is, however, that while serious doubts are not entertained by people as to the validity of geography, language-work, science, music and literature, they are concerning religion. Religion is controversial at its very roots. How can opportunities for worship be given within a framework of compulsory attendance without making the educationally illicit assumption that students and staff hold certain beliefs which they may not, and probably in our secular society do not, hold?

The answer lies in putting assemblies for worship firmly into the context of Religious Education, and sharing this educational purpose with all who take part in the assemblies; their participation can then be at one of two levels. The first level would be that of worship if the individual student or teacher happens to hold the appropriate beliefs. The second and essential level, one which is open to all, is that of participating in order to find out what religion is about. It is a conscious attempt to understand what it is like to be religious, that is, to try to get on the appropriate wave-length. Without a very sincere attempt to do this, criticism of religious people is likely to be irrelevant, because one has not understood first what one is criticising. In such an exercise the imagination is not being used to obscure the truth, but in order to understand and hopefully arrive at the truth. It is the play-method of learning shorn of its dangers and limitations because it is done consciously and responsibly, fortified by reason.

Why participation is educationally required (See Figure 24)

Participation is indeed so important that it may be helpful to discuss more fully why it is.

1 Religion will never yield its secrets to external analysis – not even science will! With regard to trying to understand religion, what may feel like play is a most valuable means of finding out. Young children learn through play but it is not always appreciated how much play must remain part of the way in which adults learn too if we want to try to extend the range of experience and understanding. Evaluation comes later, alternating with fresh 'play' sessions.

To come to terms, for example, with theistic Hinduism, a far quicker and safer route is actually to enter a Hindu temple and take part in the ritual, rather than simply to sit on the sidelines and observe, although even that is usually more satisfactory than just reading. To take part in the ritual and really try to get on the wavelength and try to affirm the experience of an actual believer whom one knows, is the best of all. This does not mean one has to become a Hindu nor that one is uncertain about one's own beliefs. Indeed the opposite is probably the case: only those who have really firm convictions do not feel threatened by stepping far outside what they know and think they can agree with.

The importance of empathetic 'play' of this nature is probably harder to put into words and harder for teachers to grasp than for children to appreciate because children are conscious of more fluidity, experiencing and finding out different things and not so concerned about commitment to them. As they get older and more self-conscious, it becomes correspondingly easier to discuss this with them.

2 It is important to note that such an involvement does not dethrone rationality and reflection but actually makes them possible. For involvement requires the exercise of a particular kind of objectivity. If beliefs need to be suspended during times of discussion and reflection, it can be argued on cogent grounds that doubts need to be suspended on other occasions especially since such doubts in fact reflect a different belief-system, albeit in a 'weak' or non-explicit form; there is no sound educational reason why only one form of beliefs should be suspended and not other forms.

Openness to evidence needs to be taken seriously. If, for example, one tastes some strange food with the thought uppermost 'I shall not like this', one is not 'open' to the evidence of one's palate! Similarly, at a more serious

Figure 24   The educational importance of assemblies for worship

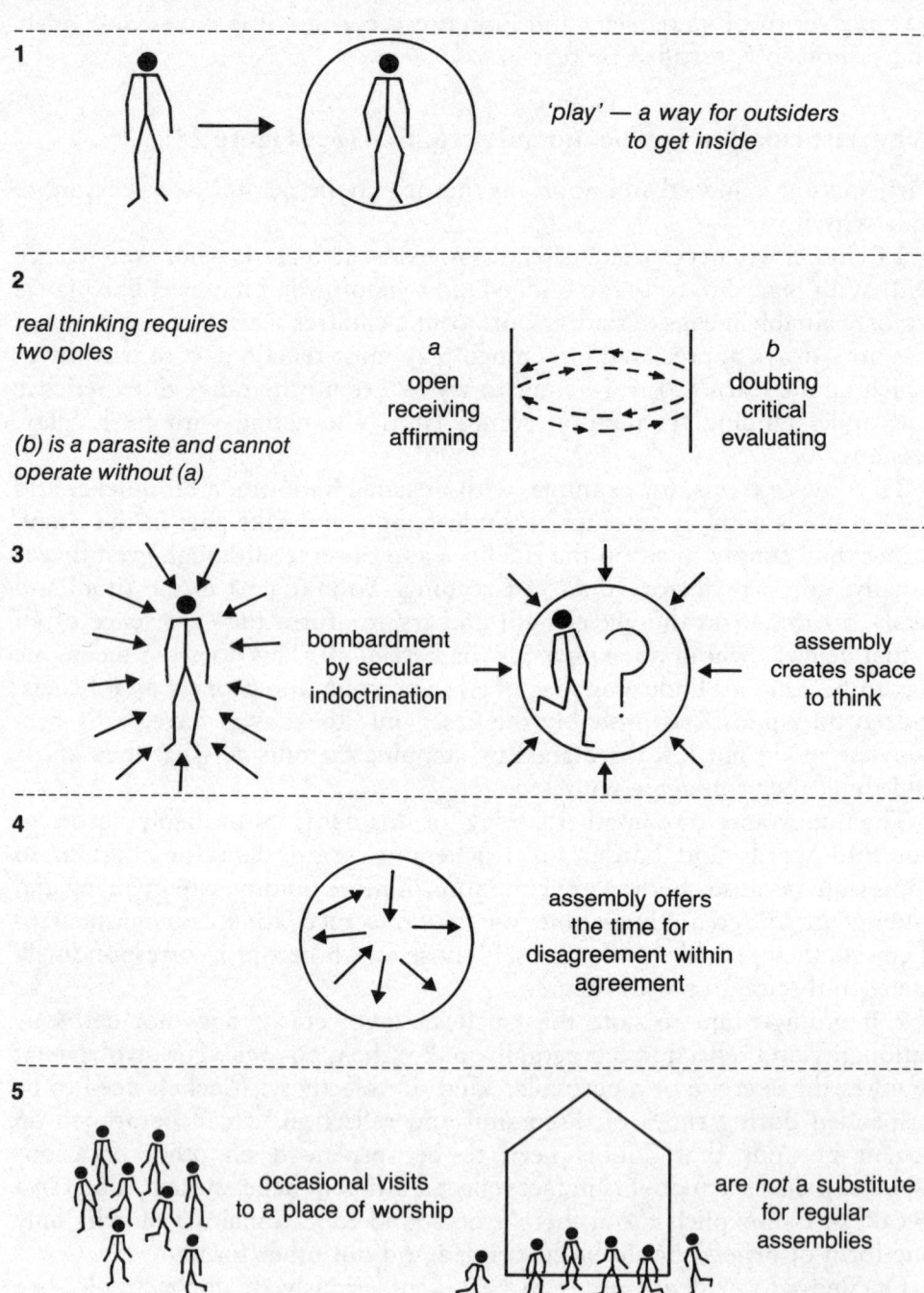

level, if one approaches a poetry-reading session with the conviction 'This is a waste of time', this is not letting the recital speak for itself. Again, in the matter of personal relationships the attempt to get to know someone is not only fraught with difficulty but actually rendered highly improbable unless one's beliefs about that person are suspended for a while, for if one only sees another person through the smoke-screen of one's own system of classification and approval, one is likely to interpret him or her wrongly and thereby restrict genuine self-expression and communication.

In order to understand what religion is, it is necessary to have occasions when one allows it, in its most distinctive aspect, to make its own impact. So far from encouraging dishonesty of thought, such experience, and such willingness to suspend judgment, is the only guarantee that one's understanding of religion is grounded in reality rather than in one's own prejudiced view – whether favourable or unfavourable.

In the three analogies referred to, it is not possible to predict what the result will be. So in the case of assemblies which offer the opportunity for worship, the requirement to suspend judgment can only result in worship if other conditions are fulfilled, but it may be that the experience of a deliberate passivity will afford some insight into the nature of worship and therefore further one's understanding of religion. Attendance at a worship assembly is therefore a demonstration of the openness which is educationally required in the classroom. Refusal to attend may betray the closed mind.

3 Because we live in a society which is predominatly secular and materialistic, we should be alert to the conditioning we have undergone and which children undergo. Agnosticism and atheism, in whose interests worship in school is often argued as inappropriate, themselves rest on beliefs which all too often are never questioned at all: namely, that this present life is all that matters, or that if one is odd or strange enough to consider metaphysical questions the world is totally explicable in terms of molecules. Worship assemblies are a valuable *anti*-indoctrinatory device, challenging the prevailing assumptions.

4 A major reason for fearing to expose children to what is acknowledged to be controversial is that people tend to cling to the idea that assembly should be a time of unity and agreement. Yet difference is part of life, and if community depends on agreement on all major things then in fact it is a lie however bravely maintained. As a society we have not wrestled with this satisfactorily; but schools should do so, and the assembly provides an ideal setting. Within the bounds of the 'shared values' the possibility of seriously different opinions should be constantly acknowledged. As Arthur Rowe expressed it: 'One of the most important lessons our democratic society has still to learn is to disagree within a mutual acceptance'.[7] There is need for a basic, civilised, disciplined atmosphere of respect for people.

5 Frequent contact at regular intervals is the best way to gain understanding of worship.

Professor Joad once made an arresting remark, that 'good music should never be heard for the first time'[8]. This is obviously impossible, but it points to a profound truth, namely that the nature and strength of the predilections and prejudices which people usually bring to new experiences is such that familiarity with the new subject must be gained on different occasions before helpful judgments about it can be made. An occasional visit to a concert does not replace listening to music on a frequent or weekly basis.

The same is truth with regard to worship. It is often argued that an occasional viewing of slides or visit to a place of worship together with work *about* it in the classroom, is adequate to introduce children to this dimension of religion. This approach is helpful but insufficient by itself because it suffers from serious educational inadequacies. Bias and fear of what is strange and unknown, combine with the sheer distracting power of interesting but peripheral details to make this kind of activity often only marginally helpful. It becomes really meaningful only when supported by the opportunity to take part in worship in an educational way on a regular basis as part of the life of the school.

Implications for the running of assemblies

The kind of assembly which is educationally appropriate needs to be implemented in a particular way. It is essential that the two possible levels of participation are constantly articulated, in one way or another, even with the youngest children. The conditioning factors operating upon children or adolescents to conform or to rebel, but not to think independently, are so great that much thought must be given to communicating these levels of involvement.

I would like to make six points about the conduct of such assemblies (summarised in Figure 25).

1 The first sentence should remind everyone of the educational nature of the assembly, that it is openly religious and that people are invited to reflect for themselves without disturbing the occasion for others. Possible opening sentences might be:

The theme for our assembly today is a religious one. Like all our assemblies, the point is to have an opportunity of thinking about something important and worthwhile. It is not that everyone will agree — we must all think for ourselves.

or

This morning Class 6 are going to give us a presentation about a religious festival . . . Let's imagine we are visitors to a Hindu temple . . . It will

Figure 25 Making assemblies for worship educational

1 Make explicit in assembly its *educational*
   function, encouraging everyone to think for themselves

2 Ensure that both content and method
   harmonise with sound educational principles and
   are therefore capable of being an *integral part
   of religious education*

3 Give opportunity for *quietness*, without any
   attempted public assessment – allowing music or
   silence to make an impact on the *affective* side
   of the personality, and giving opportunity to
   enjoy freedom from pressure

4 *Focus on what is central* to a religious
   interpretation of life – not just developing
   a general theme, or drawing attention to
   what is peripheral in religion

5 See that the assembly is suitable for people of
   all religions (and none) because it seeks to make
   intelligible what underlies religion, yet without
   requiring or expecting commitment for or against
   any religious or non-religious view-point

6 *Involve as many* people as possible in the planning of assemblies

mean *something different for each of us, but just think about it for
yourself.*

In the rest of the assembly care must be taken to avoid such phrases as 'Let us
sing hymn number . . . ' or 'Let us pray'; these must be expanded into an
invitation which articulates the alternatives available. The following are
examples of the kind of terminology which focuses attention upon the
individual's freedom to respond in different ways:

> *'Let us join in either listening to or praying this prayer.'*
> *'Let us sing these words as a hymn, or as a song, according to how we feel
> about it.'*
> *'Let us sing this hymn considering what we can, and what we cannot,
> personally agree with in it.'*
> *'Let us try to imagine what it is like to be a Christian/Muslim/Hindu as we
> sing/say these words.'*

'Let us listen to this Christian/Muslim/Hindu . . . prayer, and if we want to, silently say Amen.'
'As we sing/say this let us reflect upon (think about, consider) the meaning that these words may have for a Christian/Muslim/Hindu . . . believer.'
'Let us join together in making our own individual response to these words, remembering that real community spirit allows people to think differently.'
'No assumption is made about your reaction to this hymn/prayer. Interpret it in whatever way is sincere for you.'
'Participation in this hymn/prayer can signify either assent or empathy.'

2 It is most important that worship assemblies be seen as an intrinsic part of the Religious Education aspect of the school curriculum in which qualities of imagination, an on-going spirit of enquiry and empathy are fostered together with awareness that true community exhibits the opportunity for diversity as opposed to uniformity of belief. This will help students to respond in a responsible way, according to their age and ability, to the silent decision-making required of them in worship assemblies.

3 There should be no attempt to assess the level of response, whether this be one of worship or one of finding-out-about. This would inevitably bring pressure to bear upon the participants, and their opportunity to exercise genuine decision-making would be impaired. This indeed constitutes perhaps the most important reason for not having voluntary worship assemblies. Children's religious beliefs and non-beliefs are in a fluid state; it is not only unrealistic but unkind to expect them to declare themselves in the way that attendance or non-attendance at voluntary worship assemblies would require.

The leader in an assembly, therefore, should never ask just those who agree with a hymn to sing it, or those who can with integrity pray a prayer to say *Amen* audibly. The outward expression of involvement should be basically the same for all, whatever their inner level of involvement. Integrity is not damaged by this outer apparent uniformity because no assumptions are made about what that inner level of involvement is for any given person; the need for diversity is therefore respected.

A particularly helpful aspect of such assemblies would be silence. This would encourage genuine reflectiveness free from pressure to conform to other people's views. Silence can be deeply appreciated by children and young people as well as by staff. Suitable music can be an effective alternative, or can help to create an atmosphere of stillness.

4 The content of the assembly should focus directly on some theme central to religion. It is not playing honest with people to move from a general topic to religion, although this, unfortunately, is widely the practice in many schools which retain assemblies of a religious nature. So often the religious element appears as an unnecessary postscript. It is possible to give a lot of attention and interest to a theme such as 'birthdays' and then say 'Some

people on their birthdays like to thank God for the gift of life . . . ' But this does not organically follow from the rest; it is an interruption unless there is time to develop it properly, and it can leave a nasty impression that the rest was a 'bait', leading students to swallow the hook on which, paradoxically enough, little time could be spent.

Similarly, it is important not to deal with explicitly religious data in a superficial way, without promoting reflectiveness.

5 Due weight needs to be given by those planning assemblies as a whole to the variety of views concerning religion which are represented in the school community. In preparing assemblies it is particularly helpful to involve not only a number of members of staff but students too, so that what is presented can reflect real interest and needs. In areas where there is a significant multi-faith presence, for example, it is most important that this should be reflected in the kind of assemblies held. Some could be multi-faith, incorporating aspects of different religious viewpoints. Others could be devoted to individual religious stances.

6 Wide discussion as to the purpose of such assemblies needs to be promoted with staff, students and parents. All members of staff who wish to should be able to take an appropriate role in planning the assembly structure, and parents could be involved wherever possible or feasible. Students should be encouraged to offer suggestions, develop ideas and prepare content as well as take part in presentation.

It is particularly important that those who actually conduct the assembly are clear about its educational validity and therefore wholehearted in putting it across, whether they have religious belief themselves or not.

I believe that what has been said concerning such two-level-assemblies answers the first three objections raised at the beginning of this chapter. Such assemblies foster integrity and student-freedom, and make possible an openness which is both critical and affirming.

Two further objections and responses to them

The first objection is a pragmatic one: that school worship is exceedingly difficult to do well. What is usually offered can be open to criticism and parody, and indeed be a travesty of worship, as well as of education.

A major reason for poor practice is ill-understood theory, with a resultant lack of motivation and proper preparation. If the educational case for such assemblies giving opportunity for worship is thoroughly understood by all involved, the educational commitment to them will be such that improvement will follow.

Very often poor assemblies reflect a deeper problem of relationships in the school as a whole. For education to happen, there must be a fundamentally good atmosphere in the school – a working one, but also one that is friendly and relaxed, without strain between staff and students. This is a *sine qua non* for any worthwhile teaching. To attempt any assembly without this is to make a farce of it unless it is just a one-off entertainment.

It is also the case that much experimentation is needed as to the time of day, the place and mode of organising most conducive to establishing a mood of inner quietness.

A second objection can be raised on behalf of a religious point of view. Can what happens in such an assembly be regarded as in any way an experience of worship? If not, how does participation in it help people forward in their understanding or worship? As one person expressed it:

> Worship of God is an end in itself; whether it serves to educate others is irrelevant. To design a religious service in which the purpose of education is equal to the purpose of worship would seem self-contradictory, besides being distasteful to many religious believers. Such services might be sincere but they would hardly express worship at its deepest level. Probably they would end in being earnest, gentle and completely conventional and the non-believer would remain unexposed to the essence of worship.[9]

In reply I would say, first, that worship at its deepest is not something which can be ensured or planned anywhere, not even in church, synagogue, mosque, gurdwara or temple. If there is a God who receives worship, then true worship is known by God alone. Religious people should be familiar with the many forms of temptation which can render pious intentions hypocritical.

Second, the school cannot and, indeed, should not, aspire to being a poor relation of a church or other religious building. What it can do is to offer a means of experiencing, perhaps in a preliminary kind of way, what worship is, within a non-specialised setting. It is possible that the worship for a few of those present may be very real indeed. Perhaps for most it will not be worship at all, but only a finding-out experience. Even though this is, from the point of view of the religious believer, inadequate, it is the necessary way to trying to understand and appreciate.

An analogy with music may be helpful. In a compulsorily-attended situation in which music is played to people, the quality of musical experience may be low compared with that reached in a concert to which people have gone voluntarily. Yet it is not for an outsider to judge this with regard to any one individual attending. At least a chance to listen properly to the music was given. Similarly, assemblies giving opportunity to worship can play some part in helping people to appreciate what it is like to be on the inside of religion.

Figure 26 summarises the chapter.

Figure 26 Chapter summary

Objections   1 *hypocrisy* compromises integrity

                    2 *emotional acceptance* compromises critical openness

                    3 *indoctrination* compromises student freedom

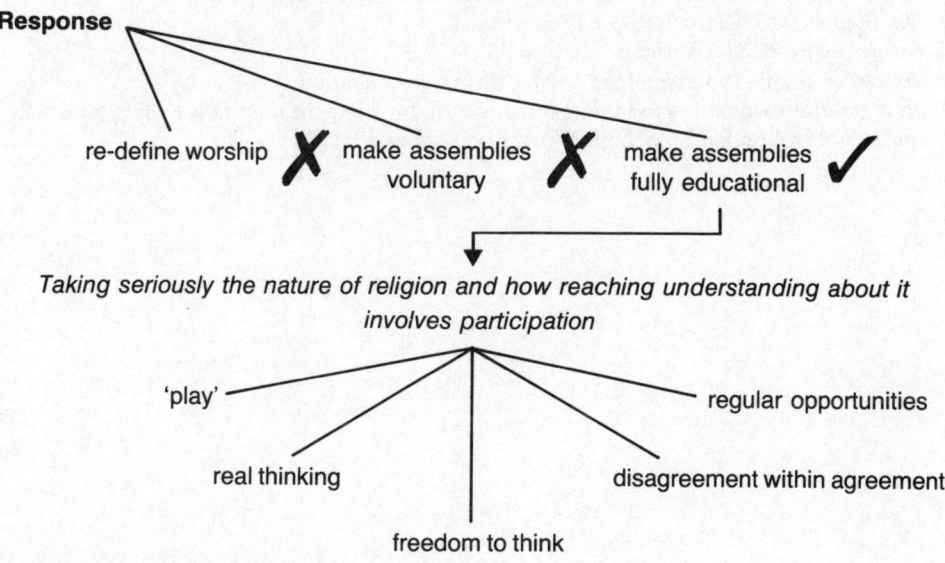

Response

re-define worship ✗ make assemblies voluntary ✗ make assemblies fully educational ✓

Taking seriously the nature of religion and how reaching understanding about it involves participation

'play' — regular opportunities

real thinking — disagreement within agreement

freedom to think

Implications for the running of assemblies

making explicit 2 levels of participation: worship level and educational level

part of RE

quietness

focusing on something central to religion

diversity of views acknowledged

involving staff, students and where possible parents in preparation

Two further objections

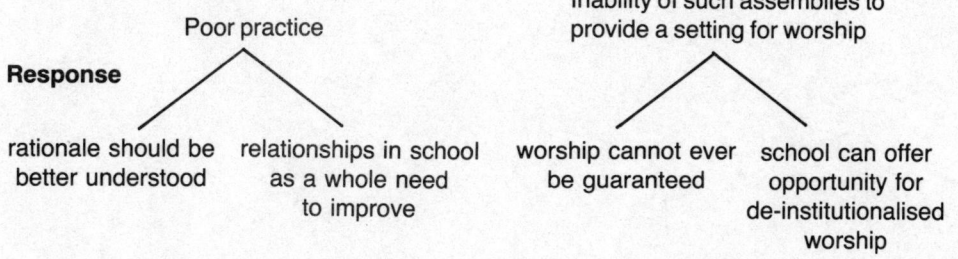

                Poor practice   Inability of such assemblies to provide a setting for worship

Response

rationale should be better understood   relationships in school as a whole need to improve   worship cannot ever be guaranteed   school can offer opportunity for de-institutionalised worship

Notes and references

1 British Humanist Association booklet *Objective, Fair and Balanced* Autumn 1975, p 28
2 Evelyn Underhill *Worship* (Nisbet, 1936)
3 John Hull *School Worship: An Obituary* (SCM, 1975) p 62
4 Harold Loukes *New Ground in Christian Education* (SCM, 1965) p 133
5 Ninian Smart *Reasons and Faiths* (Routledge and Kegan Paul, 1958) p 14
6 *The Fourth R* (SPCK, 1970) p 617
7 Arthur Rowe *BJRE* (Autumn, 1980) p 11
8 My father recalls Professor Joad saying this in conversation
9 I am grateful to Brenda Hoddinott for this written comment on a talk I gave at an ARE conference in London on School Worship, October 15 1983

C   IN THE CLASSROOM

15 Focus on Method in the Primary School 1

Religious Education in the Primary School

Primary schools lend themselves extremely well to religious education because they can sidestep many of the problems encountered in secondary schools (see Chapter 17). Among their advantages are the following:

a The practice of an integrated day instead of timetabled lessons – which is common for infants and fairly frequent for juniors – means that religion does not have to be boxed off from the rest of the children's learning experience.

b Primary children are not normally alienated from the learning situation: they are still keen and curious, and enjoy asking questions.

c The simplicity and imaginative powers of infant and junior children enable them to grasp intuitively some insights which older students and adults find difficult or incomprehensible.

d There are usually fewer distractions and competing pressures than in secondary schools.

e The teacher knows the children well and can readily establish the kind of trusting rapport which is particularly needed when dealing with so sensitive an area as religion.

Associated with these advantages there are, however, certain dangers:

a It is easy for religion to be a very unclear area, or indeed non-existent, for the children and so in effect omitted altogether. Often teachers take shelter behind the concept of implicit religious education and refrain from any explicit teaching (seee Chapter 8 for discussion of this question).

b It is easy to be lulled into imagining that children are achieving as much as they can. Yet the seeds of future apathy, indifference and inability to be reflective can be sown unwittingly. Much harm is done by neglecting to take children's questioning seriously and lead them on in their thinking.

c The quality of simplicity renders children, especially the younger ones, particularly impressionable and vulnerable. There is the danger of

Figure 27   Religious Education in the Primary School

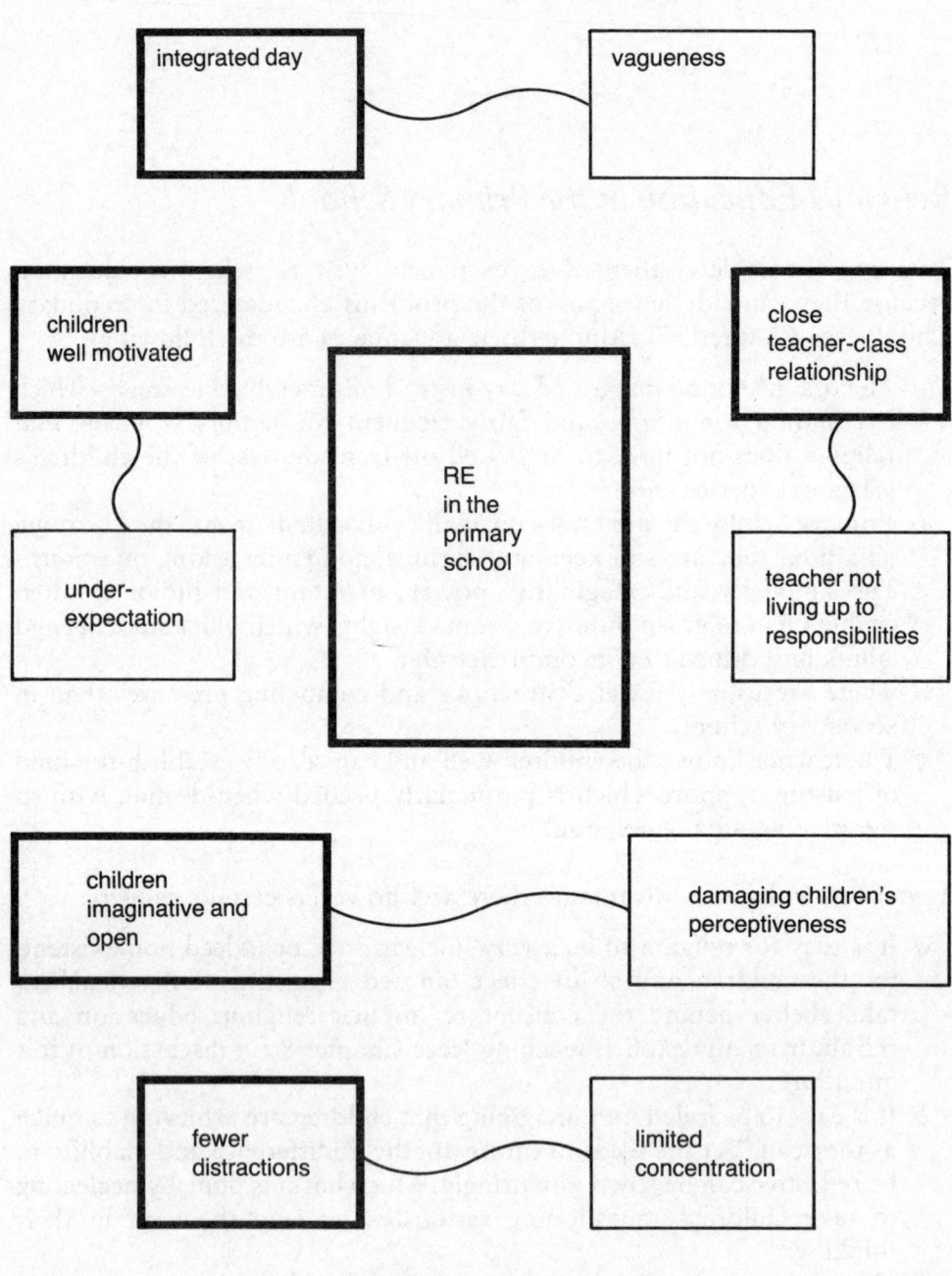

Advantages and Disadvantages

integrated day

vagueness

children well motivated

close teacher-class relationship

RE in the primary school

under-expectation

teacher not living up to responsibilities

children imaginative and open

damaging children's perceptiveness

fewer distractions

limited concentration

trampling on a child's faith, or on some insight precious to the child, and of thus doing irreparable damage.

d The younger the child, generally, the shorter the span of his or her concentration. Along with their restricted experience and limited grasp of language, children often lack the inner emotional challenge to come to grips with religion.

e When there is sustained contact between teacher and class an especially heavy responsibility is laid on the teacher actually to *be* the kind of person who commends an informed approach to religion (see Figure 27).

These dangers relate to another set of problems:

1 The primary school teacher has to be a general practitioner dealing with so many areas that any deep knowledge of religion, and of how to help children gain an understanding of it, is normally rare. Many teachers feel incompetent, unclear what they think themselves and ignorant of much about religion.

2 The primary school teacher has to watch especially carefully the problem of over-influencing children. They are extremely susceptible, and have a natural propensity for endowing what adults say with absolute authority. Many are taught this at home. Even children from homes where they receive little discipline or care have usually learnt to accept and copy what the adults around them say.

3 The primary school teacher has to tread carefully with regard to the home background of the children. 'My mum says . . . ' is a warning to the teacher not to upset the delicate balance between the child's world at home and that at school. To show disrespect to the deeply-held convictions of parents, or indeed to their unexamined assumptions, is to offend the child and risk causing inner anxiety, for the child is caught in the crossfire when disagreement between parents and teacher occurs. Some parents feel very strongly on matters relating to religion.

4 As discussed in Chapter 12, the primary school teacher has to adjust constantly to the limited experience and vocabulary of the children. This imposes a real strain: it is very difficult to simplify without being misleading. On the other hand, fear of children's not understanding can lead to failure to teach at all.

Ways of dealing with these problems are summarised in Figure 28.

Teaching method in general

The primary school sees great changes in the development of children. The changes which occur between the ages of four and ten are greater than any subsequent change at secondary level or later. Such development occurs in

Figure 28   Problems and ways of meeting them

1 *Non-specialist lacking knowledge*

(teaching by *showing how* to find out and think more; sharing with children the idea that the more one knows, the more one knows *how limited our knowledge is*)

2 *Ease of indoctrination*

(positive and constant *encouragement to children to think for themselves* and as they advance through primary school be prepared to disagree with teacher's viewpoint; showing that religion is a *controversial* area)

3 *Need for care with regard to parental attitudes*
(being concerned *to affirm them as persons*, expressing agreement with them wherever possible; where it is not being careful to treat them *with respect*)

4 *Dangers of over-simplification and absence of teaching*

(discussing with children *how difficult it is to express understanding properly*; remembering that the teacher must be *preparing children to reach the next stage ahead*, not to stop where they are now)

language skills, understanding of concepts, and interpretation of experience. There is consequently a need for the teacher to temper his or her approach sensitively to suit the stage which children have reached. Nevertheless there is sufficient similarity, in general terms, to make it feasible to discuss both infant and junior teaching together, provided its sequential nature is borne in mind.

A further point is relevant in that there can be dramatic differences in levels of ability, interest and attainment between children of the same age, often due to differences in home background. Many can be seriously deprived because they are not 'stretched' enough; they can learn damaging lessons of boredom and low standards. Others can experience a deep and almost unforgettable sense of failure or low achievement which they may carry with them for the rest of their lives. A uniform approach to the teaching of different age groups is likely to be unhelpful to many, if not most, children. In what follows, therefore, even though there is some indication of average suitability, the teacher of any age-group may find appropriate material for some of their children.

In essence, two complementary approaches are needed for Religious Education in the primary school:

- Responding to children's comments and questions;
- Initiating learning through providing an interesting and rich environment, through specific units of work and through story. Assemblies also offer important opportunities for Religious Education, as discussed in Chapter 14.

The rest of this chapter will be concerned with looking at the first of these in some depth. The next chapter will treat the second.

Responding to children's comments and questions: Religious Education through spontaneous conversation and more structured discussion

A group of infant school teachers at a recent conference summarised some general points about children's conversation and discussion as follows:

> Children learn very effectively through conversation especially if they have instigated it themselves, because the theme is relevant to their interest or concern at that moment. Spontaneous questions can be growing-points in children's understanding. More structured discussion is a development from this which can be very rewarding indeed if the teacher is really aware of the children's response and has thought enough about the theme to be able to educate through his or her own response to their comments.
>
> It is well to remember that the length of class discussion should take into account the age and maturity of the children. Very young children cannot sustain long periods of concentrated discussion in large groups. They learn to switch off if the discussion has little meaning for them, or if it is something they have not initiated out of their own interest, or if the teacher is using language they do not fully understand or making long definitive statements related to nothing very much. All these points tend to set up bad learning habits which are also incredibly wasteful.
>
> The best type of discussions are those instigated by children themselves as a result of a story, poem or event that has happened in or out of school that has affected them in one way or another. This could be developed in class discussion and followed up by the teacher when the children are engaged in small working groups in creative activities and are relaxed and at ease.[1]

Two comments from children in the same class on different occasions could be the starting-point for talking about prayer:

> Catherine, when the hens' eggs in the incubator failed to hatch, complained: 'But I have prayed to God about them and I asked Him to make them hatch.' There were tears in her eyes and she almost stamped her foot.

Julia returned to school after three weeks' absence with bronchitis. On her second day back she said she had something important to tell us: 'Last night I thought I was going to be ill again and I told God I did not want to stay away from school and I asked Jesus to make me better and here I am.'

If such remarks are not followed up, serious misunderstandings may develop. The impression may be allowed to continue that God is like some kind of magician who, on request, will change the course of scientific 'laws'. Such a God is rather like a slot-machine – put in a penny and you get what you want! This is common even among adults and the fact that they cannot get what they ask for can convince them very effectively that no God exists. Yet it is a view of God regarded as false by all the great religions. It is also mistaken with regard to the relationship between religion and science; it suggests that the way nature normally works is quite independent of how God creates and sustains it, and that God is only present when science is overruled by a supernatural intervention. This view in turn leads many to consider God as either redundant or alien to the world, and to see science as purely mechanistic, reinforcing a materialist attitude to life. This may sound complicated, but it is the kind of impression which many children can and do receive from such comments.

The teacher is therefore faced with a highly responsible task, to be able at a second's notice to turn a chance remark into valuable theological, philosophical and scientific education.

Let us, by way of example, put the opportunity for religious education presented by these children's comments under the microscope. Figure 29 gives a number of possible responses by the teacher to each of the two children's remarks. It may be helpful to try to arrange them in an order of merit according to how satisfactory they are in overcoming the dangers and problems summarised in Figures 27 and 28.

Some of these comments fall neatly into one trap or another. A number of them, however, do give the children something to think about, and encouragement to do so. The value of the comments educationally depends not on what the teachers's commitment is (for there are examples here of indoctrination from a religious, an agnostic and an atheist standpoint, just as there are examples of good teaching from a religious and non-religious perspective) but on how sound a grasp the teacher has of the essential principles or fundamental insights of religion, whether or not he or she personally affirms them. Those which have a bearing on these comments are set out below. They are numbered to suggest a logical progression round a creative circle, 10 leading to 1 again. In Figure 30, however, a different arrangement is given to show different interrelationships. The reader may like to devise yet another order.

Figure 29 Possible responses

Catherine, when the hen's eggs in the incubator failed to hatch complained:
But I have prayed to God about them and I asked Him to make them hatch.

- Well Catherine, it' a mystery, and I don't know what to think about it. It could be that God said No because it would make us lazy if God did everything for us. Or it could be that there isn't a God anyway. You go on thinking about it.
- Well Catherine, never mind, go and get your hat and coat.
- Well Catherine, there isn't a God to pray to, so perhaps you've learnt something important today.
- Well Catherine, tell me, do you think that God will always give us everything we pray for, even when we've perhaps done something stupid like not keeping the eggs in the incubator at the right temperature?
- Well Catherine, you just didn't pray hard enough. If you'd really believed God would help you He would have done.
- Well, Catherine, praying has really nothing to do with it. The eggs didn't hatch because they were not kept warm enough.
- Well Catherine, God doesn't always answer our prayers. If your little brother asked your dad if he could hold a firework or eat one of your mum's pills he would say 'No', wouldn't he? So perhaps . . .
- Well Catherine, some people don't believe there is a God to pray to anyway. But even if there is, it could be that God wants to teach us to stand on our own feet and learn about the world and how to manage it. Because the eggs haven't hatched, we're all learning how to be more careful in future to get the temperature right.
- Well Catherine, God doesn't answer silly prayers.

Last night I thought I was going to be ill again and I told God I did not want to stay away from school and I asked Jesus to make me better and here I am.

- Well Julia, perhaps God did answer your prayer but sometimes He might not – you mustn't rely on praying just to get what you want.
- Well Julia, it's a puzzle. Because you prayed you thought you would get better, and so you did.
- Well Julia, I think God answered your prayer, but some people including some religious people might say it was just chance. You must think about it for yourself – what makes sense.
- Well Julia, I'm not so sure because I don't believe there is a God anyway. But you must think about it for yourself. Religious people certainly believe that God likes people to pray, but not that God will always give them what they want.
- Well Julia, God answers prayers if you have enough faith.
- Well Julia, you only think that, because people have put the idea of God into your head.
- Well Julia, there's no need to bring God into it – the illness simply cleared up with the help of the pills you were given.
- Well Julia, people who think a lot about religion would say that perhaps God did make you well. But they might also say it was coincidence. Do you know what that means?
- Well Julia, now it's time to listen to what James has to say about his party.
- Well Julia, I think God answered your prayer, but some people including some religious people might say it was just chance. You must think about it for yourself which makes more sense. But tell me, do you think that if we're both right and there is a God, He is just someone to go and ask things from? What do you think praying is really about?
- Well Julia, I'm not so sure – but then that's because I don't believe in God. But you must not take my word for it – you must think it out for yourself.

Figure 30 Theological points

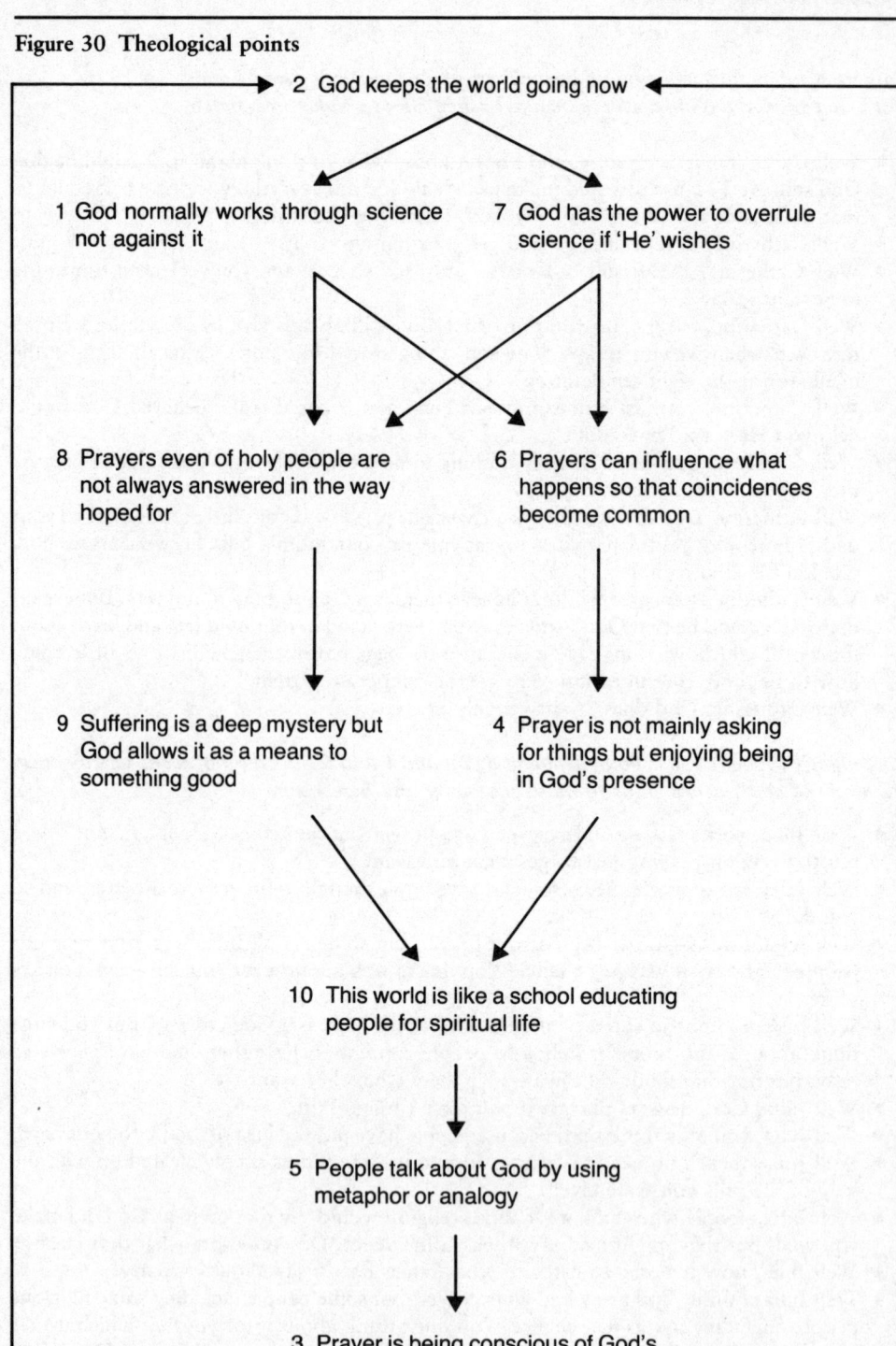

Theological points relating to Catherine's and Julia's remarks

It is necessary to be aware that most religious people believe:

1 that God is responsible for the scientific way in which the world operates, and therefore that God works in and through it. It is false to see any opposition between science and religion;

2 that God did not just create the world in the beginning but constantly maintains it in existence. Not only do religious people believe that without God the world would not be here, but also that without God the world would immediately cease to be;

3 that prayer is an activity in which people are conscious of being in God's presence. It is not that anyone is ever out of God's presence, because God is not bound by the limitations of time and space – God is, to use metaphorical language, 'everywhere, all the time'. But mostly people do not realise they are in God's presence. This is why it is valuable to pray, and why religious people believe that God wants people to pray;

4 that just as in personal relationships between people there is something drastically wrong if all that a person wants is to ask for favours, so prayer which is just asking something from God is one-sided and selfish. The highest kind of prayer is simply enjoying knowing one is in God's presence;

5 that all our thinking about God is conditioned by the limitations of our experience in this world, and the language we use. It is helpful to think of God as personal provided that we realise that God is infinitely more than what we know as personal. Thus God does not have a body, is not to be perceived by means of the five senses, etc. The analogy of person needs to be corrected by the analogy of something like life-force, power, energy.

6 that the material world is profoundly influenced by the spiritual; when someone prays, it seems, unusual things can often happen. William Temple, the Archbishop of Canterbury who died in 1944, once remarked how curious it was that 'when I pray coincidences happen such a lot.'

7 that while God is responsible for the scientific 'laws', 'He' remains free to over-rule them if 'He' wishes. To say that God *cannot* do something implies that we know better than God, or that somehow God is limited like us;

8 that there are many examples of miracles happening through people's faith in God as well as many examples in the lives of deeply religious people of prayers not being answered in the way hoped for. One of the most well-known examples is that of Jesus praying in the garden of Gethsemane that the 'cup' of suffering might be removed, and it was not;

9 that the fact of suffering, both in nature and in people, is a great mystery. Religious people cannot give any complete explanation for it, but they do show how to cope with it, overcome it and see suffering as contributing to something good, the development of persons who are wholly loving and unselfish, of strong character and spiritiual vigour;

10 that this world has to be seen in the light of eternity: it is not complete in itself but preparatory to 'something' else. All our thought-forms and concepts are inadequate to express this 'other' reality, but through imagination, poetry, art, music, luminous conversation, inner silence and so forth it is possible for people to glimpse this reality and 'know' it with absolute assurance, even though they cannot put it into words properly or prove it to anyone else.

This seemingly formidable list needs to be mastered in Religious Education as surely as the concepts of number, space, and time need to be for the proper teaching of mathematics and science. What is relevant can then be drawn on by the teacher just as the seven-eighths of the iceberg below the surface supports the one-eighth which is visible.

It is perhaps reassuring to note that it is *not* so much a *factual* knowledge of this and that which is required but an *awareness* of how these basic principles work. Seen in this light the preparation required is feasible. Once these principles have been appreciated at a simple level, the whole of life's experience can help to deepen the teacher's understanding. Whatever the beliefs of the teacher, it is failing children not to help them to think clearly about what deeply religious people in all the great religions think. To be aware of these ten points is not to gloss over important differences, but rather to appreciate first the great circle of agreement among religions beside which the disagreements can be coped with and can be welcomed. Nor is it an invitation to be dogmatic in method or approach, for in fact it opens up issues: it is inviting everyone to go to the limits of their horizons and to look beyond. Indeed it is extremely important that the children be weaned as early as possible from encapsulating their experience in dogmatic forms, so that they appreciate how difficult it is to put insights into words which are adequate.

To grasp these principles is not to be able to 'give answers' to children's questions, it is to be able to lead them constructively on in their thinking. For the controversial element needs to be openly discussed even with young children: that is, the way in which people think differently about these questions. Some useful sentences for encouraging this kind of involvement are listed in Figure 31.

Figure 31 Useful sentences

Some things we just sense, don't we? People often sense different things because they are different people and have had different experiences.

I know how you feel but I see it differently.

Perhaps some things we can only understand when we're very, very quiet.

Do you remember that incident the other day? Well, how does that fit in to what we're talking about now?

Do you think that's a good reason?

Can you both be right?

I think this . . . what do you think?

We must try not to criticise what we don't understand.

What did – – – say just now?

It is very hard for anyone to understand.

Have you thought about this?

Just because I'm your teacher it doesn't mean I am right about everything.

Some people think this . . . others think that . . .

You must decide that for yourself. See whether what I say makes sense or not.

People for whom religion is very meaningful believe that . . .

We must try to think for ourselves, not just repeat what we've heard other people say.

That's an interesting way of putting it – I hadn't thought of it like that before.

Does it make sense?

People who think deeply about religion believe that . . .

Why do you say that?

People cannot express these things properly in words.

Sometimes we just have to say nothing because we can't put what we feel into words.

A classroom conversation

It may be helpful to subject a snatch of actual classroom conversation to detailed analysis for its value as religious education.

Shazia	'Miss, if you touch God, God don't get us no sweets.
Teacher	(laughing) Do you ———
Saima	No, No, God is invisible
Teacher	Yes, we can't actually see God. Can we actually touch God do you think?
Shazia	No
Madhavi	Because he is higher
Teacher	Oh, where is he then?
Everyone	(with great feeling) He's up in the sky
Teacher	You think he's up in the sky?
Everyone	Yes
Madhavi	You couldn't reach him (lots of joint comments)
Saima	Because he's so high
Shazia	(animated telling me great news) You know the sky? – well he's up there (pointing and standing)
Teacher	Well, I wonder what he does up there?'[2]

I am very grateful to the teacher concerned for giving me a verbatim report of this class discussion she had with 5–6-year-olds in a multicultural setting. She has an excellent rapport with the children, and she was self-critical of the way she handled the conversation.

The reader will notice that in some respects the children in this extract, two Muslims and one Hindu, showed themselves as perceptive theologically as the teacher, indeed perhaps more so. Saima was quick to note that God is not to be reached through the senses, and the concept of 'higher' is one of the most unavoidable metaphors used by sophisticated adults to describe something greater than what we normally understand. It is the teacher who prompts the more spatial application of the word, to which the children readily respond, doubtless because that is what they have been taught. Instead of trying to refine the concept by introducing the children gently the use of metaphorical language to point to what is strictly beyond words, she actually reinforces the more concrete thinking by her final question (see Figure 32).

There is another point of contrast in which the children really come out better than the teacher in this snatch of conversation. The children are being genuine, involved and excited about their awareness. If Shazia is repeating the beliefs she has heard in her home environment, she is doing so because they are meaningful to her. Elsewhere the teacher described Shazia as having 'a mind that likes to make sense of things to her own satisfaction', a characteristic to which the teacher warmed. But the teacher in this conversation is very much playing the teacher-role, getting the children to

Figure 32 Metaphor

The 'up there' metaphor is not misleading if people realise it *is* a metaphor. Using a number of different metaphors helps us to build up a more mature concept of God. Even young children can begin to understand that a metaphor is like a finger pointing in a direction; it does not describe the thing itself.

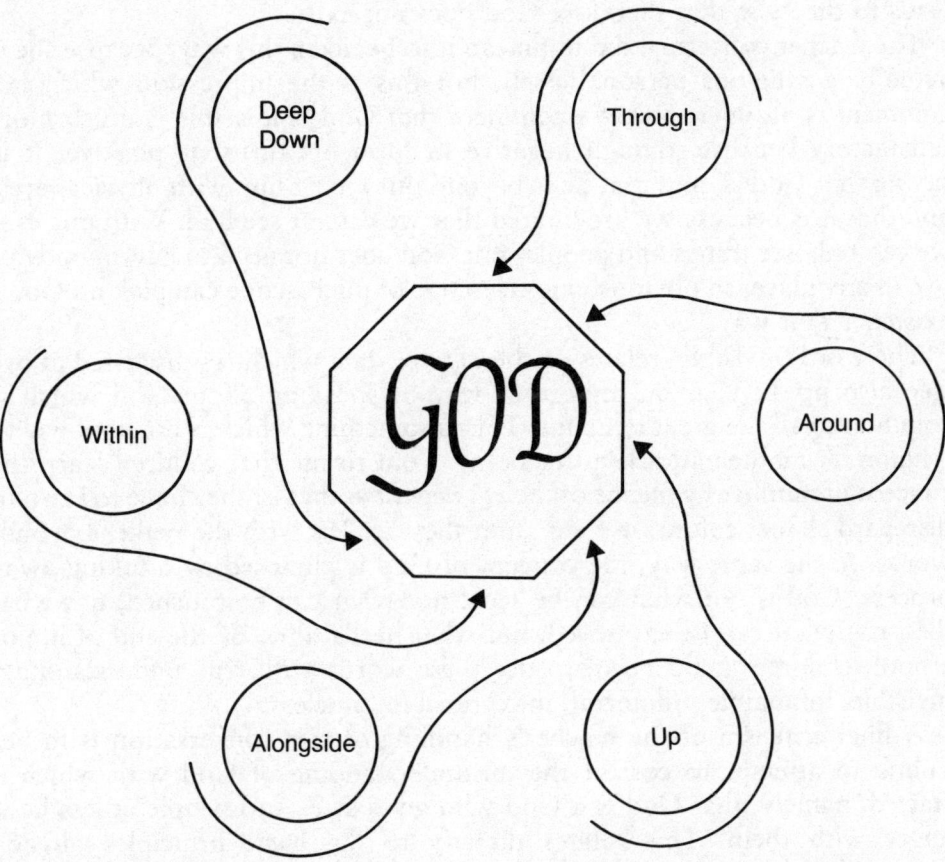

This model is probably more suitable for children of eight and upwards. However the idea, and perhaps different examples, can be introduced to younger children even if the word 'metaphor' is not used.

talk but refraining from any real involvement herself. Why did she not share what she thinks, not in order to close the conversation or to expect the children to conform, but to encourage them to reflect further on their and her joint experience?

A third point related to the above is the way in which the children are being more positive than the teacher. They are affirming something, however undeveloped and immaturely expressed, and at the age of five or six to speak of God as up in the sky may be fair enough. But the teacher should be helping them find better ways of expressing their understanding of God without the rather negative implications of her strictly correct comment that 'we can't actually see God.' This statement, for many adults as well as children, simply leads to the view that therefore God does not exist.

The teacher concerned did not mean it to be taken this way, because she is actually a religious person herself, but this is the impression which her comment could give. Saima's comment that God is invisible is much more satisfactory because, though negative in form, its thrust is positive. It is saying that God is, and that he is beyond our seeing him with physical eyes, and that it is because we are limited that we cannot see him. With our eyes we can only see things and people. But God does not need to have a body or live in any place, so obviously no telescope of microscope can pick up God's existence that way.

The word 'invisible' relates to the *via negativa* which, as discussed above (see also pp 117), is an important way of speaking about God which is common to all the great religions. This is something which is not confined to religion. A mathematics lecturer pointed out to me that children learn the concept of number by means of the *via negativa*: that is, they have to learn to disregard shape, colour, use etc, until they are left with the reality-beyond-words. In the same way, the concept of God is glimpsed by a taking-away process: God is not what can be seen, not what can be touched, not what dies, not what can be expressed, not what needs time. By the end of junior school, children could begin to use these words with true understanding: invisible, intangible, immortal, inexpressible, timeless.

A final criticism of the teacher's handling of this conversation is in her failing to attempt to correct the misunderstanding of God with which it started, namely, that God is a God who gives sweets to people unless he is angry with them. This relates directly to the basic principles already discussed with regard to Catherine's and Julia's comments about prayer (see also Figure 29). But it brings in also the question of sin, of people doing what God does not want them to do. This, as the teacher elsewhere in discussion pointed out, brings one to beliefs fraught with difficulty for the unwary. Children from religious backgrounds such as Hinduism are not protected from knowledge of this aspect of religion. On another occasion in the same class Rajesh remarked:

I saw a film about a god. The god got very angry and made the whole house burn and the people got dead.

at which point the teacher terminated the conversation

. . . in spite of the fact that the children had a lot more to say. But I cannot cope with their vengeful gods as I am far more squeamish than the children seem to be.

This honest comment points to the paradox that usually adults try to protect children from the darker side of life on the grounds that the children cannot cope with it, when in reality children are open to life in all its fullness and are aware of the dark side. Yet most children are hardly ever given any help in coming to terms with it except, significantly, in fairy-stories and much children's literature. The innocence (in the sense of ignorance) of children is perhaps more adult-imposed than we realise. Fear of raising questions about disease, animals killing each other, national disasters, and so forth is responsible for the childish, simplistic, sentimentality of a diet of only 'All things bright and beautiful'. It may be that when teachers come to take seriously the opportunities presented by the presence of children from other cultures in our schools, much greater depth in facing such questions will ensue.[3]

Teaching through conversation and discussion requires considerable professional skill but is most rewarding. The children need to feel free to comment and question without pressure or tension, knowing that whatever they say will be listened to and taken seriously. While pursuing children's red herrings and changing of subject, it is important to help them to follow up something said and think about it. With encouragement, patience and determination children can develop the ability to concentrate – they rarely will, however, if adults do not actively assist them. *Depth* is essential. This does not mean boringness but the opposite. Constant switching of subjects leads to superficiality and eventually boredom.[4]

Notes and references

1 Farmington Institute consultation on 'Teaching the Concept of God in the Infants School' 3–5 October 1980

2 Recorded conversation brought to the above consultation

3 A Muslim six-year-old, when talking about thunder, remarked 'The thunder is when God is angry. It is as if a big boy swears at a little one and God is angry with you. God sends the thunder and lightning.' It is not the case that children cannot learn to cope creatively with the fact of death, given proper support. Thus an 11-year-old girl I knew could describe her mother's death as like a snake sloughing the skin it no longer needs, while her younger sister remarked 'We can all feel Mummy's invisible cuddles but only Simba (the dog) can actually see her'

4 *Listening to Children* by Mary Ellison and Christopher Herbert (Church Information Office Publishing, 1983) records conversations by 9 to 11 year-olds in which no adult was present. It makes a plea for real listening by teachers, and letting children help to write their own Religious Education syllabus. *Does God have a Body? and other questions* by Rosalyn Kendrick (SCM 1977) faces difficult questions squarely and in an interesting way. It would make very helpful background reading for teachers

16 Focus on Method in the Primary School 2

Initiating learning

As well as responding to children's remarks it is also the responsibility of the teacher to initiate learning. There are at least three ways in which the teacher can do this.

1 By providing an interesting and rich environment for the children.

This gives them the opportunity for different types of experiences helpful for understanding religion. It is such experiences which can spark off the most meaningful of conversations. From the point of view of the person for whom life and religion are an integrated whole, anything and everything can lead to further understanding and appreciation of God. But this is not so unless there is a conscious starting-point. Putting plimsolls on, playing a recorder, doing science or painting does not of itself generate understanding of religion. So the teacher must carefully consider precisely how such situations may prove illuminating, and help children to become spiritually literate. For older juniors, watching a David Attenborough programme, for example, can become part of religious education when put into the context of the questions 'Is there a God who created this world of nature?' or 'Can a God of love have made or tolerated a world "red in tooth and claw"?'

The kinds of experiences perhaps most conducive to introducing or bringing to the surface explicitly religious questions may be seen as threefold:

a *Experiences of awe and wonder*, in which one become lost in a sense of the majesty or excitement or beauty of life. H D Lewis in his book *Our Experience of God* notes that 'Religion begins in wonder'[1] and wonder may crop up almost anywhere, but especially in connection with the arts, music and nature-study.

Such experiences can become religious education when they are related to the development of the concept of God, almighty yet near, creator and provider. It is not a question of saying to children, 'Yes, these flowers are wonderful because God made them' but rather of posing the question, 'How is it that there is such beauty?' With older children one might ask 'Is there perhaps a Mind or Purpose behind all this?' and teach them that religious people believe that God is responsible for all this beauty.

b *Experiences of self-reflectiveness* in which one becomes aware of oneself – on the one hand as being small, powerless, vulnerable and ignorant, and on the other hand being perceptive, important, responsible, free to choose and to change the way things are. In the tension and paradox of these two aspects of self-consciousness talk of religion becomes meaningful and relevant, whether it leads to religious faith or to its rejection. This is because such experiences raise ultimate questions such as 'Why do terrible things happen?' 'Where do I come from (not just mummy's tummy)?' 'What hapens to those who die' 'What's the point of it all?' 'How can I be different?' Everyday events, crises, visitors to the school, news programmes, work in different subject-areas . . . can all help to teach such awareness and discipline.

Such experiences become Religious Education when the kind of answers which are given in the great religions are discussed.

c *Experiences of limitation*, including doubting, difficulty in expressing what one means, awareness of personal inadequacy or wrong-doing and appreciation of the value of silence. All kinds of situations can give rise to these experiences. Playing with words in poetry and story, and so forth, together with struggling to understand concepts, can teach respect for the problems of communication. Listening to music, or moments of quietness in physical education, can help to develop sensitivity to another dimension of being.

Such experiences can become Religious Education when the mystical element present in all the great religions is talked about, that is, that God is beyond all that we can ever say or think or do, and that inner quietness and humility and openness in prayer or meditation are the way to being close to God; the purpose of religious words and religious objects and rituals is to point towards that which cannot be expressed in any other way.

It is clear that the interesting and rich environment which the teacher seeks to provide for the children should include plenty of explicitly religious material. Children growing up in a society in which religion is more and more banished to the periphery of life need special help if they are not to be seriously deprived. Often they are ignorant of even the most rudimentary knowledge. So religious objects, pictures of religious buildings and rituals and accounts of religious events should form part of the context for learning provided by the teacher, within which children – even in the infant reception class – can be encouraged to talk about religious happenings in their homes.

A word of caution is needed, however, in that 'facts' about religion do not

Figure 33   General Themes and Religious Education

A GENERAL THEME CAN BECOME RELIGIOUS EDUCATION

For infant education

Food

Wall pictures of foods we eat
Make books of 'I like . . . '
Make a chart to show:
  • foods good for us
  • foods we are better without
Posters of Third World countries
Discuss shortage of food
Discuss how all people need food

Idea of God as
provider of all
that is necessary
for life

Idea of God as
creator of a
world in which
people have special
responsibility to
care for other forms
of life

1 Discuss how and where
we get food – all from
nature. People can harvest
and fish but cannot
originate or create
2 Discuss idea of God as
the provider through
nature, as the creator of
nature
3 Discuss how people who
believe in God express
gratitude. Make a book of
thank-you prayers, which
they might say
4 Let children express their
own views and show what
they feel about it all
5 Discuss idea of God
working through people, so
that they are God's helpers
in seeing everyone has what
they need

For junior education
Rules

Make a chart showing road signs
Discuss what would happen if
there were no rules of the road
Discuss rules for games – why
do we have rules?
What about shool rules?
Discuss reasons for the law of
the land: freedom to act as one
chooses so long as one does not
affect other people's freedom,
freedom from burglary,
physical harm etc.

Idea of God giving
people rules for living
as a way of helping
people to become free
persons

1 Study pictures of
  • Jewish child reading
    scripture
  • Muslim child learning
    passage from the
    Qurãn
2 Why are there rules in
religion?
3 Discuss the picture of
God which can emerge
from a story like Noah's
Flood. Is this a kind of
celestial policeman? If so,
does this mean that God
hates people?

Figure 33 continued

*It is important to note
that discussion of how religious
people picture God, and of what
the idea of God in itself implies
can and should happen alongside
children being encouraged to think
out for themselves whether they
believe in God.*

4 If we don't like the idea
of God keeping order, how
can God deal with unkindness
and injustice? Is turning
a blind eye good enough? If
not, how might God change
people?
5 Can the rules of religion
be reduced to just one?
Discuss the Golden Rule as
it appears in various
religions

---

in themselves necessarily constitute Religious Education: they may be no more than history, geography, social studies etc. The kind of questions outlined in Chapter 10, on pages 138ff, are what Religious Education is really about. Figure 33 shows how two themes commonly taken in primary schools can become Religious Education.

2 By specific units of work

One way of ensuring that sufficient stimulus is given to distinctively Religious Education is by developing units of work on an acknowledged religious theme. Religion should never be dragged in by the back door, but be openly talked about, not (of course) in order to try to convert the children to this or that religious or non-religious standpoint, but in order to develop understanding.

In preparing such a unit of work on a specifically religious theme it is necessary to be absolutely clear about the specifically *religious* understanding which one hopes the children will gain from their work on the unit. It is also important to think out one's own, adult, understanding of the theme and to be involved oneself, and therefore able to lead children on in *their own* thinking. Furthermore, it is vital not to underestimate children's capacities, but to try to stimulate their further development.

With regard especially to this last point I may perhaps cite a unit of work, on the beauty of nature and the problem of suffering, consisting of slides and discussion material, which I prepared for junior age-groups.[2] This attempted to introduce children in an open way to theological thinking about how contemplation of the world of nature can raise questions concerning belief in God. It was tried out in a number of schools with encouraging results, and it may be helpful to share with the reader some of the reactions of teachers to it, and the kind of work and level of discussion it can stimulate.

A review in *AVA Magazine* Spring 1983 described the unit as providing 'a diverse and inspiring resource for teachers who are able to adapt it to their own needs.' but commented that the material was more suitable for pupils of 14 plus. Yet teachers in a trial group of primary schools felt differently.[3] One Oxfordshire teacher of nine-year-olds commented:

> I enjoyed using it very much. Ideally the work should arise out of the classroom situation. Over a year it would be sure some time to occur naturally – meeting a question about space, science fiction or the importance of science etc. I felt the scheme did move on effectively to begin to awaken the child's inner vision which tends to be starved without a vocabulary, without a sounding-box.

Another teacher used the unit with a group of twelve 7–8-year-old boys and girls. Her report shows, I believe, the danger of underestimating children's ability. In discussion about Gagarin's comment 'I travelled through space but I did not see God' one child said 'Of course he could not *see* God, he is everywhere, but he would probably *feel* God, like we do.' The teacher went on to comment:

> There was quite a lot of discussion about God in the abstract: concepts, feeling, sense of joy through things they saw. I was surprised that nobody attempted to describe God's appearance . . . The words which came through strongly were '*feeling* God through nature, God giving people *freedom* to use the natural things around them . . .'

These 7–8-year-old children are prepared to think. A number of Religious Education units could emerge from these discussions alone, following up the leads given by the children themselves. I suspect some incipient agnosticism would be voiced before long by a few of the children. If not, the teacher should raise the question, because this could help to deepen their thinking. It is important, however, that the teacher does this in a genuinely open way which is not destructive of anybody's faith, but rather, illuminating (see Chapter 5 for more on this issue).

A type of unit designed to be worked through by individuals or in groups on their own with only occasional support from the teacher may be very valuable in the primary school when different needs, interests and abilities are represented in a class.[4] There is much to be gained from letting groups of children work on various topics and then encouraging them to share their findings with the rest of the class. The actual work of thinking how to tell the other about the subject in an interesting and appropriate way helps to reinforce the learning for them, as well as providing a really authentic reason for time spent on revision.

3 Through story

With younger children especially, direct religious education can very effectively be done through the medium of story, bringing in specifically religious words, events and people. Many stories can be drawn upon from the various religious traditions. Especially valuable are stories about religious people, because children can relate easily to a person, and religion can more readily be seen as meaningful when associated with a person.

Another type of story which can be particularly valuable educationally is that centred round an illuminating conversation. Two examples are given at the end of the chapter. They are virtually self-explanatory, arresting, challenging – even for very young children – and memorable. Furthermore, they deal with aspects central to an understanding of religion. *The Little Fox*[5] brilliantly brings together two insights which religious people affirm: first, that God is Spirit, not something or somebody which can be seen with physical eyes, who requires fives senses as we do; and second that even very simple and seemingly naive religious practices may be deeply religious and acceptable to God, for we are dependent on the five senses even if God is not. *The Secret of Happiness*[6] goes straight to the heart of the matter concerning obedience to God's will. So often this is seen both by religious people and by those who reject religion as a joyless, servile, rigid requirement imposed by religion. To those, however, who have drunk deep it is the opposite: it gives happiness, freedom and an amazing adaptability. The picture of God as an alien judge or policeman has been entirely replaced by that of God as a loving friend with whom one is very close and therefore very contented and fulfilled.

These are profound religious points, yet they can be expressed through story in a way that very young children as well as adults can appreciate – if they will.

Many stories, however, which are commonly told to children as part of Religious Education are not illuminating and may even be regressive. 'David and Goliath', for instance, while being an excellent story as such, can leave children with the impression that God is only on the side of the under-dog, and that God wholly approves of violence in a just cause. Such a story, if told to children, ought to be followed by discussion which enables such misunderstandings to be cleared up, and positive points made. Perhaps a story giving a very different impression of God could be told. 'David and Goliath' could be balanced by the rabbinic story of how, after the Egyptians had been drowned in the Red Sea and the Israelites were dancing and singing songs of victory, God sent a messenger to them asking 'How can you celebrate like this when *my children* are drowning?' In this story God is portrayed as the Father of *all* people, including the enemy who has to be defeated. The two stories could be put side by side and the children invited to weigh up these two pictures of God. They could begin to think out the exceedingly difficult question of how goodness should respond to the presence of injustice. In this way, the story can help Religious Education to take on a new depth.

An objection is often raised to the idea that stories should be analysed and discussed in this way. To burden a story with comment and conversation is to spoil it beyond redemption, just as dissecting a poem can kill it stone-dead. Yet with young children the time to talk about it is often immediate – they usually want to anyway. It may be that with older children the story should be left as a story on the day of its telling, unless the children spontaneously start a discussion about it. But later – the next day or the next week – they should be reminded of it, especially if it could be a misleading story, and discussion initiated by the teacher if necessary. In this way the story can make its full impact as a story and yet proper educational mileage can be obtained from it.

An example might be the story of Noah's Ark. It would be better not to tell this story to very young children of four and five years because it might be difficult to prevent them getting misleading ideas from it. By the age of six, however, they should be able to discuss it quite well. It could first be told straight and stimulate imaginative work but, a little later on, the inadequate concept – which many children might acquire – of God as a celestial policeman who likes good people and dislikes bad people, whom he is prepared to drown, can be examined. The story can be put into context, opening up for them the question about whether it really happened as part of history or whether it was made up to teach a particular message, and, if so, what message (see Figure 34).

The distinction between stories which are historically true and stories which are fiction but true in a different sense, shedding light on some other aspect of reality, is a crucial one, and one which young children need to be helped to appreciate. Dora Ainsworth, in her research on teaching parables,[7] concluded that on the whole such parables should not be told in the infant classroom because they are very sophisticated stories and will not have their proper impact; the freshness of the parables for children at a later stage may be spoilt. Significantly, however, she believes that children *can* appreciate what a parable is if the teacher introduces it in the right context, relating it to something which has happened. She told me of how a small child who had been told the parable of the Sheep and the Goats quite spontaneously remarked to her some days later 'Did you take me home yesterday because you were doing it for Jesus?'

It may be better to develop this sense of analogy in children by most using stories other than parables of Jesus, unless some simple introduction to biblical interpretation is included. Stories like Aesop's Fables and many of the myths told in different religious traditions *can* be grasped by young children with a little prompting from the teacher, and this is a skill without which children cannot proceed very far in Religious Education. It can help to prevent a literal interpretation of what is figurative, with the tangle of unnecessary problems and misunderstandings which this entails.

Figure 34 Noah's Flood

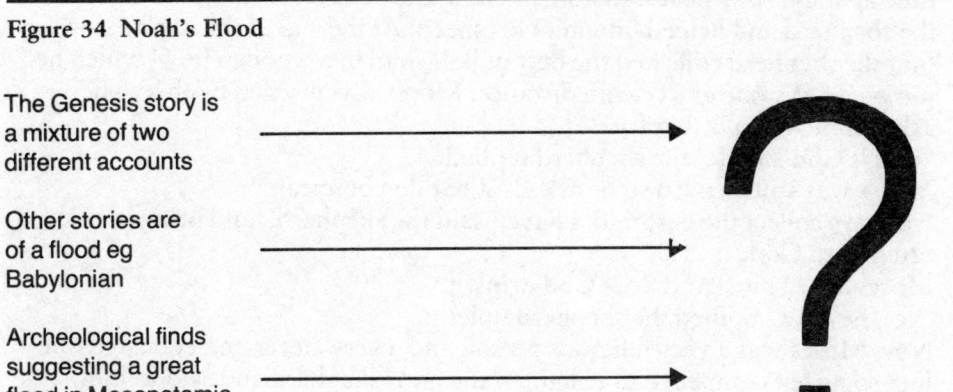

The Genesis story is
a mixture of two
different accounts

Other stories are
of a flood eg
Babylonian

Archeological finds
suggesting a great
flood in Mesopotamia
c. 4000 years ago

Some people believe the flood happened
exactly as told in the Bible

Other people believe it was a
made up story — like *Jack and
the Beanstalk* – and it isn't
true in any way

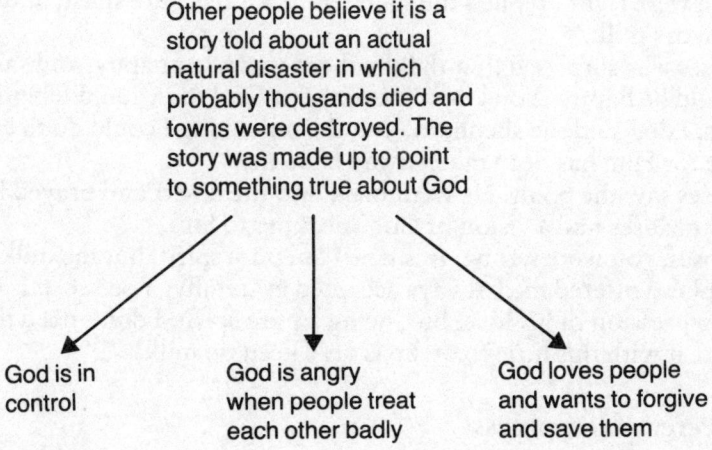

Other people believe it is a
story told about an actual
natural disaster in which
probably thousands died and
towns were destroyed. The
story was made up to point
to something true about God

God is in
control

God is angry
when people treat
each other badly

God loves people
and wants to forgive
and save them

The little fox

Moses was one of the great leaders of the Jewish people. He lived a long time ago. One day he found a shepherd in the desert. He spent the day with the shepherd and helped him milk his sheep. At the end of the day he saw that the shepherd collected the best milk he had in a wooden bowl which he put on a flat stone at a certain distance. Moses was puzzled by this so he asked him 'What is that for?'
'This is God's milk,' the shepherd replied.
Moses was still puzzled so he asked 'What do you mean?'
'I always collect the best milk I have,' said the shepherd, 'and bring it as an offering to God.'
Moses asked him 'And does God drink it?'
'Yes, he does,' replied the shepherd quietly.
Now Moses was a very religious person and a very clever and educated one too, so he felt compelled to enlighten the poor shepherd and said to him 'But God is pure spirit and does not drink milk.'
'But he does' responded the shepherd vigorously.
'No, He does not,' said Moses. 'Tonight, you hide behind the bushes very quietly and then you'll see whether God drinks the milk.'
Moses then went out to pray in the desert.
When night came, the shepherd hid very quietly in the bushes and in the moonlight he saw – a little fox come trotting from the desert. It looked right, looked left, and made a bee-line towards the milk which it lapped up and then disappeared into the dark again.
Next morning Moses found the shepherd quite depressed and downcast.
'What is the matter?' asked Moses.
'You were right', replied the shephered, 'God is pure spirit, and he does not want my milk.'
Moses was surprised that the shepherd was so unhappy, and said 'You should be happy. You know more about God than you did before.'
'Yes, I do,' said the shepherd, 'but the only thing I could do to express my love for Him has been taken away from me.'
Moses saw the point. He went back into the desert and prayed hard. In the night Moses had a vision of God speaking to him.
'Moses, you were wrong. It is true I am pure spirit, but the milk which the shepherd offered me I always accepted gratefully. You see, it is offered as an expression of his love, but, being a pure spirit, I don't need the milk, so I share it with this little fox who is very keen on milk!'

The secret of happiness

In the middle ages many people lived rather like tramps. They had no houses to live in, and hardly any possessions, and they would wander around from village to village begging for food. In a country like Germany where the weather can be cold and wet and where so many people were poor it could be a very hard life.

One day a man called John Tauler, who was a very religious person living
the life of a hermit, met a beggar. He thought he would speak to him.
'May I wish you a good day, my friend,' he said to the beggar.
'I thank God that I never had a bad one,' the beggar replied.
'Well then, I wish you a happy life, my friend,' said John Tauler.
'I thank God I am never unhappy,' the beggar responded.
'Never unhappy?' asked John in amazement. 'What do you mean? No-one
can be happy all the time!'
'Well, it's like this,' replied the beggar in a very matter of fact way:
'When it is fine, I thank God;
when it rains, I thank God;
when I have plenty, I thank God;
when I am hungry, I thank God;
and since God's will is my will,
and whatever pleases Him pleases me,
why should I say I am unhappy when I am not?'
John Tauler looked at the man in astonishment. 'Who are you?' he asked.
The beggar said simply, 'I am a king.'
'Where is your kingdom?' asked John Tauler.
'In my heart,' replied the beggar quietly.

Notes and references

1 H D Lewis *Our Experience of God* (Allen and Unwin, 1959) p 104
2 Unit of work on *The World of Nature and Belief in God* published by the Farmington
Institute, Oxford. Copies are available from 4 Park Town, Oxford, OX2 6SH
3 I am especially grateful to Betty Bartlett and Marion Greenstreet from whose written
responses I quote
4 For an example, see Brenda Watson, *The Dove and the Devil*: A scheme of work,
Farmington Institute for Christian Studies, Oxford, June 1982.
5 'The Little Fox' quoted by Metropolitan Anthony of Sourozh in *The Essence of Prayer*
(Darton, Longman and Todd, 1986) p 150f
6 'The Secret of Happiness' quoted by William Barclay in *Gospel of Matthew Vol 1* (St
Andrew Press, 1956) p 264
7 Dora Ainsworth: *An Aspect of the Growth of Religious Understanding in Children aged
between 5 and 11 years* (Manchester, 1958)

17 The Beleaguered Secondary Religious Education Specialist

Religious Education in the secondary school can be exciting, challenging and immensely worthwhile. Students are of an age when the deeper questions of life and fundamental convictions behind religion can be explored and understood at far greater depth than in the primary school. Often there can be an intensity and emotional urgency operating on students to make discussion of religious issues a top priority, fascinating and important for them. Secondary Religious Education can help to ensure that students both want and know how to pursue the ongoing search for truth and for commitments which are comprehensive and trustworthy.

Despite having much less staff-student contact time than their colleagues in primary education, skilled and thoughtful secondary teachers can play a vital role in the educational development of young people – a development which must increasingly be the students' own responsibility. In this task adolescents need time away from adults, so that they are not over-influenced by them and can find their own way.

Although there are some schools where Religious education can flourish in this way, there are unfortunately far more where enormous obstacles lie in its path. These can range from low status and impossible working conditions to negative or apathetic attitudes among students. These factors are often combined with a rhetoric of high-sounding aims and objectives concerning breadth and depth, and it would require a genius to handle them effectively. The distractions, resentment and general alienation from education common to many adolescents, all serve to heighten the challenge of teaching Religious Education.

A far from untypical situation is one in which just two specialist staff struggle in a school of 1500 students, with one 35-minute lesson a week for most classes. They may be helped by other teachers who are qualified only by virtue of some peripheral interest in the subject or by the fact they happen to have some free periods. Religious Education may have no specialist room and but a low capitation allowance, and equipment may have to be borrowed from other subject-areas. Some of the teaching may be part of integrated work in the Humanities on themes not closely related to religion. Homework periods may be few, and in any case the overworked staff would be incapable of setting and marking material properly for over 400 students each a week. Little relief is obtained through examination classes because Religious Education is a low-grade option usually chosen only by those unable to do some subject generally regarded as more rigourous, useful or relevant.

Discipline in class can be quite a problem because the work cannot be properly tailored to suit individual needs. This is both because staff do not have the time, energy or opportunity to discover what those needs are, and because constraints of a syllabus, assessment requirements and a limited number of resources which are often also educationally inadequate defeat even the most enterprising. Furthermore, staff have to tread with extreme care in teaching about a range of religions, lifestyles and contentious issues for which their training and experience have not properly equipped them.

Adminstrative chores such as the writing of reports can take an inordinate amount of time because staff teach so many classes and can know only a fraction of the students in a way which enables them to write something useful. The impersonal and rushed nature of the Religious Education thus launched on students conspires to lower their motivation for studying the subject still further with the distractions of other concerns and the subtle materialistic conditioning of society. The vicious circle therefore continues and it is with difficulty that Religious Education happens in such schools at all.

This grim picture is not uncommon. Many recent studies and reports, such as that by the Religious Education Council,[1] confirm the impression that the Religious Education teacher is in a beleaguered situtation in very many secondary schools today. Often a teacher with only a few years' teaching experience is in charge of a department. Such a person is not only liable to feel very isolated and over-worked but also may not have acquired the knowledge or skill to be able to argue forcefully for Religious Education *vis à vis* other subject-areas; as a result the subject often remains a very low priority. Because of poor career prospects many of the more ambitious and forthright Religious Education teachers move to other areas where promotion is more likely. The lack of a determined drive for the subject can be quite fatal in a time of falling rolls, cuts, and competition from other new initiatives, subject-areas and courses. Lack of enough good teaching in schools, however, causes the situation to be self-perpetuating.

What can be done to improve the chances of good Religious Education happening? In Chapter 6 I noted that many factors outside anyone's direct control are operating in schools to prevent really far-reaching reform, but that nevertheless the scope for the enterprising teacher remains impressive. This chapter will concentrate on what *can* be done.

Strong presentation of the educational case for Religious Education and its basic requirements

It is essential that the teacher understands fully the educational role of the subject in the total curriculum, both how it links with other areas and how it is distinct, so that he or she can present arguments for it clearly and vividly, without special pleading. Such representations need to be made on any and every occasion that presents itself, but especially to the Head and those responsible for curriculum planning, staffing and resources. The support of other staff, governors and parents can be very important. So many people still have outmoded ideas of Religious Education as a watered-down Sunday school input merely attired in a new pluralist outfit. Often it is regarded as a subject that only remains in the curriculum by courtesy of the law. A letter to parents or a personal visit to a well-disposed or influential governor can help to make the educational case for Religious education better known.

There is need for a certain toughness in a refusal to expect anyone to teach hundreds of students for one lesson 35 minutes a week. Two such lessons a week, together with a homework period, should be regarded as a minimum for any worthwhile education to take place, unless the group is a very small one, for otherwise it is impossible to relate to students as people.

Similarly, strong objections should be raised against anyone being expected to teach the subject if they know little about it or do not wish to teach it. A basic understanding in the teacher is a prerequisite for any subject and particularly for one which demands great sensitivity to avoid misusing the classroom situation, giving offence or purveying inaccurate, biased or misleading ideas about complex and controversial matters. If the non-specialist staff helping to teach Religious Education are numerous and inexperienced it is important to claim a more generous allowance of resources to help them than would otherwise be the case. In addition, two or three periods a week in which to prepare materials and discuss issues are necessary if staff are not to be over-worked. Good resourses are in any case needed to help improve the general image of the subject. Money for visitors and outside visits and so forth needs to be argued for, not aggressively, but firmly, as the way in which proper allowances can be agreed.

Making educational mileage out of avoiding unnecessary work

At a different level some strategy for survival is necessary to cope with the work-load and the immense demands of the subject-matter being dealt with. Such a strategy needs to be concerned both with ways of avoiding unnecessary work and with realistic selection of priorities in teaching. The following are some suggestions:

1 Make the most of resources available, even if they are old stock and poor quality, by teaching skills of criticism. A homework task, for example, could be to point out the inadequacies in a book and re-write a section of a chapter to make it more accurate, more interesting, less biased and so forth. This kind of work is valuable in encouraging students not to endow published material with automatic authority or infallibility.

2 Use homework times as an integral part of Religious Education enabling students to learn more fully how to work on their own and follow things up. Visits to libraries and buildings and talking to people in order to find out for themselves, form a valuable extension of the more limited opportunities available in the classroom for individual initiative. Sometimes, too, written work can be set. This, however, should rarely be marked by the teacher. Try to get students into the habit of assessing their own work a week or so after they have done it. This process of self-evaluation can be aided by their regularly marking each other's work, not by giving grades or percentages but by correcting, questioning and commenting.

It is important, however that the tacher reads examples of each student's written work at least once a term. If four or five homeworks a term are of this kind, and there are 30 in the class, it would mean that the teacher should read six or seven each time, preferably chosen, from the students' point of view, at random. Marking and assessment should be done with great care, so that students know in detail how well they are progressing and what their strengths and weaknesses are; they need positive encouragement to improve with regard to particular faults. In this way criticism can become creative and contribute to a student's capacity for realistic self-assessment, without loss of self-esteem. Marking many pieces of work superficially is time- and energy-consuming as well as boring and does very little to advance the student's self-knowledge. Frequently the same faults occur: for example, illogical progression of sentences, or bald statements of opinion unsupported by evidence or argument.

3 Allow plenty of scope for individual and group project work, with time and opportunity for it to be shared with the rest of the class. This has many benefits. It promotes maximum motivation by allowing students choice of subject matter and style of study and presentation. It permits a far broader spectrum to be covered than can possibly happen within the constraints of a uniform scheme of work for the whole class. It builds up each student's skills in organisation of work and communication with others. It makes the best use of scarce resources. Furthermore, it

increases a sense of community in the classroom as students become aware of others working on different topics within the same setting.

Project work has sometimes come into disrepute because incompetent teachers have used it as a fill-in, or because students have simply copied material out of books with little real learning or involvement. Moreover it has a reputation for demanding far more from the teacher than other methods, if it is to be educationally valuable. It is vital that at key points the teacher plays an advisory role and this does mean that there are peaks of activity, but normally these should be organised on some basis of rotation. Once launched, a project can prove intriguing and cumulatively valuable for students, and the good teacher knows how to let people pursue their study in their own way. Again, when the students are presenting the results of their project work to each other the teacher does not have any preparation work to do. The result is that, overall, the teacher needs to do less for far greater educational results than with a method of teaching which involves constant teacher-directed stimulus.

The key lies in first linking project work with real skills of self-discipline and self-evaluation (as has already been discussed with regard to homework); any second-hand work must simply not be tolerated. Second, real freedom of choice should be given with regard to topics. There is no reason why they all have to be within a particular area, say Hinduism, or festivals, or biblical material. It is possible to have students working on all three at the same time in the same classroom. The choice should be made on the grounds of interest, need and aptitude. Thus if there are Muslim students in the class they may wish to do one project on Islam followed by another in which they are encouraged to study a different religion and then compare how they found working on the two. Third, work must be in sufficient depth. Almost any theme can lead to the six fundamental questions about religion outlined in Chapter 10, provided the natural ramifications of what is being studied can be allowed to surface.

4 This last point relates to the crucial sharing of the educational task with the students so that they become consciously and articulately involved in pursuing their own Religious Education. The subject will then cease to be something which they think is done *to* them or *for* them, and against which they may have strong feelings of revulsion, claustrophobia or rebellion. They will experience instead an openness and non-dogmatic atmosphere in which they can feel accepted as people and encouraged to learn and progress. The teacher will be free enough to teach by example, that is, sharing with students *how* he or she learns. This is a far quicker and more efficient way of teaching than any didactic approach. It requires an acceptance of vulnerability by the teacher but can lead to very genuine respect, even from students with a tendency to be troublesome. Teachers who adopt this approach are not

obvious targets for lampooning because they make youngsters feel as if they are being treated as adults.

5 The emphasis on self-education compels the teacher really to listen to students and sense where they are educationally. Do not try to deal with questions they do not ask and are not interested in or do not see the point of, but attend assiduously to the ones they do ask. This means taking seriously what was said in Chapter 13 about syllabus. Abandon any feeling of being obliged to keep to the syllabus or get through this or that material. The syllabus is there to suggest possible starting-points or to provide reference material and ideas to be used if helpful. It takes courage to abandon all planned syllabus or work-schemes, textbooks and the like if the students are not 'biting' at them, and instead to start from where they are, but this can often achieve a breakthrough.

A student whom I had on teaching practice had prepared a good scheme of work for a mixed-ability third form group in a Salford school. It went disastrously; the youngsters did not give him a chance – they could not have cared less. So he abandoned it altogether and asked them simply 'Why do you regard Religious Education as a bore?' It turned out that these students had never before been given the opportunity to express their feelings, and actually articulate their reasons. They therefore found the experience novel and enjoyed hitting out at this, that and the other irritation. The student was able to take all this in, show sympathy with them over many of the points they raised by saying that if he were in their shoes he would equally loathe the subject, and then go on to question the validity of some of the things they had said. For example, one of them announced 'The Bible is a load of rubbish.' 'Is it; can you give me an example?' – 'All these miracle-stories; they didn't happen.' 'How do you know they didn't?' This led, with this particular class, to a discussion of miracles today, faith-healing, Mother Teresa praying for food and money which then arrived, the Shroud of Turin, and so forth. The purist would say that this was far too miscellaneous for a good lesson, but the fact remained that apart from three or four lads the students were interested, the whole class was attentive, wanting to knock the teacher's arguments down but finding his replies challenging, difficult to deal with, and interesting. Why? Because he had started where they were, on whether talk about religion can have an ounce of truth about it.

As teachers we risk not getting a hearing unless we attend to the questions which, in fact, our students are asking – probably not explicitly. This is why discussion with them in private and in class is so important, in order to get on their wavelength. In the case just cited, the student was able to plan a three-week follow-up on 'The Bible – fact or fiction?' which really got the students thinking, including the intellectually less-able.

6 A special word of warning is needed against the beguiling temptation to elaborate impressive lists of aims, objectives, skills, analysis of content and assessment methods. These can make the conscientious teacher feel good and give the indifferent teacher an illusion of achieving something, but they can scare, overwhelm, and arouse the suspicions of those with greater awareness of the complexities and controversial nature of religion. Such lists all too often constitute a virtually impermeable barrier between the teacher and those in whose interests they were ostensibly drawn up. I well remember how detrimental were the forms which college students were expected to fill up when they went to evaluate a teaching situation. There was no time for the quiet, passive taking-in of an atmosphere; the relaxing and often much-needed noticing of humorous development; or the grappling-in-the-mind with what was fundamentally amiss in a particular set-up. Attention was so fixed upon the exercise of assessment skills that what was being assessed was largely ignored.

Many people have had the same thing go wrong on organised field-trips, outings and visits. The checklist of what to look out for has been so absorbing as to be counter-productive, together with all the hard work which went into its making. The window has been so fascinating and detailed that the eye never looks through it.

Make time therefore simply to be present with a class. Insist on the discipline of quietness and maintaining an atmosphere in which people are not constantly distracting each other, and then relax in that atmosphere. Be concerned to build up only the *basic* concepts of religion necessary for any degree of understanding and evaluation, and study how to relate these concepts to the particular students who happen to be present and to their assumptions, beliefs, needs and interests. In such a spirit of simplification, be brave enough to cast off into the unknown so that the subject really can take off. Do not limit the possibilities by over-attachment to syllabuses, schemes of work or any other form of preparation laid down beforehand which may have the effect of keeping everyone anchored fast or hugging the shore-line.

Notes and references

1 See, for example, data in the Report on Provision for Religious Education published by the Religious Education Council in 1984. This remains basically accurate at the time of writing (1987) in its analysis of shortage of specialist staff and declining provision across the secondary age-range

18 Standards in the Secondary School

It may be feared that a flexible and un-trammelled approach such as that outlined in the last chapter may be detrimental to a high standard of learning and the capacity to do examination work well. I believe, however, that this is far from the case. By concentrating on students' practising skills of self-education, teachers equip them with the ability to work to some effect, and to do so much more quickly and efficiently. A tremendous amount of time and effort is frequently wasted through the wrong kind of application and working through exercises which impress ill-understood material on the mind without students really thinking about it and criticising it for themselves. Such study is empty because the students are not 'present' in it.

By developing a proper self-esteem in students, which rests not upon comparison with other people but on their own past performance and present opportunities, students lose the fear and lack of confidence with are the most inhibiting factors – preventing people from doing as well as they can, especially in examinations. It is often not acknowledged how poor an instrument of assessment examinations are, partly because of the tension and anxiety they so often cause – affecting not only performance on the day but the whole of a student's attitude to the work.

Examinations and religious education

The Religious Education specialist has to face the vexed question of whether any examination work should be offered in the subject. My own view is that, because of the high status accorded in our society to examinations, it is essential that Religious Education features among the subject on offer. Furthermore, the advantages of examination work in providing an extra something to work for and enabling the successful candidate to feel a measure of fulfilment, should not be lightly thrown aside even though motivation should not depend on examination work. A further very important reason for examination work in Religious Education is that it enables the teacher to spend more time with students and do work in greater depth; most schools allow a more generous allotment of time-tabling and resources for examination classes. It is also on the presence of good levels of academic attainment at school enabling students to go on to college and university that the future health of Religious Education depends.

It has often been said that examinations should serve education not the other way round, but in practice the cart is usually put before the horse. Students are sacrificed on the altar of the paper qualification. The new GCSE examinations show some awareness of certain unsatisfactory features of the examination system but it is by no means clear that the fundamental preoccupation with assessment is not going to continue to reduce the educational quality of what goes on in school.

The great advantage of GCSE is that it gives teachers a real opportunity to stand back and consider how they can make examination work valuable in itself. Donald Whittle, a member of the Secondary Examinations Council Religious Studies Committee, considers that

> 'the aims and objectives of the national criteria do provide an excellent base for imaginative and exciting work in religious studies offering students a real opportunity to develop their understanding and think for themselves.[1]

The new examinations have certain features which are very encouraging: breadth of content is possible, ample choice for individual needs and interests is available, the emphasis is on skills not just of factual regurgitation but of understanding and evaluation from a personal point of view. Furthermore, a mere stating of opinions is discouraged because evidence and reasoning are what is being assessed. This last point needs to be emphasised, namely that opinions as such are not awarded marks, otherwise candidates are encouraged simply to repeat acceptable views regardless of their own thinking. This is hypocritical, boring and a fundamental waste of time. Another excellent feature of the new examinations is the abandoning of norm-related criteria so that it now becomes possible for all candidates to reach their proper level of achievement without regard to competitors. In addition, greater standardisation makes the choice for the Religious Education specialist between different boards less crucial, and yet the differing syllabuses do offer differing emphases – which is as it should be.

Of course, from the point of view of good education everything depends on how the examinations are carried out in practice. The inclusion of a considerable proportion of course-work is much to be applauded, but will teachers get bogged down in assessment procedures and so concerned about such matters as balance between knowledge, understanding and evaluating that they teach in a 'safe' way, discouraging imagination, individual initiative and any real wrestling with questions? Will teachers continue to be overworked in preparing material and marking course-work – or even become more so? Will examinations which are either too easy or too difficult for large numbers of students still have baneful, inhibiting effects on learning? Will the syllabuses on offer expect too great a range of material to be covered and fail in fact to take seriously the building up of candidates' own reflection upon the material?[2]

These are questions which the coming years will clarify. Individual teachers can, however, ensure that examination work is valuable. I offer here a few suggestions which might serve also to lighten the teacher's load.

1 The three components of knowledge, understanding and evaluation, while needing to be theoretically distinguishable as an assessment exercise, in actual learning should constantly interact and dovetail into each other. Evaluation is in fact the key; it is at this level that students are most personally involved in what they are studying, and this applies to the so-called less intellectually-able candidates as much as to those more academically gifted. All students are not only capable of having opinions, but actually do have them. Many, however, need greater encouragement to learn to express them and support them with reasons. Evaluation needs to form the centre of the teacher's concern, not only because it is crucial in itself but because this is where the greatest professional skill and sensitivity is needed in helping students forward in their thinking. If prime attention is given to evaluation, knowledge and understanding will automatically be gained. Emphasis on knowledge can expect the human brain to be like that of a parrot; understanding without evaluation distances the student from the material studied. Progress in evaluation, on the other hand, gets people interested in and concerned for correct information and a proper appreciation of the relationship between different facts, problems of evidence and so forth. My own experience, and that of large numbers of teachers over the years, has convinced me that students of all abilities acquire a far fuller grasp of material if they are expected to relate intelligently to it. To facilitate this, certain precise skills can be taught, as discussed below on pages 245ff.

2 One of the problems of course-work is ensuring that, as far as possible, all candidates have an equal chance of doing themselves justice, whatever their home background. This can be resolved, to some extent, by arranging for course-work to be written in school without a rigid time-limit, but in an atmosphere where there are no distractions. Such an arrangement, together with the kind of work set, can be in line with the way in which assessment work lower down the school is approached. It is important that questions set should stimulate thinking and discourage an impersonal, second-hand attitude.[3] In the Appendix at the end of this chapter there are examples of a style of question which is extremely fruitful in testing a candidate's knowledge and understanding. For evaluation, students can then be asked to write as much as they can, explaining what they think about the subject-matter under discussion, and giving reasons for their views. This can supply a kind of template for

composing examination papers.

3 It is essential however that examination work should not be pursued to the detriment of other Religious Education work, from the point of view of either teachers or students: it should be something taken in one's stride. This can be so even if it is organised as voluntary sessions in lunch-hours or after school, provided that the responsibility for working hard is placed squarely on the students themselves, and that they have weighed the cost.

Given well-motivated students who have progressed some way in learning how to learn, and who possess a fair degree of self-assurance, as discussed above, the actual content of examination work, whether at GCSE or the present 'A' level, can be covered economically. The factual material can be largely catered for in homework periods, leaving lessons freer for discussion and evaluation and making the topics live.

This approach will require considerable planning ahead by the teacher, in reading syllabuses and studying past or recommended examination-papers carefully; selecting subject-matter wisely, allowing for sufficient but not too much to be learnt; and preparing or ordering resources. The actual way of organising the learning should not be presented by the teacher as a *fait accompli*. If arrangements for covering the material are not discussed with students and a measure of freedom given, valuable learning experience will be bypassed, and the risk of students experiencing boredom or anxiety encouraged. Moreover, this imposes a great burden of extra preparation work on the teacher. If examinations are approached in the way outlined in this section, they can make a positive contribution to education.

Religious Education and Moral Education

Personal and Social Education and the pastoral side of school organisation are two of the curriculum areas which have some concern for moral education. Traditionally Religious Education has had special responsibility for this and it still has a great deal to contribute to such courses. It can only do so effectively, however, if it stops masquerading as general education and turns attention openly to the specifically religious perspective. This is something fresh for most students, unusual, controversial and fascinating.

In Chapter 9 a particular lesson on drugs was referred to as being good educationally but inadequate with regard to forwarding any understanding of religion. Furthermore, students may be said to be deprived in their appreciation of the drug problem if the religious dimension is not introduced to them. What would have made the lesson *Religious* Education?

The ideal setting for such a lesson would be in integrated work where the

Figure 35 Moral Education and Religious Education

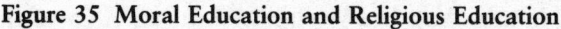

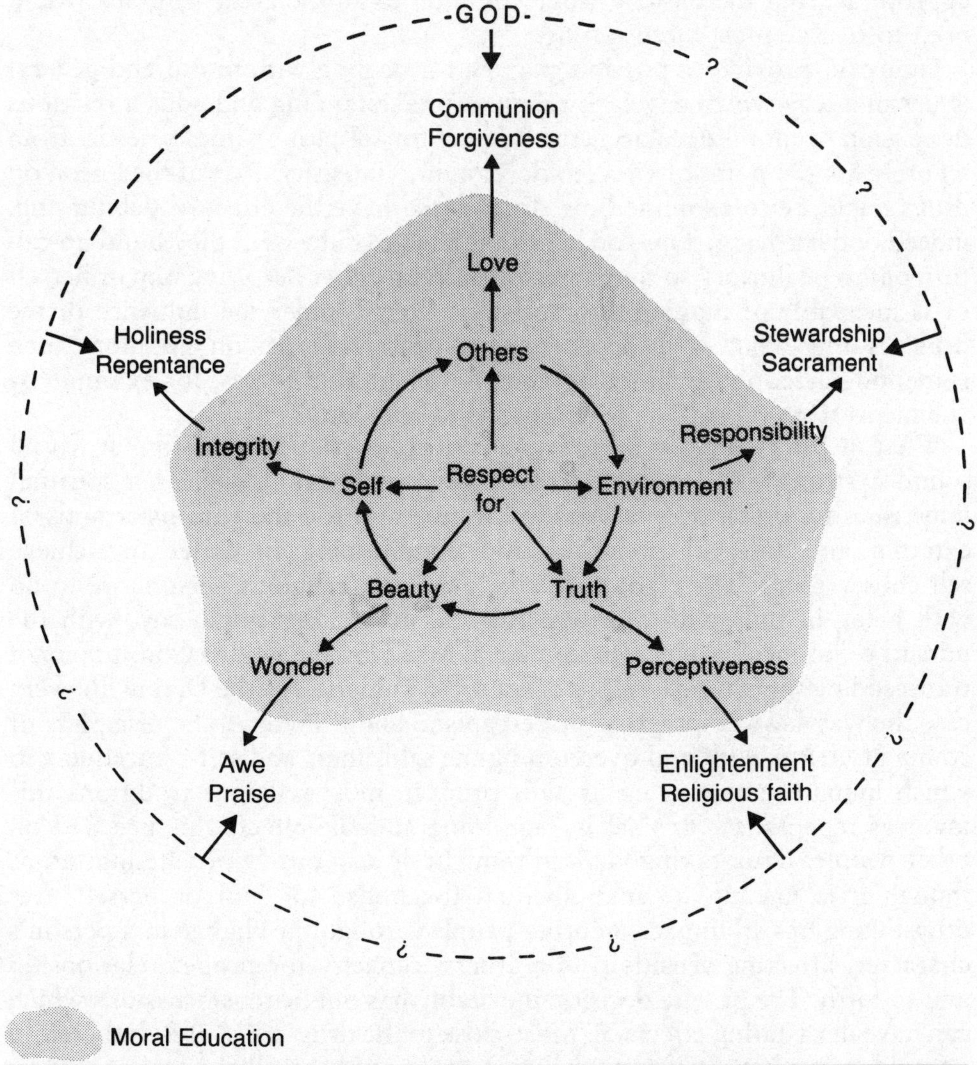

-G-O-D-

Communion
Forgiveness

Love

Holiness
Repentance

Others

Stewardship
Sacrament

Integrity

Responsibility

Self — Respect for → Environment

Beauty   Truth

Wonder

Perceptiveness

Awe
Praise

Enlightenment
Religious faith

Moral Education

human values themselves could be explored in much greater depth. The theme of drugs can and should be related to the basic attitude of fivefold respect upon which education itself rests. Religious Education could then contribute its own unique perspective to the debate, encouraging students to study and wonder what difference having a religious faith or believing in God would, could or should make. Could religion help Bob to come off drugs? Would he indeed have started taking them in the first place if he had been genuinely religious? What difference might it have made to the attitude of his parents or his girl-friend if they had been religious? In each case the distinctions between different religious stances should be discussed where appropriate, but the basic attitude common to all the great religions would need to receive most attention first.

Figure 35 provides a possible pattern for dealing with moral and general issues in a way which develops religious understanding and adds a religious dimension to moral development. Respect for self, for example, needs, from a purely human point of view, to develop into integrity. Part of the lesson on drugs might be to examine how drugs often have the effect of debilitating, indeed of destroying, a person. The high image of the 'self' they build up can turn out to be illusory so that a person ends up either despising him or herself or is incapable of making any decisions except under the influence of the drug. Is this what is meant by self-respect? Is a person no more than something acted upon either by external or internal forces, for example by chemicals from outside or reactions inside the body?

What might a religious perspective contribute to the discussion? It would sound a strong 'No' to both these questions. It acknowledges a spiritual dimension in which people learn to be free and use the various strands of external and internal pressures and conditioning in order to achieve self-chosen goals. These goals, for the genuinely religious person, are to do with being in tune with Spiritual Reality, or, as they might say, with the pursuit of holiness. Some religions speak of doing the will of God, others of transcending the physical self in order to be immersed in the Divine. In every case the way lies via integrity, not escapism, and it involves the discipline of coming to terms with and overcoming the selfishness and self-centredness to which human nature so easily falls prey. In most religious traditions this involves repentance for past wrong-doing and the effects this has had on other people. Drug-taking is often thought of as a purely private matter, as though it is just up to an individual to choose for him or herself. Yet drug-taking has an impact on other people through the change in a person's character, affecting sensitivity for others, capacity for proper relationship and so forth. The private decision inevitably has public reperscussions which can have devastating effects on those close to the drug-taker. If Bob therefore became a genuine religious believer he would be likely to experience repentance, and want to help any whom he had hurt and try to make it up to them.

These are the kind of questions and ideas which specifically Religious Education would throw up for consideration.

Teaching skills of discernment

The word 'genuine' has twice been used in the last paragraphs. Although a difficult concept to establish, it is in fact crucial to any progress in understanding religion, for the impact of many possible substitutes for religion can torpedo any appreciation of what religion is in itself, as discussed in Chapter 9.

This relates to the fourth of the questions outlined as being basic to religion: 'Is this person or action genuinely religious?' By way of example I would like to close this chapter with a detailed consideration of the kind of discussion which needs to be part of Religious Education, whether at examination or non-examination level. I would go so far as to say that without an attempt to equip students with such skills of discernment, Religious Education in school has largely failed them. The ability to discern genuineness is not simply intuitive, neither does it require special gifts. There are forms of evidence which permit discussion, even though they are not rules-of-thumb as such. Students could be asked to consider, for example, this account of an ugly incident in a New York underground.

> Just yesterday as I rode a subway train I noticed a young man carrying a Bible. He got off at the same stop I did, and I was amazed to see him attack a stranger on the platform, beating him with the Bible and trying to push him into the tracks. The transportation police stopped the assault, but I suggested to the attacker that rather than use the Bible to assail another person, he read the Gospels and put to use the message found there.[4]

No motive was suggested for the attack and the young man may have been deliberately using the Bible as a weapon to show his contempt for it, but as the observer saw it the attacker was technically a believer whose conduct was utterly at variance with the supposed content of his belief.

This is a familiar situation. The role of beliefs as ideals, guides and prodders rather than as an expression of what is, means that all belief-systems suffer to a greater or lesser extent from a debilitating flaw: there is no guarantee that people who say they are convinced Socialists, Buddhists, Marxists or Methodists actually *are*. In fact this young man's commitments may be the result of conditioning, of psychological drives leading him to seek security and protection by a group, of emotional frenzy, of calculating political or economic ambition, and so forth; he may know next to nothing of the claims which the belief he credits himself with makes upon him, and he may care even less. From the well-worn horror story of the headmaster who in assembly used to beat any boy who would not acknowledge that God loves people, to the Church lay-reader who victimises his assistants at work, the story is the same.

How is it possible to decide whether or not the Bible-bashing youth, the headmaster or the Church lay-reader are being genuinely Christian, however sincere they may claim to be? There are in fact certain criteria by which the nature of a religion or a belief-system can be evaluated. By themselves such tests are not necessarily reliable, but taken together they may provide very strong evidence indeed.

1 The first is the consistency between what is said and what is done, that is, between belief and behaviour. To claim that God is love and then without the least provocation to use violence against another human-being is an obvious mismatch. To judge the belief by the behaviour is clearly inappropriate because the person was acting not according to their stated belief but according to a different conviction, one indeed which may be only semi-conscious or unconscious. The real convictions by which the Bible-bashing youth lived were probably based on a sense of himself as the centre of the universe and a feeling, therefore, that he had the right to express his aggressive moods as and when he pleased.

2 The second is the consistency between what an individual or small group believes and what the main tradition to which they claim attachment believes. The Church lay-reader is a member of the Anglican tradition which, even in its present organisational form, is over 400 years old and in its creed and theology has always seen itself as part of the stream of authentic Christianity going back to the first days of the church over 1900 years ago. Some people may argue that because the total tradition contains within it notable examples of persecution, tyranny and inquisition, it therefore either supports the victimising lay-reader or is useless as a court of appeal because it sounds contradictory notes. Such reasoning, however, is faulty because the persecution and so forth were themselves inconsistent according to the first criterion. The church stands condemned by its own teaching, as sincere Christians are foremost in acknowledging, when it sinks to such fanaticism.

In fact the appeal to the main tradition is based on two strong considerations:

a *The test of time* Tenacious traditions cannot just be dismissed. Normally there is something valid about that which sustains human beings over a long period of time; the new, on the other hand, may prove ephemeral and of only temporary significance. In his essay on the *Development of Christian Doctrine* Newman calls this 'the test of chronic vigour'.[5]

b *Saints and scholars* Those people who attain what in religious terms is usually called holiness or sanctity, together with those who have given years of study to understanding the tradition, provide the clearest insight into what religion is about. To judge Hinduism, for example, on the basis of an impression of superstitious, priest-ridden idolatry in a remote village, and to ignore the life and teaching of a Gandhi or a Sri Ramana (a saintly guru who died in 1950 and whose ashram is still the focal-point of Hindu meditation) indicates a fundamentally unfair, indeed frivolous approach, for both Gandhi and Sri Ramana themselves perceived the naivety of the idol-worship.[6]

Figure 36 Criteria for discernment

Are there any criteria by which it is possible to decide whether someone is being genuinely religious?

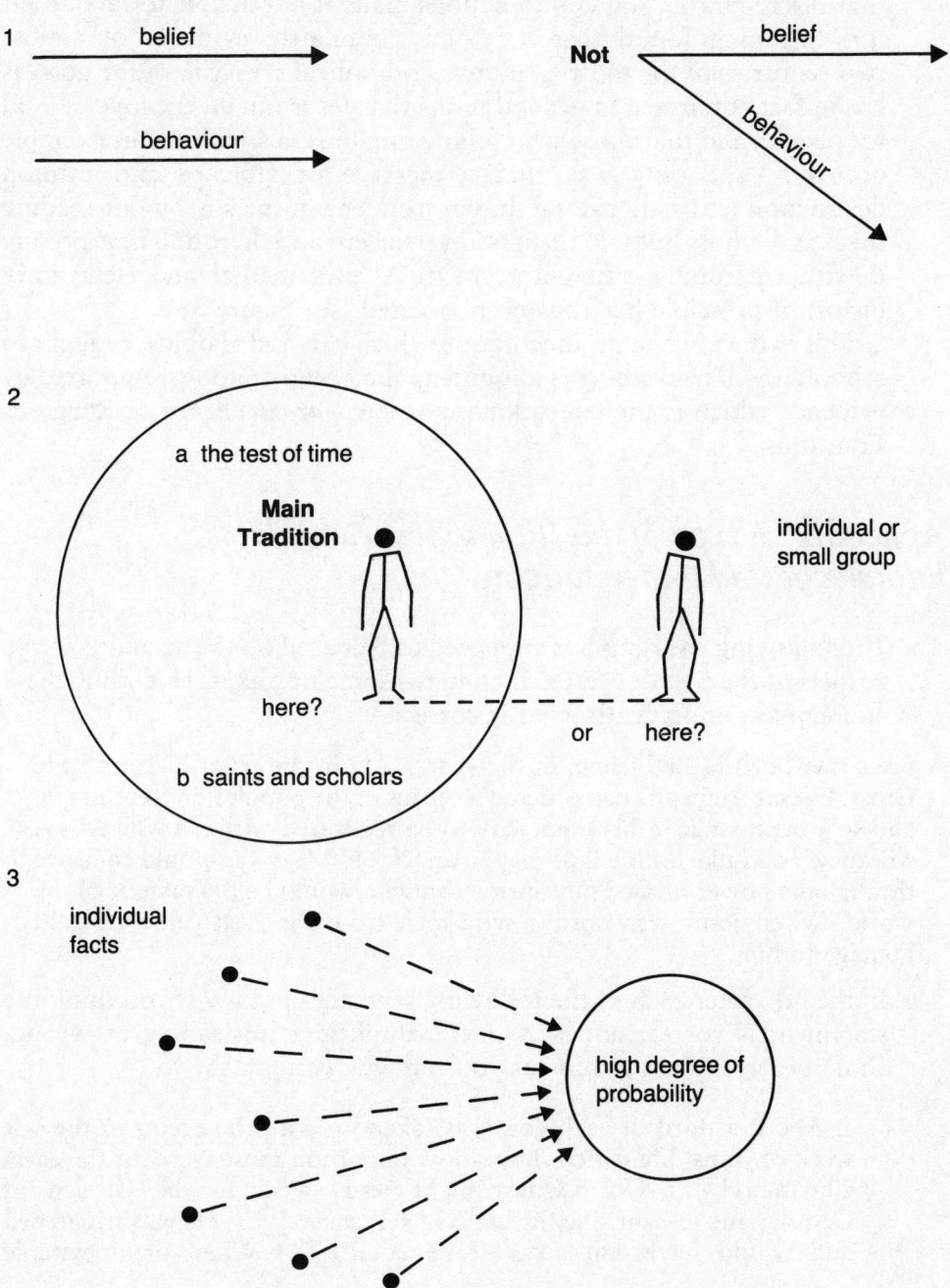

3 The third criterion or test for discerning what is genuinely religious relates to the interpretation of all historical texts and practices. In the Bible-bashing incident, the young man was asked to read the Bible and put to use the message found there. This may seem simplistic: a tremendous apparatus of biblical criticism is surely required to establish what the message is, and even so large numbers of scholars would argue that discrepancies and contradictions make it impossible to talk about '*the*' meaning found there. Yet the cumulative evidence of almost two centuries of the most assiduous and radical criticism of the gospels has in fact confirmed in general terms that Jesus taught the love of God for people, and that those who follow him must also follow his example of love.[7] The only way that a message of violence and wanton destruction and hate can be drawn from the gospels is by not reading them as a whole but taking an odd verse here and there and interpreting it within a totally different context. A fundamental and elementary historical principle has thus been violated (see Figure 36).

This is the kind of argumentation which can and should be taught in school. It will help students to build up their own opinions supported by evidence which is the educational purpose *par-excellence* of Religious Education.

Appendix: A type of question to test candidates' knowledge and understanding

a The following paragraph is supposed to be based on the accounts in the gospels of the birth of Jesus. It contains some mistakes. Underline these and explain underneath what is correct.

Jesus was born in Bethlehem in the year 1 AD in the reign of Herod the Great. Caesar Augustus had ordered a census of the population to be made, and so Joseph went to his home city to be registered with his wife Mary. Matthew and Luke both tell us that an angel told Mary she would conceive through the power of the Holy Sprit a son who would be the saviour of the world. When Jesus was born 3 wise men from the East came and did homage to him.

b In the box after each of the following sentences put a √ if you think the statement is correct and a X if you think it is misleading or wrong. Underneath explain as fully as you can why you put the X.

1 About a third of each gospel is taken up with the events in the last week of Jesus' life which shows how important these were for the early Christians.☐ 2 On his last night Jesus went to the Garden of Gethsemane just outside the walls of Jerusalem.☐ 3 He was frightened and would have run away if he could.☐ 4 When the inevitable

happened and he was arrested he gave himself up without protest.☐ 5 At his trials before Pilate and Herod he refused to say anything in his defence.☐ 6 On the cross he spoke some words in Hebrew which came from Psalm 22 and which some people think were a sign of his confidence in God's victory, and others a cry of utter despair.☐ 7 Several of his disciples were present at the crucifixion and he told them not to be afraid because he would rise again.☐ 8 All the accounts agree that Jesus was a revolutionary planning to overthrow the Roman government in Judaea.☐ 9 This was dangerous and unrealistic and therefore all the Jews except for those who were Zealots or who were his own close friends opposed Jesus.☐ 10 Pilate also thought that Jesus was guilty of treason against Rome.☐ 11 Yet Jesus did not behave like a revolutionary, for according to Luke, he prayed when he was nailed to the cross: 'Father, forgive them for they know not what they do.'☐

c The following statements relating to the Sermon on the Mount (Matthew, chapters 5, 6 and 7), are *a* right, *b* wrong, or *c* not wholly untrue but giving a false impression of the teaching in the Sermon. Under each of the statements say into which category you think it falls. If you think the category is either *b* or *c* give your reasons and what you think is the correct teaching.

   i   The sermon teaches that a charitable, humble attitude of mind is more important than a blind obedience to rigid, external rules of behaviour.

   ii   Christians should always tell other people of their own good deeds in order to set them a good example.

   iii   The Law is not important as it is too rigid and mainly taught by the scribes and Pharisees and therefore people need not keep it.

   iv   Those who are meek and do not demand their rights, bearing wrongs patiently, are happier and have more liberty of spirit than those who are held in a certain amount of fear and always get their own way because of their forcefulness.

   v   Although we cannot be perfect as our heavenly Father is perfect and love those who wrong us, at least we should not take revenge.

   vi   If we are going to offer a gift at the altar but remember that someone has something against us we should offer our gift all the more promptly and pray that the person may repent.

   vii If someone tries to wrong and take advantage of us we should resist sufficiently to keep our rightful belongings and our self-respect but go no further.

   viii We ought not to worry about maintaining our livelihood but try chiefly to obey and love God and He will care for us as He does the birds and flowers which are much less important than we are.

   ix   God will satisfy those who hunger and thirst for righteousness.

Notes and references

1 Donald Whittle 'GCSE: Progress Report' in *Journal of Beliefs and Values* 1985, Vol 6, No 2

2 See, for example, Peter Doble: 'GCSE, Religious Studies and PSE' in *News and Events* Spring/Summer 1986 (York Religious Education Centre). Blake Hemmings: 'Conceptions of Course Work in Religious Studies' in *RE News* Summer 1986 (Welsh National Centre for Religious Education)

3 Raymond Holley, for example, gives examples of examination questions designed to elicit evidence of spiritual insight. See his *Religious Education and Religious Understandings* (RKP 1978) p 152

4 Father Fehren in an article for *US Catholic* (1980)

5 See N L A Lash *Newman on Development: A study of the Essay on the Development of Christian Doctrine* (London, 1975)

6 See, for example, *Gandhi's Religious Thought* by M H Chatterjee (MacMillan, 1983) and *The Collected Works of Ramana Maharshi* edit Arthur Osborne (Rider, 1969)

7 See, for example, J Jeremias: *The Central Message of the New Testament* (SCM 1965)

Postscript

'The unexamined life is not worth living.' This Socratic maxim summarises one of the key goals of any education worthy of its name. As was argued in Part A of this book, a responsible attempt to share with young children and students knowledge and understanding of beliefs and values is central to the whole educational enterprise.

While Parts B and C focus only on Religious Education, this does not imply that every other area of the curriculum has not a decisive role to play. What this long excursion into one area does claim, however, is that if Religious Education is handled with sensitivity, intelligence and real respect for the integrity of those taught it can make its own unique contribution to education in beliefs and values. Such Religious Education can illumine, and be illumined by, other subject-areas. It can play its part in helping to make schooling a significant, pleasurable, and liberating experience for all.

Appendix: Evaluation of a School

How positive is it in its measure of the following?

General running of the school and discipline

Promoting community spirit
instilling uniformity

Inspiring a caring attitude towards others
tolerating indifference and amoral attitudes and failing to restrain disruptive behaviour

Appreciating diversity of outlooks and cultures
exhibiting exclusivism

Providing a setting in which imagination, creativity and originality can flourish
stereotyping people

Demonstrating the willingness and ability to listen, by those responsible for running the school
acting dogmatically and not prepared to discuss and really listen

Giving opportunity for genuine protest at what is deemed to be unfair
viewing any expression of dissent, complaint or anger as pernicious

Fostering mutual trust and communication at all levels of relationship
allowing cliquism, deception and non-communication

Training in self-discipline and self-control
enforcing external conformity through bribery or punishment

Teaching attentiveness and the ability to concentrate
enforcing frowning application and tension

Helping people to be aware of the distraction of too much talking and the need for silence and reflection
permitting a talkative, rushed and over-active attitude to life

Encouraging people to take a pride in their appearance and presentation
condoning slovenly habits and attitudes

Achieving an atmosphere of good humour and genuine laughter helping to dispel the pomposity which besets most institutions and those in authority
encouraging an over-serious and humourless approach to life and endowing the school with too much reverence

Emphasis in Encouraging Motivation to Learn

Seeing the school as preparing people for life and for self-education
regarding the school as training for work

Emphasising self-evaluation and desire to improve on one's own past achievement
setting up external scales of attainment and underlining comparisons with others

Developing co-operation
reinforcing competitiveness

Valuing the variety of people's talents and insights from their own unique experience
establish a model of academic, technical, athletic or cultural skills dependent especially on forms of testing which make many or most people feel inadequate

Helping people to the self-esteem which can cope with crisis and failure
hindering the development of self-esteem by stressing the desirability of total success

Developing the capacity for flexibility, adaptability and courage to relate intelligently to changing situations
imposing a pre-recorded attitude resulting in people being lodged in grooves and afraid of change

Seeking to evoke a sense of wonder
supporting only a matter-of-fact approach to life and learning, suppressing any personal response

Encouraging a basic interest in everything even though lacking time or skill to pursue it
promoting a specialist attitude which ignores or scorns most pursuits outside the specialism

Encouraging people to see links between what is functional and what is beautiful
adopting a purely utilitarian attitude which relegates the arts to the periphery

Quality of thinking encouraged at all levels

Encouraging personal engagement in exploring the truth about things
permitting the attitude that there are authoritarian set answers just to be accepted, and not thought out

Seeing everything as part of a whole
compartmentalising knowledge

Acknowledging the complexity and difficulty of issues without succumbing to inertia or inaction
reinforcing simplistic thinking or ignoring the need for action

Encouraging the development of strong, well-thought-out and educationally-appropriate convictions and comments
tolerating a sitting-on-the-fence attitude and failing to examine prejudices and assumptions

Developing the capacity to cope with doubt and levels of certainty and uncertainty
reinforcing an obsessive need for a clear-cut yes or no to everything

Accepting disagreement between people and the need for controversy on many fundamental issues
assuming agreement where agreement does not exist

Cultivating skills of critical awareness and thoughtful expression
tolerating sloppy thinking and allowing people to get away with crooked methods of arguing

Promoting emotional development alongside cognitive
either ignoring the emotional side of life or separating it from control by reason

Cultivating wisdom
being impressed only with cleverness and successful memory-work and problem-solving

Bibliography

A vast literature is available. The following is a small selection of helpful or illuminating books in addition to those already mentioned in the text or footnotes. Most of them have useful bibliographies which the reader may like to consult.

A General Issues

Abrams, M, Gerard, D and Timms, N (ed) *Values and Social Change in Britain* (Macmillan, 1985).

Boud, D, Keogh, R and Walker, D (ed) *Reflection: Turning Experience into Learning* (Kogan Page, 1985).

Macintyre, Alasdair *After Virtue* (Duckworth, 1981).

Peacocke, Arthur (ed) *Reductionism in Academic Disciplines* (Society for Research into Higher Education and NFER Nelson, 1985).

Polanyi, Michael *Personal Knowledge* (Routledge and Kegan Paul, 1958).

Pring, Richard *Knowledge and Schooling* (Open Books, London 1976).

Rogers, Carl *Freedom to Learn for the 80s.* (Charles E Merrill Publishing Company, 1983).

Stradling R, Noctor, M and Baines, B *Teaching Controversial Issues* (Edward Arnold, 1984).

Thouless, Robert H *Straight and Crooked Thinking* (Pan Books, 1953).

Tomlinson, P and Quinton, Margaret *Values Across the Curriculum* (Falmer Press, 1986).

Trigg, Roger *Reason and Commitment* (CUP 1973).

Ward, Lionel O (ed) *The Ethical Dimension of the School Curriculum* (University College of Swansea, Faculty of Education, 1982).

Wolfe, David L *The Justification of Belief* (Inter-Varsity Press, Illinois, 1982).

B Understanding of Religious Education

Barnett, James (ed) *Theology at 16+* (Epworth Press, 1984).

Cole, W Owen (ed) *World Faiths in Education* (Allen and Unwin, 1978).

Cox, Edwin *Problems and Possibilities for Religious Education* (Hodder and Stoughton, 1983).

Felderhof, M C (ed) *Religious Education in a Pluralist Society*, (Hodder and Stoughton, 1985).

Hull, John (ed) *New Directions in Religious Education* (Falmer Press, 1982).
ibid Studies in Religion and Education (Falmer Press, 1984).
Jackson, Robert (ed) *Approaching World Religions* (John Murray, 1982).
Lamb, Christopher *Belief in a Mixed Society* (Lion, 1985).
Nichols, Kevin F (ed) *Theology and Education* (Association of Teaching Religions, 1974).
O'Keeffe, Bernadette *Faith, Culture and the Dual System* (Falmer Press, 1986).
Rodger, A R *Education and Faith in An Open Society* (Handsel Press, 1982).
Sealey, John *Religious Education Philosophical Perspectives* (Allen and Unwin, 1985).
Smart, Ninian and Horder, Donald (ed) *New Movements in Religious Education* (Temple Smith, London, 1975).
Sutcliffe, John M (ed) *A Dictionary of Religious Education* (SCM, 1984).

C Relationship Between Religions

Anderson, Norman *Christianity and World Religions* (IVP, 1984).
Cracknell, Kenneth *Towards a New Relationship: Christians and People of Other Faiths* (Epworth, 1986).
Cragg, Kenneth *The Call of the Minaret* (Collins, 2nd ed revised, 1985).
The Christ and the Faiths: Theology in Cross-Reference (SPCK, 1986).
D'Costa, Gavin *Theology and Religious Pluralism* (Basil Blackwell, 1986).
Vandana *Gurus, Ashrams and Christians* (Darton, Longman and Todd, 1978).
Whaling, Frank *Christian Theology and World Religions: A Global Approach* (Marshall Pickering, 1986).

D Practical Application in the Classroom

Cole, W Owen (ed) *Religion in the Multi-Faith School* (Hulton, 1983).
Copley, Terence *RE Being Served – Successful Strategy and Tactics for the School RE Department* (CIO Publishing, 1985).
Gower, Ralph *Religious Education in the Infant Years* (Lion Publishing, 1982). *Religious Education in the Junior Years* (Lion Publishing, 1984).
Grimmitt, Michael *What Can I Do in RE?* (Mayhew-McCrimmon, 1973).
Holm, Jean *Teaching Religion in School: A Practical Approach* (OUP 1975).
Thornecroft, John K *Religious Education through Experience and Expression* (Edward Arnold, 1978).

E Textbooks

Examples of recent textbooks which positively encourage students to develop detective-skills and to think for themselves are:

Jesus: An Enquiry by David Naylor and Ann Smith. (Macmillan Education, 1985).

Jesus and the Shroud by Ray Bruce and Ian Wilson. (Holt, Rinehart and Winston Ltd, 1982).

Investigating Jesus by K R Chappell. (Edward Arnold, 1982).

For examination work:

Comparative Religions: A Modern Textbook ed W Owen Cole (Blandford, 1982).

Dimensions of Christianity An approach to the NEA's GCSE in Religious Studies – Sister Anne Burke (Kevin Mayhew, 1986).

Religions of Man J R S Whiting (Stanley Thornes, 1983).

Six Religions in the Twentieth Century W Owen Cole with Peggy Morgan (Hulton, 1986).

The topic approach is much favoured in textbooks. An example of a useful and well-produced series for primary and lower secondary is that on *Exploring Religion*. Teacher's Guide and Books by Olivia Bennett on 1) *Festivals* 2) *Worship* 3) *Writings* 4) *Signs and Symbols* 5) *Buildings* 6) *People* (Bell and Hyman).

A useful series of booklets for upper age-groups in secondary schools relating scientific, moral and religious issues in an open way is *Studies in Christianity and Science* (OUP, 1985) edited by Peter Hodgson.

Index